CALL OF DUTY
ADVANCED WARFARE

SINGLE-PLAYER SPECIALIZED TRAINING

Call of Duty®: Advanced Warfare makes big changes to traditional *Call of Duty®* gameplay with the addition of the exoskeleton. Players can now perform boost jumps, dodges, aerial maneuvers, and a host of other powerful skills thanks to their Exos. These additons drastically alter the way the game is played.

A few of the bigger changes in *Call of Duty®: Advanced Warfare* are as follows:

>> **Exoskeleton Abilities.** The player's exoskeleton gives him numerous abilities that open up all kinds of possibilities on the battlefield.

>> **Exoskeleton Upgrades.** An upgrade system allows you to improve your Exoskeleton as you complete challenges.

>> **Grenades.** For most of the Campaign, you carry two grenades, each of which has three different uses.

>> **Heads-Up-Display.** All of your weapon information has been placed on your weapon.

>> **New Advanced Weaponry.** New weapons and tactical equipment, such as directed-energy rifles and a hovertank, make for some exciting gameplay.

READ THE MANUAL, USE THE TUTORIALS

The purpose of this chapter—and this guide as a whole—is to supplement, not replace, the in-game tutorials and user's manual that accompany the game. Our goal is to expand on the information those sources already provide and help you understand some the game's finer elements before you charge into battle. The following pages touch upon fundamental aspects of the game, devoting special attention to the changes made in *Call of Duty®: Advanced Warfare*.

CAMPAIGN BASICS

This section covers the basics of *Call of Duty®: Advanced Warfare*. You can find detailed information on the Exoskeleton abilities and upgrade system after the basics. If you are a veteran of *Call of Duty®*, you may want to skip this part.

OBJECTIVE MARKER

Whenever you have an objective, a yellow circle with a dot in the middle appears where you need to go next. If it is off screen, a yellow arrow points in its direction. If you ever get lost and don't know where you should go, look for the yellow indicator, or wait for one to show up.

YOUR HEALTH

There is no health meter or number to represent how much health you have. Blood splatter on the screen represents your general well-being, and a blood smear shows up when you are hit. Its arc represents the direction from where the attack originates.

As you continue getting hit, the blood splatter gets thicker until the words "You are Hurt. Get to Cover!" show up on screen. Move behind cover, and the screen clears, showing that you are recovering.

STANCE

There are three stances in *Call of Duty®*: stand, crouch, and prone. Press the Crouch button to lower your profile. This allows you to move under obstacles, makes you a tougher target, and steadies your aim.

Hold the Crouch button to go prone. This provides the same benefits as the crouched position, but you are even tougher to hit.

SPRINT

Pushing in on the Left Stick causes your character to run faster. Sprint between pieces of cover to become a tougher target to hit.

DODGE

Your Exo Suit gives you the ability to dodge in any direction. Simply click the Left Stick while pressing in the desired direction. This is strictly an in-air maneuver.

MELEE

When you find yourself face-to-face with an enemy, press the Right Stick in to perform a melee attack. This won't always result in a kill, but it is good to get in the habit of using it when you are near a foe. You can use a silent attack when you are cloaked, or when quietly approaching a hostile from behind.

WEAPONS

Call of Duty®*: Advanced Warfare* has a huge selection of armaments to choose from. However, in the Campaign, you are limited to your initial loadout, drops from enemies, and guns found lying around. There are six types of weapons:

>> Pistols

>> Submachine Guns

>> Assault Rifles

>> Shotguns

>> Sniper Rifles

>> Heavy Weapons

Each type has its own pros and cons with specific attributes, including accuracy, damage output, range, fire rate, and mobility. Many will come with different optics and attachments, such as scopes, extended mags, a foregrip, an improved stock, and more.

Try out each type as you progress through the single-player game to figure out your own preferences.

Keep an eye out for new advanced weapons like the EM1 heavy weapon, a directed-energy gun that fires a constant beam until it overheats. The IMR assault rifle is equipped with built-in 3D printing technology, constantly creating another clip of bullets until it fills up. The Tac-19 shotgun is a powerful directed-energy weapon that is great in close combat.

LOADOUT

At the start of each Campaign level, you are given a specific weapon loadout. This most often consists of two guns, two grenades, and your Exo Suit. As defeated enemies drop their weapons, you get the opportunity to switch to other options. In the Campaign walkthrough chapter, this guide lists your initial loadout at the start of each mission.

AMMUNITION

The current amount of ammo in your clip and reserve are shown on the back of your gun. Keep an eye on these numbers. Reload whenever you get the opportunity, and look out for a new gun when your reserves get low.

You can often find ammo stashes on the battlefield, giving you an opportunity to restock your reserves, as well as your grenades. This either looks like a big stack of ammo boxes with a bright icon on the side or a small duffel bag. Keep an eye out for these, and use them whenever you get a chance.

AIM DOWN SIGHT (ADS) VERSUS HIPFIRE

There are two ways to discharge your weapon: aiming down the sight or firing from the hip. ADS greatly improves the accuracy of your shots, while hipfire is much quicker. It is best to limit the latter to close combat, where accuracy is not as important. Shotguns against a nearby enemy work great when fired from the hip.

GRENADES

During the Atlas mission, you are taught how to use the new Tactical and Lethal Variable Grenades. With these in your arsenal, you have six different grenade types to choose from. The number of grenades you are carrying is shown on the left side of your gun, with Lethal displayed along the top and Tactical displayed just below. Grenades are restocked when you use ammo stashes.

TACTICAL VARIABLE GRENADES

Hold down the Exo Ability D-pad button and then tap the Use button to cycle through the following three grenade types. With your desired type selected, aim your toss, and release the button.

Threat

Threat Grenades reveal the locations of enemies within the area, with all enemies being affected. For times when you are unsure where hostiles are hiding, toss one of these to highlight them all in red. This is great when foes hide behind weak cover, as you can then take them out while they believe they are safe. Note that the Threat effect wears off after a time.

Flash

Toss a Flash Grenade into a group of enemies to blind them, causing them to stagger and not return fire for a few seconds. However, this can also affect you if you are not careful. If you are blinded, you cannot see your surroundings until the effect fades away. There is no lasting damage to you or hostiles.

EMP

The EMP Grenade disables specific technology in the game, destroying nearby drones and shutting down ASTs. An affected AST hunches over for a short while before continuing his pursuit.

LETHAL VARIABLE GRENADES

This grenade is all about destruction. Hold down the Lethal Variable Grenade (RB) button and tap the Use button to cycle through the following types. With your desired type selected, aim your throw, and release the button. Note that these grenades damage both enemies and allies, so be careful where you throw them.

Smart

When you throw a Smart Grenade, it hovers in front of the player for a few seconds before homing in on the target. This may take some getting used to, as it isn't what you target when the explosive is thrown, but the enemy that your reticle rests on when the grenade starts to move toward its intended target. Get used to the timing, since most situations do not allow you to remain idle while the grenade hovers.

Contact

A thrown Contact Grenade explodes as soon as it makes contact with a surface. This area of effect damages both enemies and allies.

Frag

This is your typical Frag Grenade. It explodes a few seconds after you throw it. You can cook Frag Grenades, giving you more control over when and where they explode.

GRENADE DANGER INDICATOR

The enemy soldiers will use grenades of their own against you, so be ready when one drops nearby. A grenade danger indicator appears on screen when one is close, along with an arrow that points in its direction. The icon appears gray and smaller when you are farther away and red and larger when a grenade is closer to you. If possible, move over to the grenade, and hold the Right Bumper to pick it up.

Quickly aim toward a foe, and let it fly to send it back their way. If there isn't time for this, dodge out of the area, or put cover between you and the explosion to avoid getting hit with the blast. The specific icon that appears denotes the type of grenade you're encountering.

USING COVER AND PENETRATION

Taking cover in *Call of Duty®* is essential to survival. Crouch and move behind a wall or object that gives you protection from weapon fire. When you are injured, quickly get behind something so that you can recover health.

Your bullets easily go through softer materials like wood doors and furniture. Higher-powered weapons, such as light machine guns, penetrate through even thicker surfaces. The penetration of your bullets works well with a Threat Grenade.

IMPROVISED DOOR SHIELD

The occasional automobile on the streets of *Call of Duty®: Advanced Warfare* has been left with its doors wide open. Walk up to a door, and press the Use button to rip it off the car. Face in the direction that you wish to block incoming fire, and it automatically shields you. Press the Fire button to throw the shield once you are done with it.

BREACHING

Throughout the Campaign, there are times where you must breach a doorway or some other opening. To start a breach, press the button shown on screen. At that point, you are moved inside automatically as time slows down. This allows you to focus on taking out the enemies inside.

A Mute Charge, used on several occasions in the Campaign, allows you to breach rooms and take out hostiles without alerting nearby enemies. After activating the charge, all player activity is muted. You can only perform this at certain points in the Campaign where an outline of a Mute Charge is shown on the floor. Hold the Use button to plant the charge, and quickly take down anyone without fear of being heard.

EXO SUITS

The newest addition to *Call of Duty®: Advanced Warfare* is the exoskeleton suit. This gives players movement that has not been seen in the series previously. Big double jumps and quick dodges in any direction, along with some great tactical abilities, make this a significant game changer.

Each Campaign mission starts you out in a specific Exo Suit type with a selection of Exo abilities. This guide's Campaign chapter lists your Exo loadout at the start of each level. The next section of this chapter dives deeper into the Exo Suit and its abilities.

TACTICAL EQUIPMENT

In the single-player Campaign, you are given numerous opportunities to operate tactical equipment, including Mute Charges, security cameras, a Mobile Turret, Mobile Drone Shields, a Sniper Drone, and a variety of vehicles such as an SUV, a powerful hovertank, a fighter jet, dive boat, and an AST suit. The Campaign chapter covers each of these, with helpful tips on how to utilize them in the best way.

INTEL

Each mission in the Campaign contains three hidden Intel. Collecting these contributes to an upgrade challenge, two Achievements/ Trophies, and unlocking Audio Logs. Once you have found an Intel in a mission,

you can listen to its corresponding Audio Log from the Campaign menu. Refer to the Campaign chapter for details on how to find all 45 collectibles.

EXO SUITS

Every level in the Campaign involves some kind of Exo Suit that varies in its purpose and equipped abilities. This information is given to the player at the start of each level.

EXO TYPES

Two types of Exo Suits are used through nearly the entire Campaign, Assault and Specialist. The Assault type is equipped with Boost Jump and Sonics abilities, while Specialist comes with Riot Shield and Overdrive. You are also always given the Stim ability or an ability that is necessary to get through the level, such as Grapple or Cloak.

EXO ABILITIES

The following abilities are only available in specific missions. Use them to your advantage, as they can be lifesavers when battles get overwhelming.

BOOST JUMP

First Level Seen: Induction
Controls: Double-tap the Jump button.

This double jump allows players to reach greater heights with their jump.

EXO SLAM

First Level Seen: Induction
Controls: Press the Crouch button in the air.

Jump into the air, and find a target on the ground. Push in his direction, and press the Crouch button to perform a quick slam move that takes the enemy out with a direct hit.

LAND ASSIST

First Level Seen: Induction
Controls: Press Right on the D-pad to activate. Hold the Use button to slow Mitchell's fall.

This Exo ability allows you to slow your fall, minimizing the impact when you reach the bottom. You are limited in the amount that you can use this ability, so conserve its usage until you approach the floor. The Fuel meter that appears next to the weapon represents this supply.

OVERDRIVE

First Level Seen: Atlas
Controls: Press Up on the D-pad to toggle on and off.

This ability slows down time and heightens perception, giving you an easier time targeting the enemies. This consumes battery somewhat quickly, so use it sparingly. Toggle it on for a tough situation, and immediately toggle it off once things become clear again.

RIOT SHIELD

First Level Seen: Atlas

Controls: Press Down on the D-pad to bring up a shield.

Using this ability brings up a shield from your left arm. Weapons are unusable at this time, but you can move around. This consumes battery, so use the shield sparingly. If you find yourself badly hurt without cover to duck behind, bring up the shield to protect yourself. Be careful if you're surrounded, though; the shield only protects in front of you. You are able to melee enemies with the shield out.

CLOAK

First Level Seen: Bio Lab

Controls: Press Right on the D-pad to enable and disable.

Only available in the Bio Lab level, the Cloak makes the player invisible. As you move, the battery runs down fairly quickly. The faster you move, the quicker it depletes. Standing still slowly recoups it, while uncloaking gets it back in just a few seconds. Use this for short periods while sneaking past an enemy or group of foes.

GRAPPLE

First Level Seen: Utopia

Controls: Press the Tactical Variable Grenade button with the grapple icon present.

Used in only three missions, the Grapple allows the player to attach to a ledge from a great distance and pull himself up to it. This only works on ledges that show the grapple icon when aiming that way.

GLOVES

First Level Seen: Traffic

Controls: Hold the Use button next to a climbable wall. Move up the surface with the Left Stick.

These gloves allow the player to scale specific metal walls in the Campaign. When standing next to a climbable surface, a message appears on screen.

SONICS

First Level Seen: Induction

Controls: Press Down on the D-pad.

This ability releases a sonic pulse that stuns enemies as it travels straight ahead. The pulse makes them stagger for a short time, leaving you with a great opportunity to take the hostiles down.

STIM

First Level Seen: Atlas

Controls: Exo Ability D-pad button

With this ability equipped, the player receives a health boost.

EXO UPGRADE SYSTEM

Earn Upgrade Points during a mission by completing four challenges: Kills, Headshot Kills, Grenade Kills, and finding Intel. You then spend these points between missions to improve your Exo Suit.

These challenges award you one point each time you complete one, and they are cumulative. Once you complete one, the next tier of the challenge will begin tracking toward your next Upgrade Point. Note that Grenade and Headshot Kills also count toward the Kill count, so it is good to go for the head any chance you get and use grenades whenever available.

Once you complete a level, an After Action Report displays your progress on the four challenges. Press the Use button to access the upgrades. Upgrades each have two levels. The first level costs one point and two points for the second upgrade. There are 11 upgrades total, so 33 points are required to fully upgrade Mitchell. You can also replay levels to score more Upgrade Points. Some upgrades require another to be purchased first.

The upgrades are listed here, along with their requirements. If no requirement is listed, it is available from the start.

Upgrade	Requirement	Level	Description
Resistance	—	1	Reduce explosion damage by 25%
		2	Reduce explosion damage by 50%
Detection	Resistance	1	Activate grenade detection
		2	Increase threat detection duration
Armor	Resistance	1	Increase health by 10%
		2	Increase health by 25%
Lethal Variable Grenade	—	1	Increase Lethal Variable Grenade capacity by 1
		2	Increase Lethal Variable Grenade capacity by 2
Tactical Variable Grenade	Lethal Variable Grenade	1	Increase Tactical Variable Grenade capacity by 1
		2	Increase Tactical Variable Grenade capacity by 2
Sprint	—	1	Increase sprint time by 50%
		2	Increase sprint time by 100%
Recoil	—	1	Reduce weapon kick by 10%
		2	Reduce weapon kick by 20%
Flinch	Recoil	1	Reduce flinch when shot by 40%
		2	Reduce flinch when shot by 80%
Reload	—	1	Increase reload speed by 25%
		2	Increase reload speed by 50%
Quick Aim	Reload	1	Increase aiming speed by 25%
		2	Increase aiming speed by 50%
Battery	—	1	Increase Exo ability uses by 1
		2	Increase Exo ability uses by 2

SINGLE-PLAYER WALKTHROUGH

INDUCTION

LOCATION Seoul, South Korea   **DATE** July 10, 2054 — 0500 hrs   **MISSION DETAILS** Push the North Korean attackers out of Seoul.

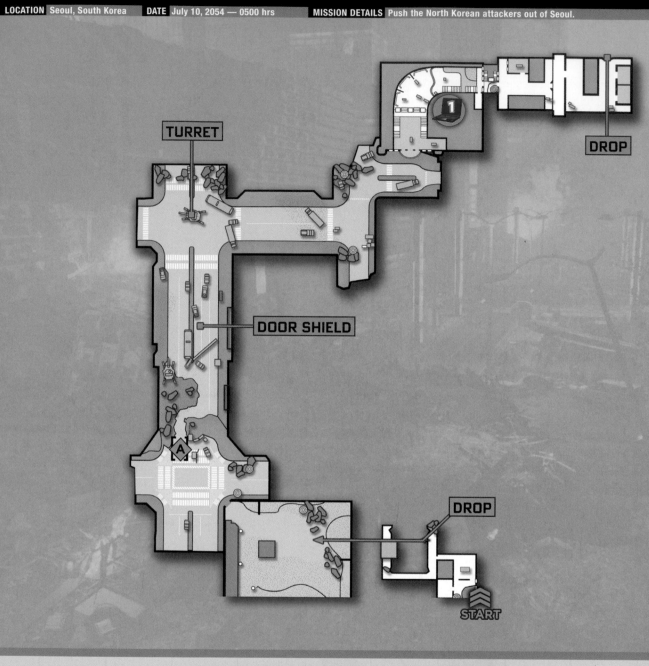

TURRET

DROP

DOOR SHIELD

DROP

A

START

FACTION

U.S. MARINES

SQUAD MEMBERS

Will Irons

Cormack

MISSION OBJECTIVES

◇A Regroup with Demo Team One
◇B Pick up the Demo Charges
◇C Destroy the Havoc Launcher

LOADOUT

PRIMARY

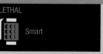

IMR Red Dot Sight

SECONDARY

Atlas 45

GRENADES

LETHAL	TACTICAL
Smart	Threat

EXO ABILITIES

EXO TYPE
ASSAULT

◦ BOOST JUMP
◦ SONICS
◦ LAND ASSIST

"THE ONLY DANGER IS THAT ONE DAY, YOU MAY HAVE TO OPEN YOUR EYES." —*Mitchell*

In *Call of Duty®: Advanced Warfare*, you play as Mitchell, a new recruit of the U.S. Marines. Friend Will Irons, Private Jackson, and Sergeant Cormack join you in a drop pod as you head into war-torn Seoul, South Korea. North Korean forces have invaded the capital, and your squad is called in to help repel the North Korean invasion of Seoul.

The pod takes a hit and the hatch opens prematurely, threatening to pull Jackson to his doom. Rapidly press the Use button to pull the lever and close it back up. Once the vessel comes to a stop on the edge of a busted sky-rise floor, tap the shoulder buttons to release your harness. Then, walk over to the door and press the Melee button to break it open.

 OBJECTIVE

A REGROUP WITH DEMO TEAM ONE

Follow the team into the kitchen ahead, and look down the hall toward the open door. As four enemies enter the room, aim down the sights of your rifle. Keep the gun trained on the doorway until you've eliminated all of them.

IMR ASSAULT RIFLE

You start out equipped with an IMR Assault Rifle, which features built-in 3D printing technology. This means that it is constantly creating another clip of bullets until the weapon reaches its maximum of 540. Therefore, you never completely run out of ammunition. If you begin to run out of ammo, take cover and let the gun produce more.

KNOW YOUR ENEMY

Differences in the U.S. Marines and North Korean troops' equipment make the two sides easy to distinguish. Note that a name appears next to a soldier when he is on your side.

| ALLY | ENEMY | ENEMY |

Just through the door, there is only one way to go: down. Jump off the ledge, and use your Land Assist ability to slow your descent as you approach the ground floor. Exit the building through the entrance ahead.

EXO ABILITY: LAND ASSIST

Press Right on the D-pad to activate Land Assist. This Exo ability allows you to slow your fall, minimizing the impact when you reach the bottom. Hold the Use button as you drop to slow yourself down. You are limited in the amount that you can use this ability, so conserve its usage until you approach the floor. The Fuel meter that appears next to the weapon represents this supply. If you hold the Use button from the start, this empties your supply, and you will take damage when you hit the ground.

Follow your leader into the tent at the intersection to find your next destination. Exit out the other side and follow the trench, pausing just long enough to let the spider tank pass overhead. Once you are back in the open, take cover and eliminate the North Korean soldiers ahead.

As you push onward, take note of the two cars with their doors wide open. When a swarm of drones appears farther down the street, grab one of the doors, and use it to shield yourself from the drones.

IMPROVISED DOOR SHIELD

At certain points throughout the game, you find a car with its doors wide open and a surrounding highlight to signify that you can use it as a shield. Hold the Use button to grab it and move around, keeping it between you and the enemy to block incoming attacks. Once you are finished with the shield, press the Fire button to throw it straight ahead. You can even take out enemies with a well-placed toss.

At the next intersection, move over to the tank, toss the door aside, and enter the turret. Track the drone swarm with the gun, taking down as many as you can while the tank's EMP system reboots. Once the "EMP Ready" message appears, press the button displayed on screen to release the electromagnetic pulse. This instantly shuts down any remaining drones and causes them to fall to the street below.

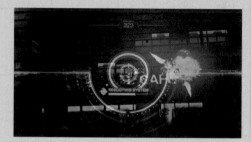

ACHIEVEMENT/TROPHY

NOT ON MY WATCH
Prevent the drone swarm from destroying the walking tank. If you take down the drone swarm with the tank's EMP, you earn this Achievement/Trophy.

Perform a Boost Jump to get over the delivery van just behind the tank as you follow your squad into an open building slightly beyond another intersection. As you ascend the stairs inside, more enemy troops drop in ahead. Use the steps as cover while taking them on, being sure to back away before taking too much damage.

BOOST DODGE

Press in on the Left Stick as you press in the desired direction to quickly move to the side, back, or forward. This makes you a tougher target for your enemy, and the maneuver is also great for clearing away from a grenade. Boosting forward works only in the air, as the same input while on the ground makes you sprint. You can earn the Escape Artist Achievement/Trophy by dodging 20 grenades with the Boost Dodge, so it is a good idea to get in the habit of avoiding grenades with this move during the campaign.

As you take out the first group of enemies, move farther into the room as more adversaries show up along the balconies and the top of another set of stairs. Use a Smart Grenade or two to take your foes down quicker. When you've cleared out the area, run up the steps to a broken window.

SMART GRENADE

Pressing the Right Bumper tosses a Smart Grenade. This explosive hovers in front of you for a short while before homing in on your target. Place your weapon reticle on the enemy that you want to take out.

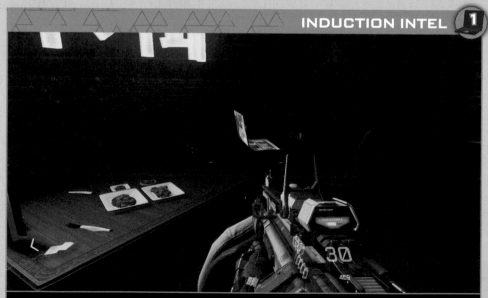

INDUCTION INTEL 1

Once you've dealt with the enemy threat around the steps, move up to the second landing and enter the restaurant on the right. The first Intel rests on the table in the corner. There are three Intel in each campaign level. Collecting them contributes to one of the challenges and unlocks audio logs. Access these recordings by selecting Intel from the Campaign menu.

"NOTHING LIKE BASIC, HUH, MITCHELL?" —*Will Irons*

Activate Land Assist and jump out of the window. Hold the Use button to hover across the gap, landing inside a neighboring building. Follow your squad as they jump into an office building, again using Land Assist to safely descend inside.

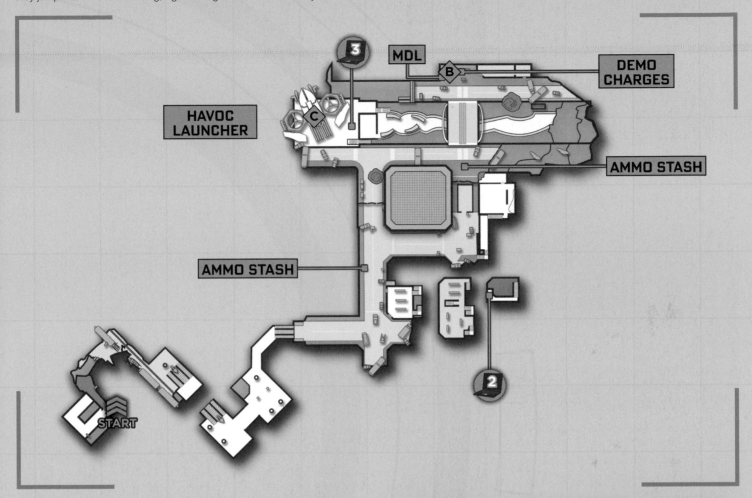

At the other side of the floor, make sure your Land Assist is still activated, and drop off to a lower level. At that point, you receive more information about your target, a Havoc Launcher—including its location and destination.

Follow the squad members over a concrete beam and down another floor. As enemy soldiers and drones enter the subway ahead, take cover at the next concrete barrier. If you have any Smart Grenades available, use them to thin out their numbers. Stay put until you've eliminated them all.

Continue to the far wall, and then follow it to the right before entering the open train car. There is an ammo stash and a Bulldog shotgun before the train. Move ahead until you reach an open door. Toss a Threat Grenade to locate the enemies ahead, and take them out by shooting through their cover.

THREAT GRENADE

Tap the Left Bumper to toss a Threat Grenade. This grenade reveals the location of adversaries within the area, giving them a red glow. No harm is done, but all enemies are affected. This is especially effective when foes are hiding behind weak cover.

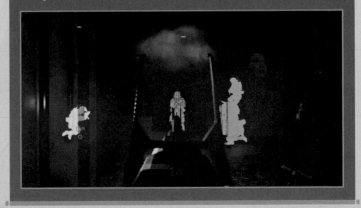

Move up the escalator, proceed through the turnstiles to the left, and approach the gate that blocks the corridor ahead. Hold the Use button to attempt to open it, as ally soldiers drop in. After exchanging pleasantries, follow Cormack up to the street.

"WANTED TO SERVE MY COUNTRY, NOT MY OLD MAN." —*Jackson*

A small group of North Korean soldiers patrols the intersection. Line one up in your crosshairs, and take him down to start the short fight. Stay on the move while your team eliminates the foes, as there isn't much cover. Watch out for additional enemies positioned on the second floor of the far-left corner.

Boost Jump into the second-floor restaurant, and mow down the opposition ensconced inside. As you move into the bar area ahead, be careful; troops drop in under the cover of a Smoke Grenade, and more fight from the balcony across the street.

INDUCTION INTEL 2

Before exiting the bar, climb the stairs at the back of the room and circle around the balcony to find the second Intel lying on the floor.

A technical fires its mounted machine gun on the street below. Use your vantage point to pick off its operator, along with any other enemies you can target, before you hop down next to the truck.

Use the cover on each side of the street as you fight your way toward the next intersection. Be extra mindful of the rocket launcher on the street as well as one in a second-floor window on the right. An ammo stash rests in front of the Japanese Noodle House, so be sure to stock up on ammunition for your weapons and grenades.

AMMO STASH

You can find big ammo crates throughout the campaign levels, so keep an eye out for them and take advantage whenever possible. A bright ammo icon shines from a distance, informing you that you can top off your ammunition there. Walk up to one and hold the Use button to max out the ammo in your weapons and your grenades. No need to worry about your supplies at these locations; let the grenades fly.

Around the corner, another Smoke Grenade reveals more troops. Toss a Threat Grenade in to spot their locations. After clearing the street of the opposition, follow your squad up the stairs ahead. Continue to the third floor, where you can see your target out the far window.

OBJECTIVE

B PICK UP THE DEMO CHARGES

You pull out a pair of binoculars, focusing in first on the target and then on the demo charges needed to complete the task. Once you gain control, spend a little time surveying the area, spotting the enemies who guard the launcher. Use the Left Stick to zoom in and the right to look around.

Canal Fight

Before hopping down to the street, take some time to snipe as many foes as possible. An ammo stash sits just below, so don't worry about using up your grenades. When you drop down, be sure to use Land Assist to soften the fall.

CARMA

Kill an enemy by throwing a car door at him. A vehicle sits on the near side of the bridge with its doors wide open. Grab the door, and shield yourself from enemy fire as you head to the opposite side of the street. Move toward the closest soldier, and throw the projectile at him to score this award. This Achievement/Trophy is not specific to this level; you can earn it during any mission where a car door is available and an enemy patrols nearby.

Be careful as you move across the bridge, as more enemies emerge from the far building. Fight your way over to the demo charges that lie on the ground. Resting on a crate nearby is an MDL grenade launcher, which may come in handy as you finish out the mission.

OBJECTIVE

C DESTROY THE HAVOC LAUNCHER

With the explosives in hand, follow Will Irons down into the canal, where several North Korean soldiers are holed up. As you take them out, a couple drones drop in. Fight from behind cover as

much as possible as you clear out the opposition. Don't forget the troops who fight from the upper level.

Continue behind Will as he takes on the final soldiers on the landing above. Use the concrete barrier at the top of the waterfall to finish them off. Join Will at the launcher, and hand him the charges.

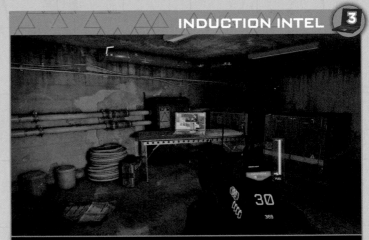

INDUCTION INTEL 3

Before exiting the canal and climbing back up to street level, move through the waterfall to find a hidden room. The third Intel sits on a folding table inside.

EXO UPGRADES

Once you complete a level, an After Action Report displays your progress on the four challenges. For each one completed during the mission, you earn an Upgrade Point. Press the Use button to access your upgrades, and spend the points to improve your Exo. Refer to page 7 in this guide for more information on Exo Upgrades.

SEOUL MATES

You earn this Achievement/Trophy once you complete Induction.

ATLAS

LOCATION Arlington, Virginia and Denver, Colorado, USA **DATE** July 24, 2054 — 0930 hrs **MISSION DETAILS** Train at Atlas Corporation.

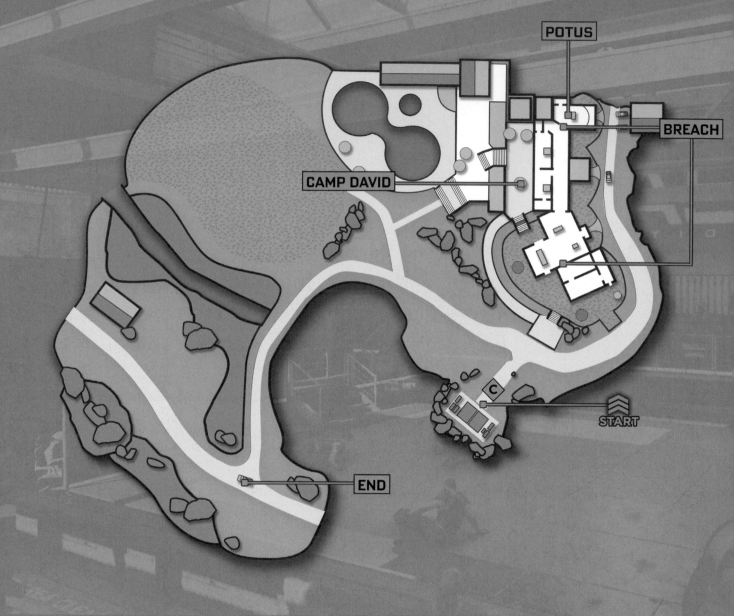

POTUS

BREACH

CAMP DAVID

C

START

END

FACTION

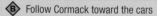

ATLAS

SQUAD MEMBERS

Joker   Gideon

MISSION OBJECTIVES

- Ⓐ Pay Your Respects
- Ⓑ Follow Cormack toward the cars
- Ⓒ Rescue the President
- Ⓓ Follow Gideon
- Ⓔ Complete the Firing Range
- Ⓕ Follow Gideon
- Ⓖ Complete Grenade Training
- Ⓗ Follow Gideon
- Ⓘ Rescue the President

LOADOUT

PRIMARY

Bal-27 Custom

SECONDARY

Atlas 45 Suppressed

EXO TYPE

Specialist

VARIABLE GRENADES

LETHAL	TACTICAL
Smart	Threat
Contact (at grenade range)	Flash (at grenade range)
Frag (at grenade range)	EMP (at grenade range)

EXO ABILITIES

EXO TYPE SPECIALIST

- RIOT SHIELD
- OVERDRIVE
- STIM

A PAY YOUR RESPECTS

The second level starts out at a funeral. When prompted to do so, pay your respects to the deceased. You must be near the casket and press the Action button.

B FOLLOW CORMACK TOWARD THE CARS

Follow Cormack toward the cars as he attempts to console you. Soon, Will's father, Jonathan Irons, offers you an opportunity that you really cannot refuse.

C RESCUE THE PRESIDENT

Next thing you know, you have both arms on a mission to rescue the President at Camp David, Maryland. Move toward the house, and take down the three enemies on the terrace.

KNOW YOUR ENEMY

The Atlas soldiers wear black under their Exo Suits. This is a big contrast from the camouflage that the terrorists have on.

ALLY — ENEMY

EXO ABILITY: RIOT SHIELD

In several missions, your Exo Suit is equipped with a Riot Shield. Hold Down on the D-pad to bring it up. This consumes battery, so use the shield sparingly. If you find yourself badly hurt without cover to duck behind, bring up the shield to protect yourself. Be careful if you're surrounded, though; the shield only protects in front of you.

Enter the house through the kitchen on the right, and meet up with Joker at the next door. When he opens the door, toss a Threat Grenade inside to reveal the terrorist locations, and quickly take them down.

Move down the hallway to the corner, and plant a Mute Charge just in front of the right door.

BULLET PENETRATION

Your bullets easily go through softer materials like this wood door and furniture. Higher-powered weapons, such as light machine guns, penetrate through even thicker surfaces. Take advantage of this ability when enemies hide behind cover, as it's especially handy when you use a Threat Grenade.

MUTE CHARGE

A Mute Charge allows you to breach rooms and take out hostiles without alerting nearby enemies. After activating the charge, all of your activity is muted. You can only perform this action at certain points in the campaign where an outline of a Mute Charge displays on the floor. Hold the Use button to plant the charge, and quickly take down anyone without fear of being heard.

Four enemies are located inside: one rests in the chair on the right, another stands in the middle of the room, the third stands next to the President on the left, and a fourth emerges from the bathroom seconds later. Quickly take them down before escorting POTUS out of the house.

"MULTIPLE HOSTILES BY THE POOL. DROP 'EM."

—Joker

When you reach the living room, you spot drones on the back patio. Pause until they are gone, and then continue outside. Several foes occupy the patio, near the house and next to the pool. Use the short wall as cover and take them out.

INCOMING GRENADES

The enemy soldiers can use their own grenades against you, so be ready when one drops nearby. A grenade danger indicator appears on screen when one is close, along with an arrow that points in its direction. The icon appears gray when you are farther away and red when a grenade is closer to you. If possible, move over to the grenade and hold the Right Bumper to pick it up. Quickly aim toward a foe, and let it fly to send it back their way. If there isn't time for this, dodge out of the area or put cover between you and the explosion to avoid getting hit with the blast. The specific icon that appears denotes the type of grenade you're encountering.

As you move down to the pool and then to the left path, clear out any remaining terrorists. When prompted to do so, hold the Crouch button to go prone and move into the foliage so the enemy patrol doesn't spot you.

Once they move past, follow Joker down the sidewalk on the left until you run into more enemy forces. Fight them off until your vehicle arrives. When it arrives, the enemy will be covered in smoke. You can use the Threat grenade to detect them. Run over to the passenger side and open the door.

OBJECTIVE

D FOLLOW GIDEON

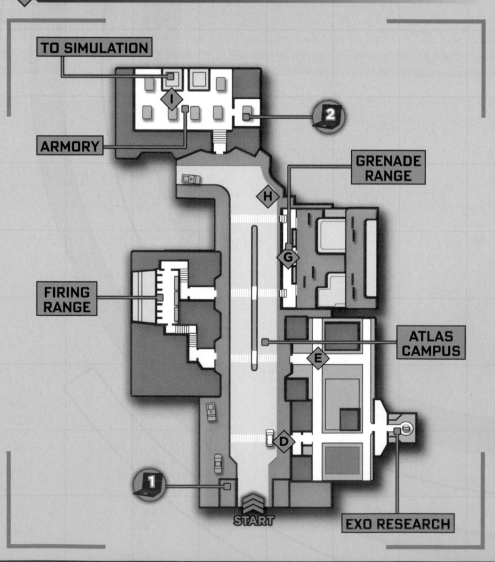

Gideon instructs you to enter the vehicle. Climb into the back seat to take a tour of Atlas Corporation's Tactical Training Facility building. Many of the technologies you see around the campus become available later in the campaign. After exiting the vehicle, follow Gideon into the building on the right. He explains your Exo Suit as you follow him through the facility. Enter Exo Research ahead to get fixed up. Follow the on-screen prompts to complete the tests before returning to Gideon, who waits in the main room.

"TECHNICIAN'S WAITING FOR YOU. GET THAT THING FIXED UP, AND MEET ME OUT HERE." —Gideon

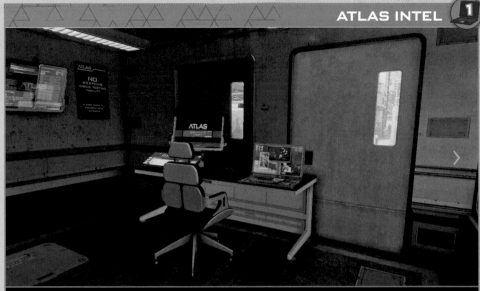

ATLAS INTEL 1

When the vehicle stops, turn around and enter the small building to the right of the gate. The first Intel sits on a desk inside.

OBJECTIVE
E COMPLETE THE FIRING RANGE

Follow Gideon back outside and into the Holographic Range. A selection of assault rifles sits on a couple of racks in the back of the room. If you prefer a specific sight, grab a rifle that has it equipped. Move over to one of the shooting booths. Hold the prompted button to begin target training.

Green and red targets appear at various points in the hologram, some stationary and some moving. Shoot the red hostiles while avoiding the green innocent bystanders. Each target is split into five parts: the head, body, two arms, and legs. Hitting the head awards maximum points, while appendages score the lowest. Hit an innocent target, and the same score is subtracted from your total.

TARGET SECTION	SCORE
Head	100
Body	75
Arms	50
Legs	50

EXO ABILITY: OVERDRIVE

Your Exo Suit is equipped with the Overdrive ability, which can make certain firefight situations easier to handle. Press Up to activate it, and everything will slow down, giving you an easier time targeting the enemies. This consumes battery somewhat quickly, so use it sparingly. Toggle it on for a tough situation, and immediately toggle it off once things become open again.

As the test advances, the situations become tougher, with both red and green targets moving across the stage. Use your Overdrive when they are next to each other, attempting to focus on headshots when possible. When you complete the test, you receive a rating, and your score is displayed on a leaderboard on the back wall.

ACHIEVEMENT/TROPHY

DEADEYE

Score "Excellent" in the shooting range. To earn the Deadeye Achievement/Trophy, you must score at least 2000 at the firing range. You can restart the firing range as long as you pause before it is over and select "Restart Checkpoint." Otherwise, you must play back up to that point.

OBJECTIVE

F FOLLOW GIDEON

Follow Gideon back outside and across the street to the grenade range.

OBJECTIVE

G COMPLETE GRENADE TRAINING

Gideon instructs you to activate the console. Press the Use button to get things started at your second test. The grenade range runs you through use of your Threat, EMP, and Smart Grenades. First, you are shown how each of these is used. Toss a Threat Grenade into the range to highlight two enemies behind the upper wall. Take them out with your assault rifle. Next, three drones fly into the area. Select the EMP Grenade, and toss it toward them. This disables the foes, causing them to drop and explode as they make contact with the ground or building. Lastly, a target moves from side to side along the roof. Toss a Smart Grenade its way while keeping your weapon's reticle on the moving board. The explosive homes in on it and takes it out. Now you are ready to try your hand at the training session.

TACTICAL AND LETHAL GRENADES

With your Atlas loadout, you are equipped with Tactical and Lethal Grenades, giving you access to six types in all. The Tactical Grenades can be used as a Threat, Flash, or EMP Grenade. Lethal can be a Smart, Contact, or Frag Grenade. Hold down the Left Bumper and tap the Use button to cycle through the Tactical Grenades. Holding down the Right Bumper allows you to cycle through the Lethal Grenades. You are equipped with five of each type, as represented by the display on the left side of your gun. The upper row shows your Lethal Grenades, while the bottom denotes the number of Tactical Grenades left. For more information about each type, check out the Basics section of this guide.

Enemies, drones, and moving targets soon show up around the range. Use the three types of grenades as you just learned to take out as many of the "targets" as possible. Be sure to shoot the enemies when they appear from the Threat Grenade. Also, when using a Smart Grenade, remember that it targets the enemy that your weapon's reticle is pointed at as the foe begins to move that way. While the grenade hovers in front of you, it doesn't matter what you are doing. Just be sure to move the reticle on top of your target when it heads away from you.

If you run out of grenades, step up to the console to restock. Each "kill" scores 100 points. Once you finish the training, the leaderboard to the left displays your score.

ACHIEVEMENT/TROPHY

GRENADIER

Score "Excellent" in the grenade range. You earn this award by scoring at least 1700.

THIRD TEST RANGE

There is a third test range for controlling the remote drone. Gideon doesn't point it out, so it is more of a discovery for attentive players than a mission objective. It is on your right after you exit the grenade range. The test is to control a drone for a set amount of time and destroy boxes placed throughout the test area.

OBJECTIVE

H FOLLOW GIDEON

Follow Gideon into the armory on the left, where a wide selection of weapons is available. There are assault rifles, shotguns, handguns, and sniper rifles, so select the ones that you want to use. Your next test is to run the "rescue the President" simulation again, but this time, things are a tad tougher. Gideon puts the simulation into assault mode and takes point himself.

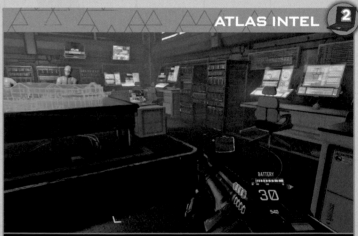

ATLAS INTEL 2

Before hopping into the elevator, enter the computer room to the right of the gun racks. The second Intel rests on the small cabinet, just right of the table.

OBJECTIVE

I RESCUE THE PRESIDENT

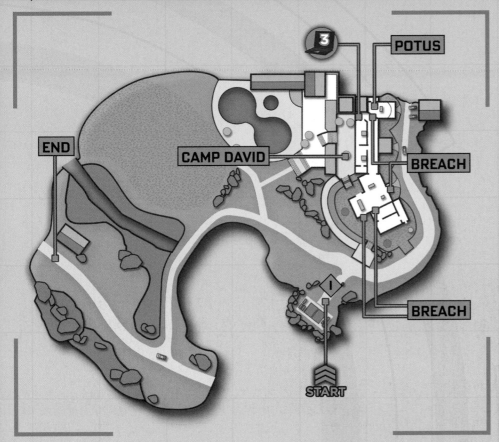

END

3

POTUS

CAMP DAVID

BREACH

BREACH

I

START

Once you have chosen your weapons, step into the elevator in the far corner (the left elevator that Gideon is not in), and ride it up to the simulation. This time, several enemies are standing on and around the terrace. Use Overdrive to give yourself time to pick off as many as you can before they assault your position.

Once you've cleared out the foes, you must breach the house. This time, there are three doors to choose from. The leftmost doors put you in the dining area, with a flanking position on most of the terrorists. The kitchen offers the same breach point as before, allowing you to fight from the doorway. The main door on the right side of the house places you directly in front of the foes, ready to be torn apart.

Once you've cleared out the living room, fight your way through the hallway, and enter the bedrooms on the left. More enemies occupy these rooms; take them out before returning to the hall.

ATLAS INTEL 3

Before breaching the room with the President, enter the second bedroom on the left side of the hallway, and go into the bathroom. Find the final Intel on the vanity.

Press the Melee button to breach the media room, and take out the three terrorists who hold the President captive. Return to the living room as drones enter the dining area. Toss an EMP Grenade to take them out before you exit out the back door.

Twenty enemies occupy the patio area near the pool, but this time, you have a drone to aid in their removal. Press Left to deploy the drone, and mow down the terrorists who occupy the area. Move out toward the pool to reach a van that sits at the end of the path.

DRONE CONTROL

Use the Left Stick to move the drone around and the Right Stick to aim the reticle. Hold the Aim button to zoom in, and fire the turret with the Fire button. Use the bumpers to move the gun up and down. The top of your HUD lists the number of enemies in the area.

Once the Threats Detected number reaches zero, move down to the pool, and follow the path out to the exfil vehicle. Open the door to get the President inside. Your extraction point is farther down the street, though.

Enemy soldiers and drones fill the street, firing from all angles. Use Smart Grenades to thin out the numbers, and toss an EMP Grenade to knock the drones out of the air. Use the Riot Shield when needed to recover your health. Once the aircraft lands ahead, run over to it to end the mission.

ACHIEVEMENT/TROPHY

WELCOME TO ATLAS

You earn this Achievement/Trophy after you complete the Atlas mission.

TRAFFIC

LOCATION Lagos, Nigeria   **DATE** March 7, 2055 — 0745 hrs   **MISSION DETAILS** Rescue the Nigerian Prime Minister.

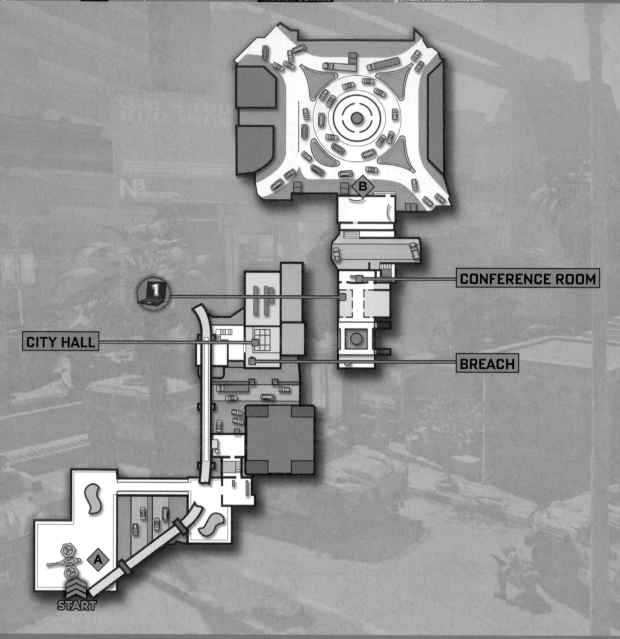

B

CONFERENCE ROOM

1

CITY HALL

BREACH

A

START

FACTION

ATLAS

SQUAD MEMBERS

Gideon

Joker

Captain Ajani

MISSION OBJECTIVES

- **A** Rescue the Prime Minister
- **B** Stop the KVA Hostage Truck
- **C** Rescue the Technologist

LOADOUT

PRIMARY

ASM1 Hybrid Sight

SECONDARY

Tac-19

EXO TYPE

Specialist

VARIABLE GRENADES

LETHAL	TACTICAL
Smart	Threat
Contact	Flash
Frag	EMP

EXO ABILITIES

EXO TYPE
SPECIALIST

- RIOT SHIELD
- OVERDRIVE
- MAG GLOVES

"TRY NOT TO GET US KILLED OUT THERE, EH, ROOKIE?"
—Gideon

Activate the Fly Drone, and it automatically enters City Hall, canvassing the building for KVA terrorists. You can pan the camera left and right with the Right Stick as the drone flies through the building. It ends up at the conference room, where enemies are holding the Prime Minister hostage. Once you gain control, use the Left Stick to move the Fly Drone around. Circle it around the KVA leader as the scene plays out.

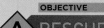

OBJECTIVE

A RESCUE THE PRIME MINISTER

"THEY'LL KILL HIM ANYWAY. WE'LL GET HIM OUT OF THERE." *—Gideon*

Upon witnessing the fallout of the conversation, Gideon decides it is time to rescue the Prime Minister. Two weapons are available for exchange in the starting location: the SN6 Red Dot Sight and the Bal-27 Hybrid Sight. Follow the team into an apartment complex, turn left, and take the stairs up to a roof access. Knock down the door to find yourself on a rooftop across the street from City Hall.

Hop onto the left platform, and follow Gideon until he stops. Leap across the small building below, and approach the objective marker on the side of City Hall. Hold the Use button to attach to the wall with your gloves, move around the window, and continue to the rooftop above.

To the right is a breach point above the meeting room where the Fly Drone spotted the terrorists. Plant a Mute Charge before Gideon sets off a special cutter that drops you inside. As you fall, take out the enemy straight ahead while your squad eliminates the rest.

KNOW YOUR ENEMY

You fight alongside his Atlas comrades in their black and gray gear. A member of the Nigerian Army fights alongside your squad in his green fatigues. This mission's enemies are members of the KVA terrorist group. They are outfitted in less formal attire, such as jeans and a camouflage top.

| ALLY | ALLY | ENEMY | ENEMY |

TRAFFIC INTEL 1

After breaching City Hall, move through the left door and enter the office ahead. Just past the copier, the first Intel sits on the corner desk.

Follow the others out of the room, and approach the Lagos City Hall insignia on the far wall. Plant the Harmonic Device just to the left. This allows you to see silhouettes of people and objects on the other side. Tag the four terrorists in the conference room by placing the reticle on each one to highlight them, and then pressing the Fire button. Targets are highlighted green when you hover over them and they highlight red when you tag them.

There are two terrorists on this side of the table and another two on the other side. The targeted person's heart rate is displayed on screen. Innocent bystanders have a quick pulse in the 150s, while the terrorists are calmer at around 90 bpm. Studs in the wall interfere with the process, so be sure you keep the reticle between the beams. If you take too long, a hostage is killed, so be quick. Once you have tagged all four enemies, press the Use button to lock in the targets and fire at one by pressing the Fire trigger. The rest of your squad eliminates the others.

Enter the conference room, and free the Prime Minster from his restraints by pressing the Use button.

OBJECTIVE

 B STOP THE KVA HOSTAGE TRUCK

Traffic Circle Fight

ENEMIES DROP IN

RPG

ENTER

"WE HAVE A TRAFFIC CAM FEED ON A WHITE BOX TRUCK..." —*Command*

Exit the room out the side door, and descend the stairwell until you are back outside. Cut through the lobby of the building next door, and enter the busy roundabout ahead just as an enemy starts to cause havoc with his rocket launcher.

Duck behind the short wall, and take down the enemy who stands atop the far bus. Adversaries surround much of the circle, and more drop in from the road above. Overdrive allows you to slow things down a bit, but watch your battery. The Riot Shield can be a bigger help if you take too much damage. Stay on the move. Once you've reduced the threat a bit, dodge in and out of the cars as you eliminate the remaining foes.

Once the roundabout is void of the opposition, follow the team into the Famolue Shopping Centre, ducking behind the fence on the left when you spot an opening. More terrorists occupy the next intersection. The left building offers some cover as you clear out the area. Watch out for the terrorists on the balconies, as they have the better angle on your squad.

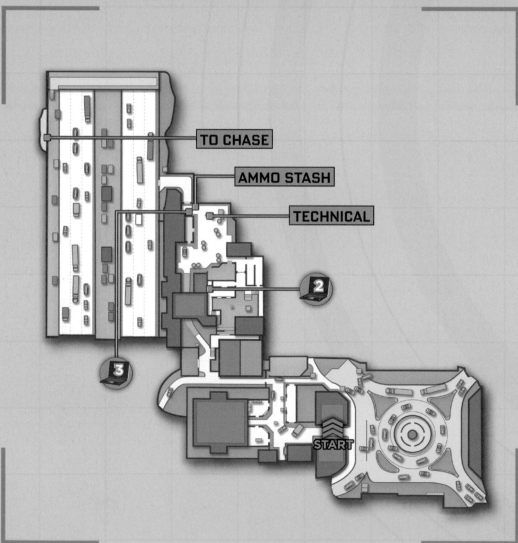

TO CHASE

AMMO STASH

TECHNICAL

2

3

START

"ONCOMING! HOOK RIGHT! HOOK RIGHT!" —*Gideon*

TAC-19 SHOTGUN

If you haven't swapped out your secondary weapon, you are still wielding the Tac-19. This is a very powerful shotgun that is great for close combat. It isn't very effective in these medium- to long-range gunfights, but pull it out as you move between locations and cut through buildings. It deals a quick death to anyone who gets in your way.

Follow your group to a gate ahead as Joker opens the way for you. As you reach the next intersection, a technical shows up. Quickly turn right and run up the steps to avoid its gunfire. More enemies pour out from the upper floor ahead, so take cover. Pick off as many of the hostiles from your current location as you can before hopping down into the courtyard.

Enter the far building, next to the technical, and take out the soldier in the back of the truck, along with any remaining enemies. Rejoin your team who wait at the next gate.

TRAFFIC INTEL 2

Once you have defeated the enemies around the courtyard, take the left stairs, and follow the balcony into a break room. Find the second Intel lying on the floor in front of the vending machines.

Take out any remaining foes as you enter the room in the far corner. Exit out the other side, where you come face-to-face with the technical. Quickly duck behind the left building until it passes.

The armored turret sits on the far side of another open area. You must flank its operator and take him out before he does too much damage. Duck into the left building and take out any enemies that you can get to from the relative safety inside. Continue around the perimeter and kill any remaining foes that get in your way. Be careful, though; innocent bystanders also populate the area.

TRAFFIC INTEL 3

With the area clear of opposition, search behind the pile of crates in the far corner for the last Intel.

"GET ACROSS THE STREET." —*Gideon*

Restock your weapons at the ammo stash, and then use your gloves to climb over the closed gate. Around the next corner, you reach a busy divided road with KVA enemies positioned in the median. Use the planters for cover as you pick them off from your side of the street. Be careful that you do not shoot the civilian vehicles as they pass by.

Cross the first street to the middle area, as more enemies show up on the far side, including two Dobermans. Use the planters and barricades for cover as you eliminate the remaining threat. Continue to the far side of the highway. Watch out, as a final foe may still remain to the right.

ACHIEVEMENT/TROPHY

LOOK BOTH WAYS

Kill all the KVA in the traffic section without shooting a civilian vehicle. Cut through the traffic before you dispatch the KVA terrorists. Take cover on the left side at the median and the far side. Using the single-shot assault rifle MK-14 is a good option. It has the range to reach across the street.

At the chain-link fence, Gideon creates an opening, so climb onto the wall. As a bus drives by, jump onto its roof when prompted.

KVA SUVs continually pull alongside the bus, attempting to keep you away from the box truck. Jump over to another bus that drives in the center lane, and concentrate gunfire at the enemies.

Vault over to a third bus when it appears next to you. As you hold onto the side of the vehicle, use your handgun to take out the two foes behind an armored truck. From there, on-screen prompts get you back on the bus.

A helicopter shows up just ahead. Fire at the chopper as you hop onto another bus. Once you've downed the chopper, continue on to another bus before moving onto your target vehicle. Be ready with a press of the Use button, and then take out the two terrorists inside with your handgun.

OBJECTIVE

C RESCUE THE TECHNOLOGIST

Immediately, move toward the box truck and open the back when prompted. Follow Gideon to complete the mission.

ACHIEVEMENT/TROPHY

LIFE IN THE FAST LANE

You earn this Achievement/Trophy after you complete Traffic.

FISSION

LOCATION Seattle, Washington, USA   **DATE** April 28, 2055 — 1520 hrs   **MISSION DETAILS** Stop an attack on a U.S. nuclear power plant.

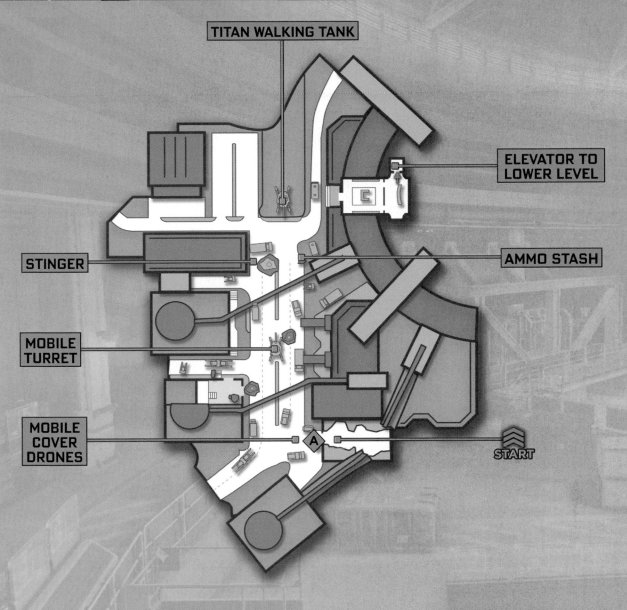

TITAN WALKING TANK

ELEVATOR TO LOWER LEVEL

STINGER

AMMO STASH

MOBILE TURRET

MOBILE COVER DRONES

A

START

FACTION

ATLAS

SQUAD MEMBERS

Gideon   Joker

MISSION OBJECTIVES

Ⓐ Shut down the Reactor

Ⓑ Escape the Power Plant

LOADOUT

PRIMARY

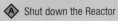

Bal-27 Custom

SECONDARY

EM1 Red Dot Sight

EXO TYPE

Assault

VARIABLE GRENADES

LETHAL		TACTICAL	
Smart Contact Frag		Threat Flash EMP	

EXO ABILITIES

EXO TYPE **ASSAULT**

BOOST JUMP
SONICS
STIM

> "THERE'S AN OLD MILITARY SAYING: YOU TREAT YOUR MEN LIKE YOU WOULD YOUR OWN BELOVED SONS, AND THEY'LL FOLLOW YOU INTO THE DEEPEST VALLEY."
> —Jonathan Irons

OBJECTIVE

A SHUT DOWN THE REACTOR

As you approach the landing zone, KVA terrorists fire from the rooftops below. Eliminate the enemies, and when prompted, hold the Use button to grab your zip line. Aim at the ground, and fire to join the fight already in progress. Note that when aiming the zip line, you cannot fire it if the circle is red.

EM1

Your secondary weapon slot holds the EM1 with Red Dot Sight. This is a directed energy weapon, which fires a constant beam until it overheats. A meter on the back of the gun shows how close you are to this point. Ease up on the trigger, and the gun regenerates. You have an unlimited supply of ammunition and never require a reload. However, if you let the weapon overheat, you must wait for its cool-down period.

> "ALPHA, WE HAVE BOOTS ON THE GROUND. COMING IN AT YOUR THREE O'CLOCK."
> —Gideon

Team Alpha is already engaged with the enemy, so move out and help with the fight. There are a couple pieces of equipment that can aid in the battle, but neither is forced on you. You decide how you handle the encounter, though you can earn two Achievements/Trophies if you follow this guide's walkthrough.

Link up to one of the Mobile Cover Drones at the start of the area, and move toward the KVA terrorists. Whenever you spot an enemy, lower the shield on the drone, and take him out.

MOBILE COVER DRONE

Step up to one of these shields, and hold the Use button to link up to it. It stays in front of you wherever you go until you unlink it in the same manner. The shield acts as an enhancer, highlighting enemies behind cover in red. Aiming at an adversary automatically lowers the shield. Use this mobile cover to absorb the enemy's weapon fire, only letting the shield down to take them out.

ACHIEVEMENT/TROPHY

RIOT CONTROL

Kill 20 enemies while linked to the Mobile Cover Drone. Sweep from side to side as you slowly progress forward to take out this many foes.

Two MD Turrets move down the street alongside you. When you hear that one of the operators is down, move over to the left one and climb inside. Take down the KVA soldiers who litter each side of the area. As you move forward, knock down the helicopter that hovers ahead. Eventually, the terrorists take out your turret. Exit the turret, and find cover on the left side of the road.

MD TURRET

Hold the Use button to climb into a MD Turret. The Analog Sticks let you move and look around, just as always. Holding the Use button while inside a turret allows you to exit. The Fire button shoots the turret, while the Frag Grenade button sends the missiles. There are four missiles represented by the four icons along the bottom of your HUD. These gray out when unavailable. Hold down the Frag Grenade button while targeting enemies to lock on to up to four targets. Releasing the button fires the missiles.

FIRE AND FORGET

Kill 10 enemies with the Mobile MD Turret missiles. Use the missiles whenever available for the greatest effect.

The tank has a trophy system, which knocks some of your projectiles out of the air. Keep firing rockets at the Titan until it finally falls. You can take the Stinger with you if you want, but it may not be as effective inside the power plant. Restock your weapons if needed, and follow your team into the reactor building on the right.

KNOW YOUR ENEMY

Your allies from Atlas and the enemies of KVA wear outfits that are very similar to the previous mission.

ALLY

ENEMY

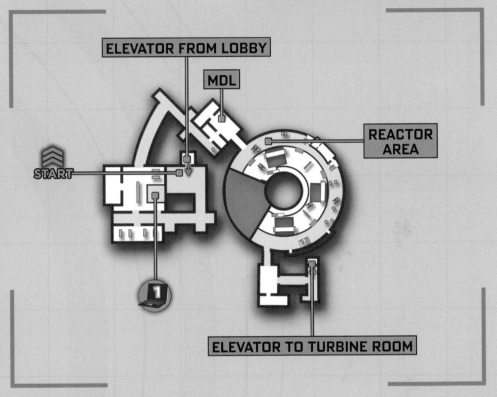

ELEVATOR FROM LOBBY

MDL

START

REACTOR AREA

1

ELEVATOR TO TURBINE ROOM

"COPY THAT, BRAVO. WE'VE GOT EYES ON A LAUNCHER NEAR YOUR POSITION." —Command

An enemy Titan tank rolls in just ahead. Your current weapons have little effect on it, but you spot a Stinger rocket launcher just ahead. Grab the heavy weapon that lies on the left side of the street, just before a white van. Fire the remaining rockets at the tank before moving to an ammo stash on the opposite side of the road.

STINGER M7 ROCKET LAUNCHER

The Stinger M7 rocket launcher fires four rockets at a time. Aiming the weapon brings up a full-screen display that allows you to lock on up to four targets. White icons represent the targeting process. If you quickly fire the gun, the projectiles fly straight ahead, hitting whatever gets in their way.

Once the elevator is open, step inside to slide into the basement. Turn right until you enter a laboratory. Exit out the opposite side, take another right at the junction, and then move through a prep area until you reach a short tunnel.

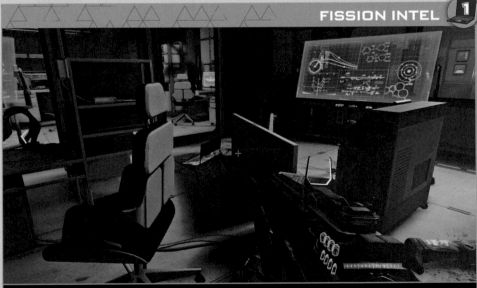

FISSION INTEL 1

Inside the basement of the reactor building, enter the first room on the right, and search behind the overturned table to find the first Intel.

If you want to swap out one of your weapons, you can grab the MDL on the ground; it's a powerful and versatile grenade launcher. Once Carter gets the security door open, step into the reactor area.

Reactor Area Fight

ENTER

ACHIEVEMENT/TROPHY

GENIUS

Kill four enemies with a single Smart Grenade. There is a great opportunity here to get this Achievement/Trophy. Not long after you enter the room, four adversaries fight from a platform just to the left. Toss a Smart Grenade their way to collect the award. But time your throw carefully, as the terrorists may disperse after a while.

Enemies are abundant in this long room, positioned on the main floor as well as on the right walkway and left balcony. Take your time as you move through the area, using Smart Grenades on the small groups. When drones pop up farther inside, use EMP Grenades to knock them out of the air.

EXO ABILITY: SONICS

Your Exo Suit is equipped with the Sonics ability, which releases a sonic pulse that stuns enemies as it travels straight ahead. This area is a great place to test this out. As you meet up with a group of foes, press Down on the D-pad. The pulse makes them stagger for a short time, leaving you with a great opportunity to take them down.

There are all kinds of cover and hiding spots that offer up recovery opportunities. Continue fighting your way around the room until you reach an exit on the outside wall.

Follow your team to the left until you reach another elevator. Access the console, selecting Level B1 to reach the turbine room. As you ascend to the higher floor, your team deploys mobile cover.

A lot of enemies occupy the next room. Fortunately, you have access to the Assault Drone used in the previous Atlas mission. Press Left to deploy it. The controls are the same as before. As you fly the entire length of the area, mow down any terrorists you see. Remember that the Right and Left Bumpers allow you to move up and down. Stay on the move to avoid being shot down. When the "Threats Detected" indicator reaches zero or you lose the drone, move out of the elevator. If foes remain, hunt them down.

EXFIL

3

B

CONTROL ROOM

ELEVATOR

TURBINE ROOM

START

2

Threats Detected : 32

Zoom   Shoot

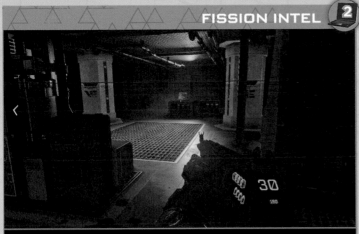

Inside the turbine room, search between the first and second turbines. The Intel rests on some equipment.

When you reach the hangar, just before returning outside, follow the walkway on the right to find the final Intel resting atop a spool.

Climb up to the walkways above, and exit through the door on the opposite side from the elevator. Follow Carter into the next corridor, and enter the control room on the left. Activate the console opposite Gideon as he works to stop the meltdown.

"CORE TEMPERATURE IS CRITICAL! ABORT!" —*Command*

OBJECTIVE

B ESCAPE THE POWER PLANT

Follow the team out of the room and into a hangar.

You encounter resistance as you exit the power plant, so fight back as you run outside. Continue gunning down the opposition as you head toward exfil. If you get badly injured, duck behind a vehicle or debris to recover.

ACHIEVEMENT/TROPHY

RADIOACTIVE
You earn this Achievement/Trophy after you complete Fission.

AFTERMATH

LOCATION Detroit, Michigan, USA   **DATE** August 5, 2059 — 2400 hrs   **MISSION DETAILS** Capture Dr. Pierre Danois.

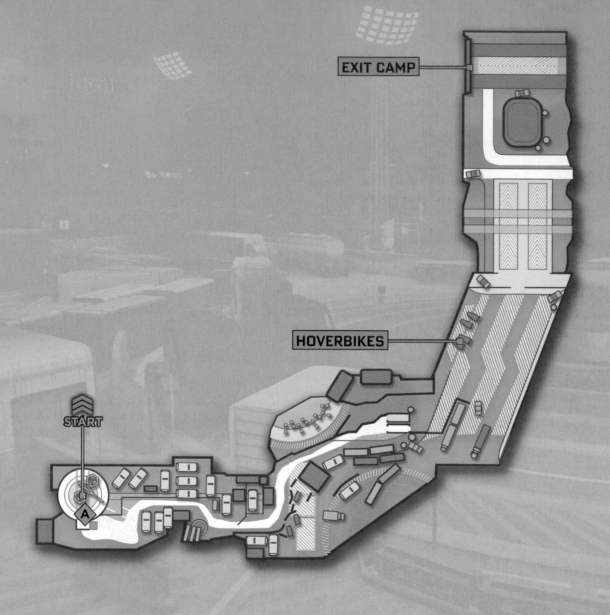

EXIT CAMP

HOVERBIKES

START

A

FACTION

ATLAS

SQUAD MEMBERS

Gideon

Joker

Torres

MISSION OBJECTIVES

- ◇A Follow Gideon
- ◇B Regroup with Gideon
- ◇C Reach the Hospital
- ◇D Capture the Doctor
- ◇E Escape with the Doctor

LOADOUT

PRIMARY

Bal-27 Custom

EXO TYPE

Specialist

VARIABLE GRENADES

LETHAL		TACTICAL	
	Smart		Threat
	Contact		Flash
	Frag		EMP

EXO ABILITIES

EXO TYPE
SPECIALIST

- ○ RIOT SHIELD
- ○ OVERDRIVE
- ○ STIM

"WHO ARE WE? WE'RE THE WAY FORWARD." —*Advertisement*

A FOLLOW GIDEON

After getting dropped off at the Detroit Refugee camp, Gideon gives you a guided tour of how Atlas has been helping citizens rebuild their lives. Along the way, you meet up with Joker and then Torres, who waits near four hoverbikes. Hop onto the closest one, and it starts driving automatically behind Gideon.

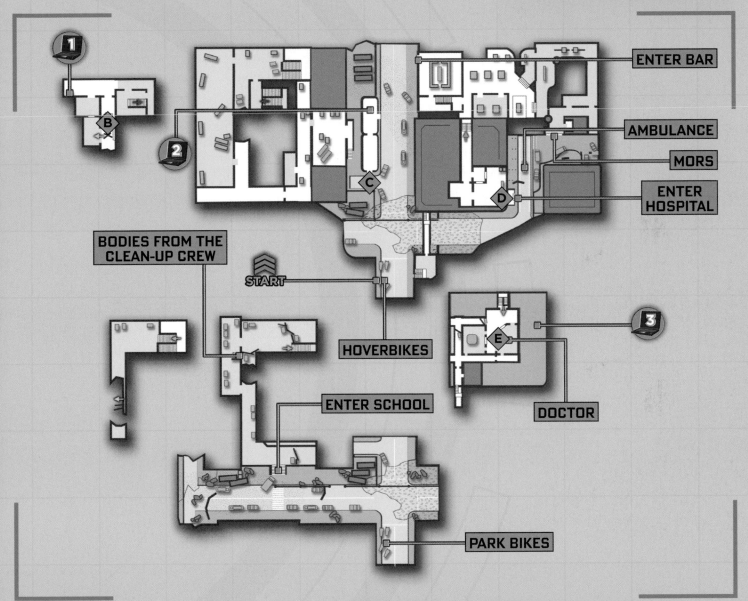

ENTER BAR

AMBULANCE

MORS

ENTER HOSPITAL

BODIES FROM THE CLEAN-UP CREW

START

HOVERBIKES

ENTER SCHOOL

DOCTOR

PARK BIKES

The team hops off their bikes at a parking garage exit, as Joker and Torres split from the group. Enter the school across the street and to the left. Follow Gideon into a classroom. When instructed to do so, open the next door to return to the hallway.

Continue behind your partner up two flights of stairs and onto a very narrow ledge. Sidle your way across until the floor gives way and you end up in the basement.

KNOW YOUR ENEMY

The Atlas team is equipped with the usual black gear and Exo Suits. The opposition is outfitted in hazmat suits ripped off of a clean-up crew, making them easy to distinguish.

ALLY

ENEMY

OBJECTIVE

B REGROUP WITH GIDEON

Now you are alone without a weapon, and the KVA forces are present throughout the school. Wait where you landed until an enemy stops just to your left. Sneak up behind him, and hit him with a melee attack. Grab his gun, and move to the far wall.

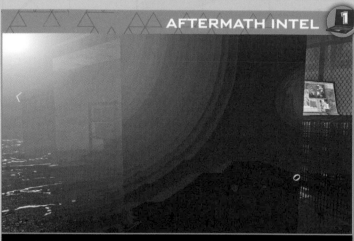

AFTERMATH INTEL 1

Just after falling into the school basement and taking out the first enemy, move to the far wall, turn left, and grab the Intel that sits in the corner.

STEP-BY-STEP BREAKDOWN

1 Quietly, sneak to the right until you find another enemy on the other side of the fence. Quickly take him down.

2 With a second gun now in your possession, move up the stairs to the second floor.

3 Let the enemy pass by the opening, and then trail him through the left door.

4 In the next room, exit through another door on the left, and keep following the corridor.

5 After another left turn, cautiously approach a hole in the wall, where a KVA member grabs ahold.

6 Press the Use button as it appears on screen to take him down.

7 One more adversary patrols the area, so either wait for him to come to you, or just go get him in the hallway.

8 Enter the classroom on the right, climb through the busted window, and hop off the fire escape to meet back up with Gideon.

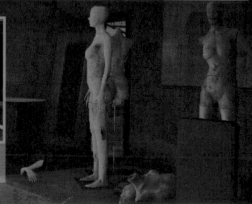

OBJECTIVE

C REACH THE HOSPITAL

"WE NEED TO ACCELERATE OUR TIMELINE. GET READY TO DROP 'EM." —*Gideon*

AFTERMATH INTEL 2

Just after exiting the school and regrouping with Gideon, enter the trailer on the left. Search its far side to find the second Intel sitting on a desk.

Two men in hazmat suits patrol the street just ahead. Pick your target as Gideon takes care of the other. This brings more enemies out of the far building, including two Dobermans.

Be ready for the charging dogs, and then hole up in the trailer as you eliminate anyone you can. Just be ready to take care of incoming grenades or clear out of the room.

Move into the bar across the street to clean up any remaining foes, watching out for another dog that attacks as you approach the door. Lobbing a Threat Grenade through a window helps with assessing the situation inside.

DON'T FORGET THE SHIELDS

Open car doors out on the street offer protection from the enemy gunfire, as does your own Exo Shield. Be ready to use one if you get badly hurt.

Proceeding through the right door and up the stairs puts you and Gideon in a business area. Take cover behind the desks or equipment as enemies pour in from the opposite door. As you eliminate the threat, watch out for enemies in the conference room.

Office Building Fight

ENTER

With the center of the building open, it is easy to get surrounded in the next area. Move into the doorway cautiously. Enemies fight from the far side and the left. However, another opening to the left allows you to get a jump on the nearby foes.

As you move around the floor, more hazmat foes appear on the balcony above, as well through the far door. These foes have sniper weapons, which do more damage. Retreat if things get hairy, using the Exo Shield as cover to avoid dying on the way out. Remember that you also have the Stim ability.

After you clear out the office building, continue around the floor until you reach a busted-out window that overlooks your meeting point with Torres and Joker. A MORS rests against a couch.

MORS SNIPER RIFLE

The MORS is a powerful single-shot rifle with great accuracy. It can dispatch most enemy soldiers in one shot, though its one bullet per clip and low reserve mean that it doesn't last long.

Spend some time sniping the enemies who encroach on your allies' location before you join them on the ground. Move to the alley on the right as Gideon tips an ambulance onto its side.

You can continually push the ambulance down the alley for cover. Make sure to pick off foes first though, as you'll be vulnerable while pushing.

OBJECTIVE

D CAPTURE THE DOCTOR

At the hospital entrance, cut through the lobby, and follow Gideon up a stairwell to the right. When you reach the second floor, watch out, as a Flash Grenade detonates. Take cover at the doorway until you get your bearings.

KVA soldiers flow into the area. Hole up in the stairwell as you take care of them. Find the open door behind the desk and move through the offices, keeping an eye out for more enemies.

AFTERMATH INTEL 3

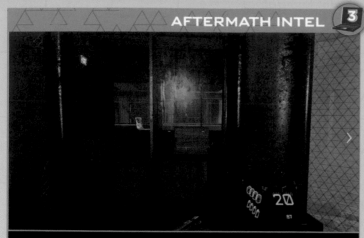

In the hospital, clear out the enemies around the nurses' station, and then move into the room behind the desk. The final Intel sits on a cabinet in the back-left corner.

Down the hallway and to the left, Gideon waits for you to start a breach of an office. Once you open the door, get ready to counter a terrorist's melee attack. Two more foes surround the doctor near the far window. Once you've taken care of them, grab the doctor, who cowers behind the desk.

"YOU HAVE NO IDEA WHAT HE'S CAPABLE OF. YOU ARE ALL DEAD. WE ARE DEAD. DEAD!" —Doctor

OBJECTIVE
E ESCAPE WITH THE DOCTOR

Return to the hallway, and follow Gideon up another stairwell and onto the roof. Run between the tracks and descend more steps, ending up in the corner room of another building. You will encounter a random task force telling you to continue the mission with the doctor.

Another stairwell leads out to the hoverbikes. Climb onto your bike. This time, your bike is not synced to Gideon's, so you must guide your own way back to camp.

HOVERBIKE CONTROL

Move the bike forward and back with the Left Stick, and steer it with the Right Stick. Ease up on the acceleration to make the tight turns, and keep your eyes on the road ahead.

To complete the level, you just need to drive your hoverbike back to camp. Unfortunately, narrow corridors, tight turns, big jumps, rockets, machine gun fire, and oncoming trains get in your way.

After the first checkpoint, enemies fire four rockets from a partially destroyed building. Dodge left, right, left, and right to avoid their blasts.

As you exit the building, line up your jump with the center of the hanging cargo container to avoid missing the tracks on the other side. After you avoid the first train on the tracks, quickly slide to the left to miss the gunfire from the helicopter. Immediately past the next turn, move right and then left to miss more trains. When you see the chopper again, there are two tight left turns, followed by a slalom section before finishing through the camp gate. Slow your speed here to avoid taking any damage.

ACHIEVEMENT/TROPHY

WHEELMAN
Finish the hoverbike sequence without hitting any walls, obstacles, or taking damage. Since you may get left behind, you can't take too long through this hoverbike segment, but you can drive cautiously. Be careful on the turns, and be ready to dodge the rockets and turret. There are a few checkpoints throughout the drive, so if you need to restart, do it as soon as you make a mistake. Otherwise, you may need to restart from the beginning of the mission.

ACHIEVEMENT/TROPHY

MOTOR CITY
You earn this Achievement/Trophy once you complete Aftermath.

MANHUNT

LOCATION Santorini, Greece   **DATE** September 13, 2059 — 1130 hrs   **MISSION DETAILS** Assassinate the leader of the KVA.

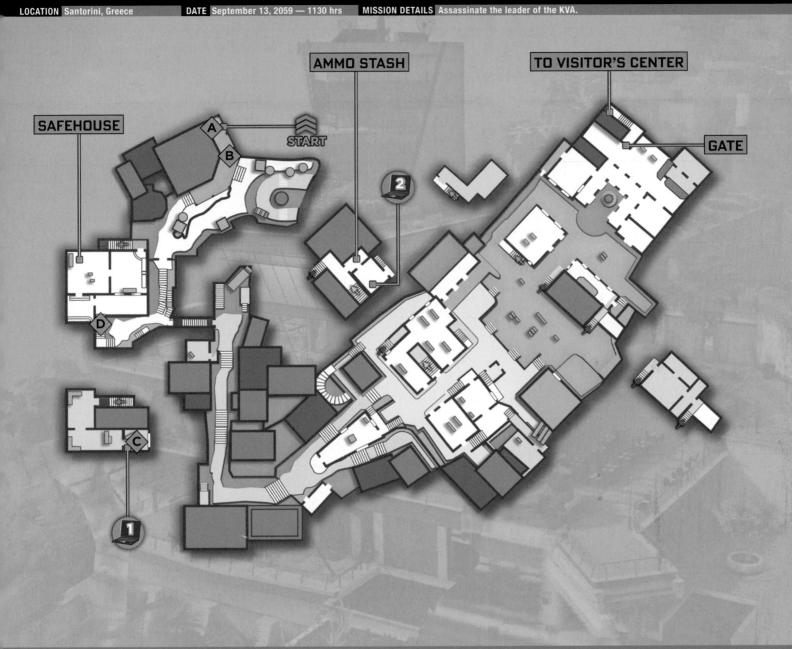

SAFEHOUSE

AMMO STASH

TO VISITOR'S CENTER

START

GATE

FACTION

ATLAS

SQUAD MEMBER

Ilona

MISSION OBJECTIVES

Ⓐ Find the KVA Key Man

Ⓑ Infiltrate the Safe House

Ⓒ Sniper Support with the WASP

Ⓓ Intercept Convoy

Ⓔ Eliminate the KVA Sniper

LOADOUT

PRIMARY

Atlas 45 Custom

EXO TYPE

Specialist

VARIABLE GRENADES

None

EXO ABILITIES

EXO TYPE
SPECIALIST

○ RIOT SHIELD
○ OVERDRIVE
○ STIM

> **"ATLAS IS AN INTERNATIONALLY REGISTERED, PRIVATE COMPANY. WE DON'T NEED CONGRESS."** —Jonathan Irons

OBJECTIVE A — FIND THE KVA KEY MAN

Ilona joins you at a café in Greece, where you search for a key member of the KVA who is reported to be nearby. When you receive the tablet, initiate a scan to bring up a view from the first camera.

Three cameras located around the market give a full view of the area. On Hardened difficulty, you have a minute and a half to find this person. This time changes based on the difficulty you select.

You can scan the area by moving around, and the Grenade buttons switch between the three cameras. The map on the left side of your HUD shows the camera you currently operate and the direction in which it is pointed. Hold the Aim button to zoom in. Zooming in is the only way to get a proper scan, so it is best to look around this way.

When the cameras are zoomed in, possible matches display a light outline around the person. Additionally, a message appears, letting you know that a potential target has been located. At this point, hold the Fire button to perform a scan. Once scanned, the outline turns red to let you know that the target in question is not your man.

Not long after two negative scans, a man in a leather jacket cuts directly through the middle of the market. Scan him to find the KVA member.

OBJECTIVE B — INFILTRATE THE SAFE HOUSE

KNOW YOUR ENEMY

The KVA wear similar attire as previous missions. You fight alongside Ilona through most of the level. Numerous innocent civilians also get in your way, so avoid harming anyone who doesn't carry a weapon.

| ALLY | ALLY | ENEMY |

Sneak up behind the KVA soldier and press the prompted button to snap his neck. You are given the Atlas 45 custom pistol. If you fire a shot here, before entering the safe house, you will fail the mission. Once inside the safe house, wait for Ilona to highlight the enemies. Quietly move behind the nearest one, taking him down with a melee attack. Two more foes in the next room are easy targets as they discuss plans. Let Ilona take care of the fourth foe, and then wait until the last man disconnects from a conversation with his boss before dropping him with a headshot.

Step up to the table, and switch into your Exo Suit before moving out to the balcony.

MANHUNT INTEL 1

After taking over the KVA safe house, step outside on the balcony, and grab the Intel that sits on the wooden bench.

OBJECTIVE

C SNIPER SUPPORT WITH THE WASP

"MITCHELL, I'LL CALL YOUR TARGETS. SHOOT THE TWO ON THE OVERWATCH." —Ilona

1 Take control of the WASP to switch to a view from its camera. Zoom in to the upper floor of the building ahead, and find your primary target standing in the middle of the room.

2 As a delivery truck pulls up below, wait for the two guards to approach, and then pop the rear one when instructed to do so.

3 Next, Ilona wants you to take care of the two men on the overwatch. Zoom in on the far one, and kill him before quickly targeting the near one. Any misses here will alert the KVA to your presence, so fire carefully.

4 Move around to the left side of the building, and focus on the overwatch level. As an enemy attacks Gideon, quickly take him out.

5 Next, kill two of the guards on the lower level as Alpha cleans up anyone remaining.

6 As Alpha moves into position to breach the structure, slide around to the glass side of the atrium. Your team plants a Mute Charge and waits for you to signal when ready. The Mute Charge gives you only 20 seconds on Hardened difficulty, so you must work quickly. Line up a shot on one of enemies on the balcony before starting the timer. Concentrate on the most distant foes from Alpha first. Go from the balcony to the group just below, and then to the guards near the window.

7 Move your reticle up the stairs to the top level to find two enemies together, making it easy to eliminate them in one shot.

8 Continue around to the rear parking lot, where three guards patrol just ahead. Hitting a car sets off an alarm, causing them to investigate. This isn't necessary, though, as you can just take them down with as little as one shot with a well-timed button press.

9 Spin around to your original position so that you have a clean shot on the boss. Once you get the signal, drop him.

SITTING DUCKS

Kill three enemies with one shot of the Sniper Drone (WASP). The best opportunity to get this Achievement/Trophy is when you encounter three guards on the balcony area to the right of the atrium where the Mute charge is placed. Here you can line up a shot and kill them at the same time.

KVA opposition converge on the location from multiple directions. Six enemies fire from rooftops on the right, while a Technical pulls up in the parking lot, with several soldiers around it. Concentrate first on the foes in the parking lot, especially the turret. They represent the biggest threat to Alpha.

Swing around to the other side of the parking area to spot two more Technicals on the ground below. Take them out as a KVA convoy moves out of the area. At this point, enemy drones down the WASP.

D INTERCEPT CONVOY

Follow Ilona to the bottom floor of the safe house, taking out the two enemies who appear outside of the windows. This triggers a chase as the convoy tries to get away.

As you move through the streets and alleys of Greece, always keep an eye out for KVA terrorists ahead. They fire from around corners, behind cover, and on balconies above.

When you reach Kretæs, the real fight begins. To the left, civilians are fleeing in your direction. Carefully take out the foes while avoiding the innocent.

Courtyard Fight
AMMO STASH

"WE'RE CRAWLING WITH KVA. KEEP PUSHING FORWARD..."
—*Gideon*

Multiple lanes offer up a variety of routes to your destination. Along the left side, find the Playful Dolphins Restaurant, and take the inside or outside staircase up to the second floor. From here, you can reload your weapons and take on the opposition in the courtyard ahead.

Use Overdrive to get an edge against the enemy, ducking back inside to recover when needed. Use this vantage point to pick off as many of the enemies as possible before moving back outside.

MANHUNT INTEL 2

Take the stairs up to the bedroom above the Playful Dolphins Restaurant. The second Intel rests on the floor on the other side of the bed.

Continue through the city, watching out for enemies around every corner. As you near the fountain, watch out for the rocket launcher on the balcony. Note that two enemies in particular take extra damage and can inflict increased damage to you when you approach the gate to open it.

Rip off the gate on the other side of the area to reach the Visitor Center. You are then updated on the convoy location and a sniper who has set up in a bell tower.

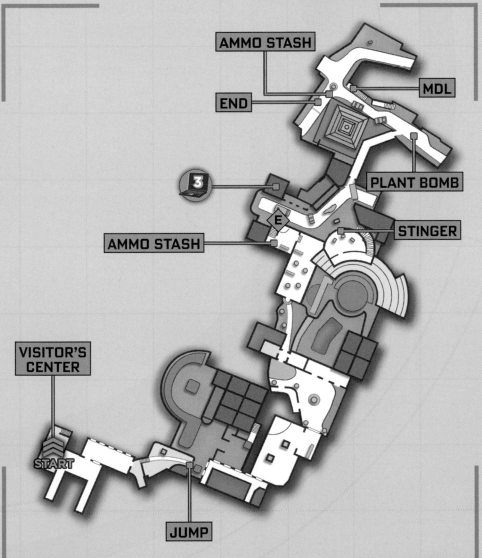

AMMO STASH

END

MDL

PLANT BOMB

3

AMMO STASH

E

STINGER

VISITOR'S
CENTER

START

JUMP

At the exit, you run directly into the sniper's line of sight. At first, you have a smoke screen to cover your movement. Take advantage of this as you jump into the window ahead and sprint down the hall.

Here, you are given a choice. From this location until you reach the ground below, you can sprint and jump over the ledges, or you can shoot at the sniper in the bell tower to suppress his fire.

In the street, drones attack from ahead as you are sheltered from the sniper. Throw an EMP Grenade high above them to knock them out of the air, and then continue through the opening.

Follow Ilona through a restaurant and into the lobby. Reload your weapons at the ammo stash on the bench before exiting back out to the street.

OBJECTIVE

E ELIMINATE THE KVA SNIPER

"WE NEED THAT STINGER. LET'S MOVE." —Ilona

More drones pester you outside, so toss an EMP Grenade to eliminate them before heading to the right.

MANHUNT INTEL 3

After learning about the Stinger and leaving the restaurant, move around the van on the street, and enter the jewelry store. The third Intel sits on the counter on the left side.

Run up the narrow ramp just past the ATM machine. Grab the Stinger M7 that rests next to the right ledge, and fire it at the bell tower. With the sniper out of the way, you can return to intercepting the convoy.

Return to the street, and help Ilona move the delivery truck out of the way. Follow the path and jump into the next street.

Press ▲ to ⟳

Move over to the plant location, and set the charge on the street. When the first truck drives over the explosive, press the Aim button to detonate it.

Grab the MDL on a nearby planter if you want some more explosive firepower. Move down the hill, taking out any KVA soldiers you encounter. Balconies on both sides of the street offer good points to fight from. Don't forget about your Overdrive and Riot Shield Exo abilities.

Once you've cleared out the area, approach the overturned truck next to the far building, and open the door. From there, follow the on-screen prompts to finish the mission.

ACHIEVEMENT/TROPHY

BORN TO DIE

You earn this Achievement/Trophy once you complete Manhunt.

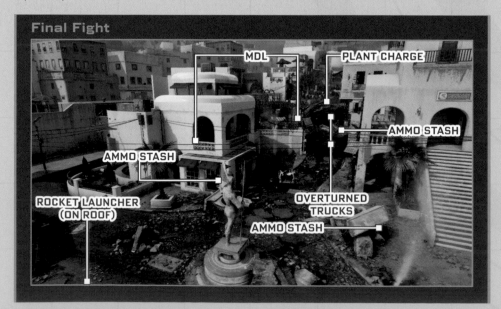

Final Fight

MDL

PLANT CHARGE

AMMO STASH

AMMO STASH

ROCKET LAUNCHER (ON ROOF)

OVERTURNED TRUCKS

AMMO STASH

UTOPIA

LOCATION New Baghdad, IRAQ **DATE** November 9, 2059 — 1630 hrs **MISSION DETAILS** Escape from New Baghdad.

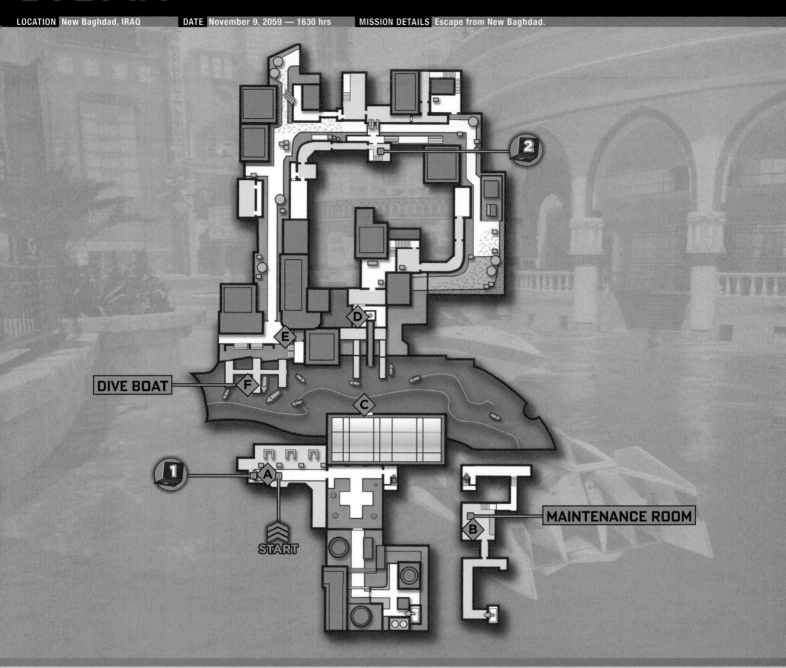

2

D

E

DIVE BOAT **F**

C

1

A

START

MAINTENANCE ROOM

B

FACTION

ATLAS

SQUAD MEMBER

Ilona

MISSION OBJECTIVES

- A Follow Gideon
- B Escape the Atlas Building
- C Follow Ilona
- D Reach the Docks
- E Kill the AST
- F Escape in the Dive Boat
- G Reach the Extraction Point

LOADOUT

PRIMARY

SN6 Red Dot Sight

EXO TYPE

Specialist

VARIABLE GRENADES

LETHAL		TACTICAL	
	Smart Contact Frag	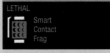	Threat Flash EMP

EXO ABILITIES

EXO TYPE
SPECIALIST

- RIOT SHIELD
- OVERDRIVE
- MAG GLOVES
- GRAPPLE

"HOW DOES IT FEEL TO BE THE HERO OF THE WORLD? DON'T LET IT GO TO YOUR HEAD." —*Gideon*

A FOLLOW GIDEON

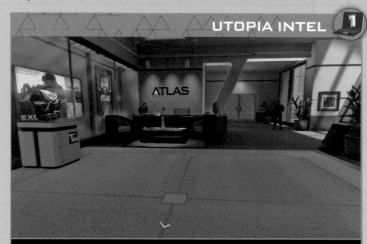

UTOPIA INTEL 1

Before following Gideon, turn around and search the reception desk for the first Intel.

Catch up with Gideon, and walk with him as you report to Ilona in the maintenance room. Watch the scene until an icon appears on the guard's leg, and then press the corresponding button. Quickly aim at the second guard and take him down.

B ESCAPE THE ATLAS BUILDING

Follow Ilona through the hallway, and step into the elevator shaft as soon as the door opens. Use your gloves on the right wall, and climb onto the roof.

Numerous drones are released into the air. As you won't be able to destroy them, sprint directly behind Ilona, following the walkway and sliding under the venting. After mantling pipes and a ledge, you end up in the courtyard. Sprint across the yard, and hop the rail to slide into the canal.

C FOLLOW ILONA

Quickly swim behind Ilona as she cuts through a drainage pipe, surfacing when you see daylight above. If you take too long, you will drown.

Climb the ladder next to your partner, and open the manhole to emerge onto the street above.

D REACH THE DOCKS

To reach the docks, you must cut through the Old Town area. Guards are scattered throughout this location, so stay alert. You can cut through the buildings on either side of the street or run straight down the middle of the road. Stairs indoors and debris outside allow you to switch levels often.

In case you get overwhelmed, you have a Exo Shield available, but try to conserve your battery as you approach the docks.

UTOPIA INTEL 2

After the first left turn in Old Town, look for the round blue sign on the left side of the street. Enter the building, and grab the Intel that sits on a coffee table to the left.

After a few left turns, you approach a narrow alley with several guards occupying the balconies and the street below. The docks are located just past the next straight path.

E KILL THE AST

Docks Fight

DIVE BOAT

A.S.T.

ENTER

The AST has a weak point in the center of its back. You can get to it only if the AST is EMP'd; this takes it down much faster.

ACHIEVEMENT/TROPHY

WHERE ARE YOU GOING?

Stop an AST with an EMP Grenade. You earn this award the first time you bring an AST to its knees with an EMP Grenade.

At the docks, an AST joins several guards. Take cover behind the short wall, and eliminate as many of the troops as possible before the AST shows up. Overdrive allows you to squeeze in more shots before that happens. An EMP Grenade stops the AST suit in its tracks. While it is motionless, toss a couple Contact Grenades toward it. Stay well ahead of the AST as you circle around the area, hitting it with everything you've got.

F ESCAPE IN THE DIVE BOAT

With the AST taken care of, run over to the dive boat and climb inside.

DIVE BOAT CONTROLS

Use the Left Stick to control the boat. Hold the Fire button to throttle, easing up to make the tight turns. Press the Jump button to dive underwater. You are underwater for a very short time, so you must time these dives well.

Carefully guide the watercraft through the canal. Keep your eyes on the water ahead, watching for any obstacles in the way, incoming missiles, and the location of the objective marker.

Dive to avoid both civilian vessels and incoming missiles. After passing under a bridge and making a right turn, line your boat up with the small ramp to avoid running into the wall.

When an aircraft starts firing at you, go underwater for a short respite. Eventually, you plow into a building.

OBJECTIVE

G REACH THE EXTRACTION POINT

"THE BOAT'S FINISHED. WE'RE ON FOOT." —Ilona

To get out of the city, you must reach the extraction point at the top of the building. Now you get to test out your newest Exo Ability: the Exo Grapple.

Follow Ilona outside, and press the Tactical Grenade button to grapple to a platform above. Continue up again and then to a rooftop on the right, where guards have discovered your location.

Take cover, and eliminate as many enemies as you can before continuing. Watch out for the moving containers, as they can knock you off the building. Fight your way across the rooftop to the tower ahead.

UTOPIA INTEL

After clearing out the guards on the rooftop, approach the nearest corner of the tower. On the left side, an Intel sits just inside the building. Bust the glass to get to it.

Look straight up, and grapple to the narrow ledge high in the air before moving to a small platform above. Step in front of Ilona, and use the gloves to climb the metal wall.

Follow your partner along another precarious, narrow walkway, grappling over to a platform before dropping down into the sky bridge.

More guards enter from the far side, so take a little time to defeat them before crossing to the other high-rise. Keep your guard up as a couple more men fire from behind the glass ahead.

Exit up the stairs on the right. Climb onto the crane above, which swings around as you move forward. When the Jump icon appears on the metal wall below, press the Jump button to finish the mission.

ACHIEVEMENT/TROPHY

BETRAYAL
You earn this Achievement/Trophy once you complete Utopia.

SENTINEL

LOCATION Undisclosed Location   **DATE** January 3, 2060 — 0100 hrs   **MISSION DETAILS** Gather intel at a private estate.

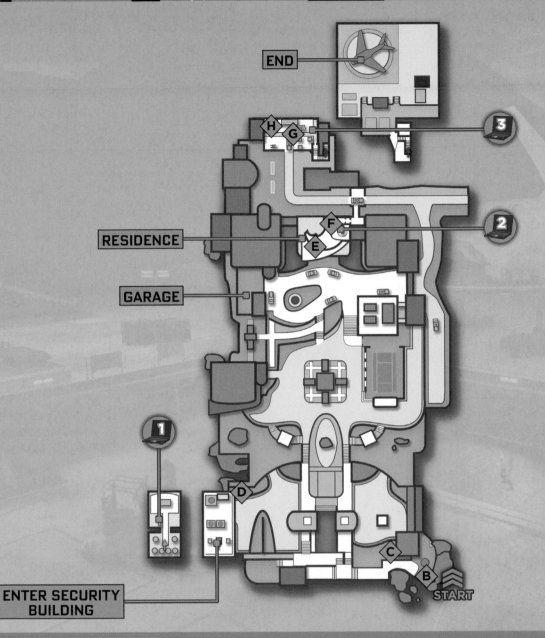

END

H G

3

RESIDENCE

F

E

2

GARAGE

1

D

ENTER SECURITY BUILDING

C

B

START

FACTION

SENTINEL TASK FORCE

SQUAD MEMBERS

Cormack

Ilona

Knox

MISSION OBJECTIVES

- Ⓐ Follow Cormack
- Ⓑ Infiltrate the Estate
- Ⓒ Access the Security System
- Ⓓ Regroup with Cormack
- Ⓔ Search the Database
- Ⓕ Infiltrate the Hangar
- Ⓖ Record the Meeting
- Ⓗ Plant the Tracker on the Plane

LOADOUT

PRIMARY

KF5 Custom

SECONDARY

MP443 Grach Suppressed

EXO TYPE

Specialist

VARIABLE GRENADES

None

EXO ABILITIES

EXO TYPE
SPECIALIST

○ RIOT SHIELD
○ OVERDRIVE
○ GRAPPLE

> **"I KNOW THIS IS DIFFICULT, BUT I NEED YOU TO MOVE PAST THAT. THIS IS BIGGER THAN ANY OF US."** *—Cormack*

The guards around the estate are in Atlas gear, while your team is decked out in Sentinel attire.

ALLY

ENEMY

OBJECTIVE

A FOLLOW CORMACK

You and Ilona are taken to a hangar area, where Cormack is giving a briefing on the current mission. Follow Cormack as he grapples up the cliffs, cutting through the waterfall to reach a higher point on the right. A few more ledges lead you to the private estate.

DETECTION METER

When an enemy hears or sees movement in your location, a meter appears onscreen. The meter fills up the more suspicious they become. Quickly duck into a planter or grapple to another location to avoid detection. When the guards are fully alerted to your presence, an alarm sounds, and you must restart at the previous checkpoint.

When the meter is full, enemies will detect you.

TARGET TRACKER

Once Knox brings your Target Tracker online, you can tag enemies and civilians. Aim at a person or drone to mark them automatically. This allows you to keep track of movement much easier, which is extremely important for this stealth mission. Enemies are outlined in yellow, while civilians show up as a bluish-green.

Move in toward the bushes ahead, and whistle to get the lone guard's attention. When he gets close enough, a grapple icon appears on him. Press the button to perform a concealed kill.

Press **+** to Whistle

OBJECTIVE

B INFILTRATE THE ESTATE

After marking the guards below, grapple over to the railing, and wait for them to pass.

GRAPPLE KILLS

Using your Grapple ability to perform a concealed kill on a guard, with nobody looking, is a great way to better your chances of going undetected. However, it isn't necessary for completing the mission. You can play through the first part of this level without killing anyone else, but there is an Achievement/Trophy available for taking out 20 enemies this way. Although Knox or Ilona will let you know if you are clear after a kill, it is still best to look around before performing the maneuver.

When an enemy stands near a ledge, you can perform a Grapple kill on him. Because this move leaves you exposed for a short while, be sure he is well in the clear before doing so. Also, note that this tactic only works against the guards; do not attempt to take on the drones.

OBJECTIVE
C ACCESS THE SECURITY SYSTEM

As you negotiate the estate grounds, the way you go and the enemies whom you take out can vary greatly. This walkthrough gives you the option with the fewest number of confrontations.

As you move through the area, use your Target Tracker on anyone you encounter. Turn left toward the objective marker, and grapple over to the planter. Wait for the guard ahead to move away, and quickly hop the rail into more bushes.

As you continue forward onto a rooftop, watch the drone on the left. If the detection meter appears at all, move back into the brush. Move forward, and then grapple to the rail on the right. Watch the nearby guard's movement, and then move over to the left planter.

"TIME TO SEE IF THE PRINT WE GOT WAS WORTH THE PRICE." —Knox

Grapple up to the roof of the security building ahead, ducking down to avoid being seen by a drone that emerges from inside. Step over to the bomb highlight, and plant the EMP. Once inside, access the security system. You only have two minutes to complete the task and get out, so be quick. Once done, immediately grapple out the way you came in.

SENTINEL INTEL 1

While inside the security building, grab the first Intel that sits on the left desk.

OBJECTIVE
D REGROUP WITH CORMACK

Back outside, turn around and move over to the ledge just ahead. Follow it around to the left, and drop into the foliage at the far wall.

ACHIEVEMENT/TROPHY

PARTY CRASHER

Kill 20 enemies with the Grappling Hook. You must spend some time moving around the property to collect this many kills. Watch patrol patterns of the guards and drones as you quietly make your way from one to another. If you are spotted, quickly duck into foliage, or grapple to a different location. Once you have your 20 kills, make your way to the house. This is not cumulative; all 20 kills must occur during one playthrough of the mission.

Two enemies occupy the balcony ahead, with a drone patrolling the left perimeter. Wait for the far foe to move away, and perform a Grapple kill on the other. Immediately duck into the bush on the right.

When the guards and drone are not looking, continue into the next planter, and then grapple up to the shelter around the corner. Cautiously grapple over to the garage rooftop. There are many guards, civilians, and drones around, so target as many as you can and watch their movements.

Look over the garage ledge toward your destination, and spot the patrolling drone and the pool below. When clear, grapple down to the right ledge. If you duck underwater, a second drone shows up to scan the water. Before it arrives, quickly grapple to the upper balcony.

OBJECTIVE
E SEARCH THE DATABASE

Step inside to meet up with Cormack.

SENTINEL INTEL 2

Before searching the database with Cormack, grab the second Intel that sits on the counter to the left of the desk. If you have collected every Intel up to this point, you earn the History in the Making Achievement/Trophy.

Access the computer on the desk.

"WE'RE IN. LET'S SEE WHAT WE CAN FIND." —Cormack

OBJECTIVE
F INFILTRATE THE HANGAR

Move around the shelves, and eliminate the two men who enter the hallway. Follow Cormack down the elevator shaft. A third and fourth guard come in after you.

Stand next to your partner until he instructs you to move. Step behind the vehicle, go prone, and crawl underneath. When you come to a stop, move into the hangar next door.

OBJECTIVE
G RECORD THE MEETING

Follow Cormack up to the top of the shelving on the left, and drop behind him to get into position. Step up to the railing, and record the meeting.

OBJECTIVE
H PLANT THE TRACKER ON THE PLANE

SENTINEL INTEL 3

You can get this Intel as soon as you exit the vehicle. Before you grapple up to the top shelf, you can reach the Intel by going behind the shelf. You will not be caught.

Grapple up to the top of the storage racks. Follow Cormack down to a walkway, up the stairwell, and out the exit.

Aircraft Fight — D DRONE

GRAPPLE ONTO WING

Several enemy soldiers and a couple drones attempt to keep you from reaching the plane. You can spend a little time fighting from behind cover, but it is best to simply hightail it to the aircraft. Use your Grapple to reach the railing quickly, and then attach to the wing as soon as the icon appears underneath.

ACHIEVEMENT/TROPHY

CRATES ON A PLANE
You earn this Achievement/Trophy once you complete Sentinel.

CRASH

LOCATION Antarctica   **DATE** January 3, 2060 — 1730 hrs   **MISSION DETAILS** Recover the Manticore sample.

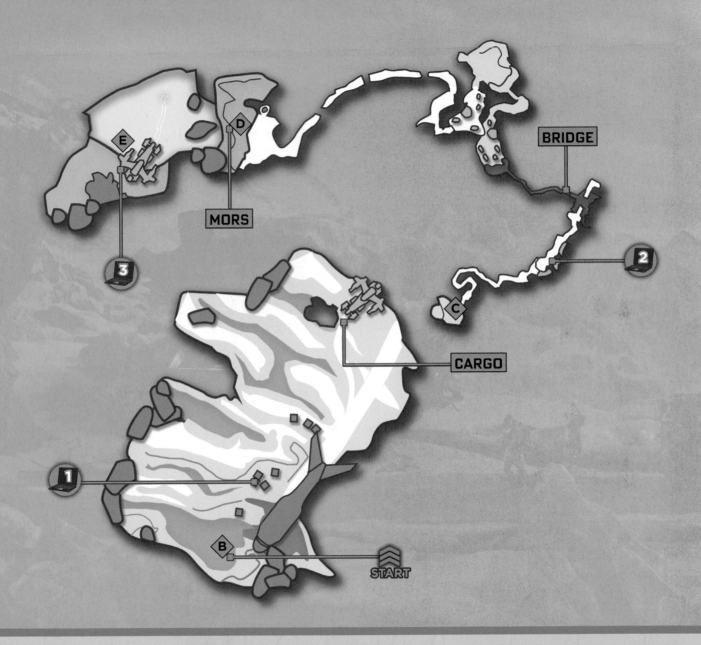

BRIDGE

MORS

E

D

3

2

C

CARGO

1

B

START

FACTION

SENTINEL TASK FORCE

SQUAD MEMBERS

Cormack   Ilona

MISSION OBJECTIVES

- Ⓐ Plant the Charge
- Ⓑ Reach the Cargo
- Ⓒ Follow Cormack
- Ⓓ Recover the Cargo
- Ⓔ Destroy the Warbird

LOADOUT

PRIMARY

HBRa3 Target Enhancer

SECONDARY

KF5

EXO TYPE

Assault

VARIABLE GRENADES

LETHAL	TACTICAL
Smart	Threat
Contact	Flash
Frag	EMP

EXO ABILITIES

EXO TYPE
ASSAULT

- BOOST JUMP
- SONICS
- MAG GLOVES

"YOUR PRIMARY OBJECTIVE IS THE CARGO. ALL OTHER ASSETS ARE EXPENDABLE."

—Kingpin

OBJECTIVE

A PLANT THE CHARGE

You start out alongside Cormack as you both approach an airplane. After landing on the wing with your gloves, move forward until you are prompted to plant the charge. The explosives are detonated, and you land safely on Darwin Glacier in Antarctica.

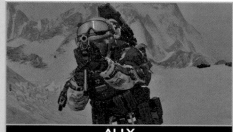

OBJECTIVE

B REACH THE CARGO

Everything seems to be going as planned until enemy soldiers show up just ahead.

KNOW YOUR ENEMY

Both your team and the opposition are decked out in cold-weather gear. Use the targeting outlines, as well as the names above your allies' heads, to make the differentiation easy.

ALLY

ENEMY

ENEMY

Ilona supplies you with an HBRa3, use it along with your Exo Ability Sonics to push back against the surprise assault.

Snow banks and cargo containers work as cover as you trade shots with your enemies. MDLs and HBRa3 grenade launchers lie around the containers, so grab one for a little extra firepower.

Hold ❌ to swap HBRa3 Grenade Launcher

CRASH INTEL 1

A pile of crates sits in the snow just to the left of the Pandora. The first Intel lies next to them on the left side.

Continue pushing the enemy back, moving forward when it is safe to do so. Once you have fought your way to the target cargo, help push it into the aircraft.

More soldiers drop in, along with ASTs and a Titan. This proves to be too much for your squad, and at that moment, the ice underneath Ilona, Cormack, and you gives way.

OBJECTIVE

C OBJECTIVE: FOLLOW CORMACK

Deep below ground, Ilona knocks down an ice wall, which reveals a narrow tunnel. Follow Cormack until you run into a group of enemies who search for your squad.

"HOLD YOUR FIRE. MOVEMENT AHEAD."

—*Cormack*

After Cormack gives you instruction on whom to take out, shoot the two foes on the ledges ahead while your allies clean up the rest.

CRASH INTEL 2

After falling underground and following the dark tunnel, take out the two foes ahead. Then, jump over to the right ledge, and pick up the Intel.

Drop down to the lower area, and fight your way deeper into the cave. Eliminate the few enemies at the bridge before crossing. When you're half way across, an AST charges toward you. Rapidly tap the Use button when prompted, and then move onto the bridge.

"I'LL TAKE LEAD. MITCHELL, BEHIND ME. ILONA, COVER OUR SIX." —*Cormack*

Follow the water until you reach a dead end. Dive under, and swim behind Cormack. Do not surface before he signals to do so. Time slows as you rise out of the water. Five enemies stand just ahead, with a sixth on the ledge above.

Once you've eliminated the first group, more foes drop in. Remember that you can use Sonics to stagger nearby foes. Fight your way around to the left, where your Boost Jump comes in handy with ledges on both sides above the ground level.

A couple more turns through the cavern get the team back outside. Slide down to the right, and carefully jump across the narrow ledges on the side of the mountain. When the drones show up, hit them with an EMP Grenade to drop them out of the air.

Follow Ilona and Cormack through a small hole in the ground, and then follow the short tunnel back outside, where you can see your objective just ahead.

OBJECTIVE
D RECOVER THE CARGO

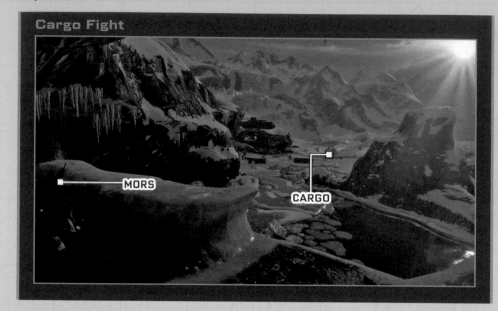

Cargo Fight

MORS

CARGO

CRASH INTEL 3

After you are helped out of the water, run around to the far side of the crashed plane, and grab the Intel that sits in the charred wreckage.

OBJECTIVE
E DESTROY THE WARBIRD

Pick up the Stinger M7, and take up position between Ilona and Cormack. Target the Warbird as it heads your way, and let the rocket launcher lock on. When you get the go-ahead, fire to bring down the aircraft.

Grab the MORS that rests against the ledge, and survey the enemies who surround the cargo. Pick them off as your squad moves in. When the rocket launcher foe shows up, take him out immediately. The enemy deploys mobile cover, making your shots a little tougher.

Drop down to the ground, and join your team as you keep fighting off the soldiers. In the meantime, the cargo is taken away, and then the ice gives way, dropping you into the freezing water. Swim up to the light.

Immediately hop off the ledges, and sprint over to the cargo as it slides down the hill. Grab ahold of the handle to get the sample, and then quickly Boost Jump up to the helicopter that arrives to whisk your squad away.

ACHIEVEMENT/TROPHY

THE DESTROYER RETURNS
You earn this Achievement/Trophy once you complete Crash.

BIO LAB

LOCATION Strandja, Bulgaria   **DATE** April 4, 2060 — 0300 hrs   **MISSION DETAILS** Infiltrate the facility and neutralize the Bio weapon.

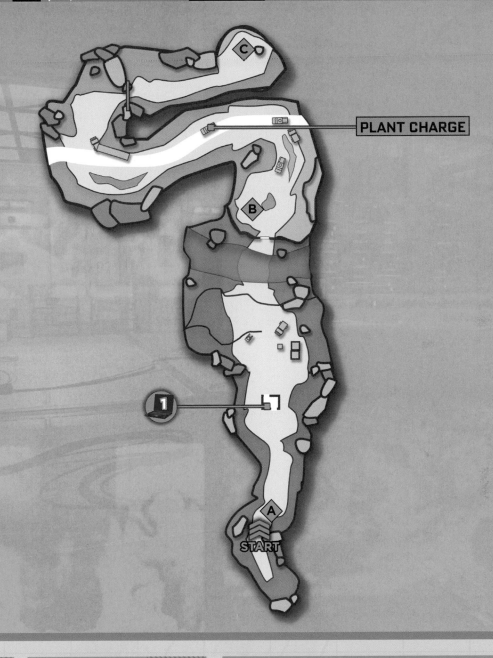

PLANT CHARGE

START

FACTION

SENTINEL TASK FORCE

SQUAD MEMBERS

Cormack

Gideon

Knox

MISSION OBJECTIVES

- Ⓐ Escape the Sniper
- Ⓑ Regroup with Cormack
- Ⓒ Infiltrate the Facility
- Ⓓ Gather Intel on Manticore
- Ⓔ Neutralize the Manticore Supply
- Ⓕ Locate the Tank
- Ⓖ Disable the Scrambler
- Ⓗ Locate the Tank
- Ⓘ Escape the Facility

LOADOUT

PRIMARY
None

EXO TYPE
Specialist

VARIABLE GRENADES
None

EXO ABILITIES

EXO TYPE
SPECIALIST
- RIOT SHIELD
- OVERDRIVE
- CLOAK

A ESCAPE THE SNIPER

"DON'T LET THAT SNIPER DIAL US IN."
—Gideon

Immediately sprint behind Gideon as a chopper fires down on the two of you.

BIO LAB INTEL ❶

From the very beginning of the mission, stop at the small shack, and collect the Intel that lies on the floor.

Hop over the trees and fence before trudging through a stream. Climb up the cliff, pressing the necessary buttons as the onscreen prompts present themselves.

Tap Right on the D-pad when prompted to do so to use the Exo Cloak ability. After the chopper leaves the area, press the Aim and Fire buttons to reach solid ground.

B REGROUP WITH CORMACK

Remain cloaked, and hit the deck when a drone heads your way. Drones cannot detect you unless you are moving, so stay still until it exits the area.

EXO ABILITY: CLOAK

Pressing Right on the D-pad enables and disables your Cloak ability. As you move, your battery runs down fairly quickly. Standing still slowly recoups it, while uncloaking gets it back in just a few seconds. You are completely invisible to the enemy when cloaked, but since you are synced with Gideon, a blue outline gives you Gideon's position.

KNOW YOUR ENEMY

Your squad wears the typical gray gear with Exo Suits. The enemies in this level wear the familiar black attire with Exos or hazmat suits.

ALLY	ENEMY	ENEMY

Run behind Gideon as he takes off, coming to a stop next to him when he slides behind cover. Slowly approach the far enemy, and hit him with a melee attack when close enough. You grab his HBRa3, but do not use it unless it is completely necessary.

Keep following your partner through the woods until you reach a guard with his back turned. Wait for a second enemy to pass, and then knock out the first foe. Take your cue from Gideon, and fully charge your battery.

Plant a Mute Charge where indicated behind the vehicle ahead, and then use a melee attack on a guard standing outside the passenger side.

Trail Gideon along the path, pausing to charge your Cloak when he stops. Another pause when a convoy passes gives you another opportunity to charge.

"FIVE ASTS APPROACHING. FORGET ABOUT SHOOTING OUR WAY PAST THIS ONE." —*Gideon*

Farther down the road, crouch beside your teammate, and wait for a group of ASTs to pass. Continue behind him as he moves over to a log pile, where you spot a Seeker ahead. Your Cloak is useless against it, so avoid letting its beam touch you.

After the patrol passes, step away from the cover so you can see the beam, and get ready to run. As it scans away from you, sprint up the road and duck behind the rock.

When Gideon says, "Okay, now," sprint directly behind him to the other side of the dirt road. Continue straight along the trail, ducking and going prone when necessary. Eventually, you find Cormack and Knox on a cliff that overlooks the facility. Note that at this point, you gain Lethal Grenades, as well as a Silenced HBRa3 and a Silenced KF5.

OBJECTIVE
C INFILTRATE THE FACILITY

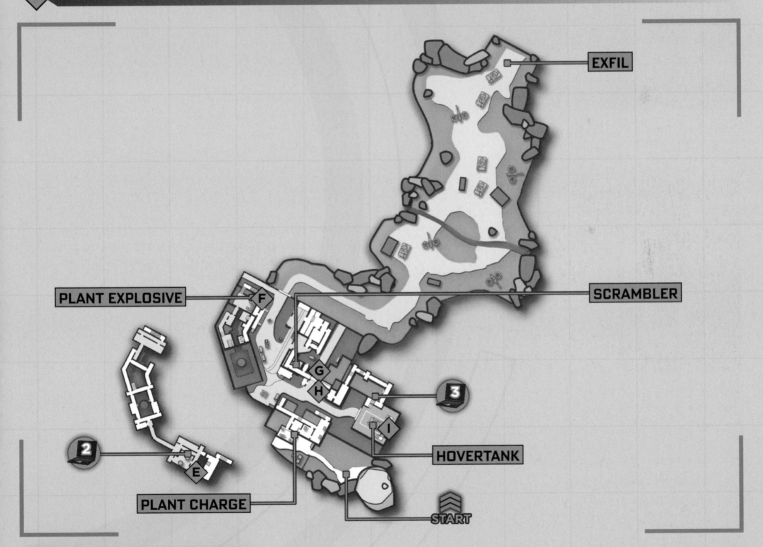

EXFIL

PLANT EXPLOSIVE   F   SCRAMBLER

G

H   3

2   I

HOVERTANK

E   START

PLANT CHARGE

Step up to the ledge, and hold the Use button to rappel off the side. On the ground, move toward the facility. Go invisible, and take out one of the guards ahead with a headshot.

Plant a Mute Charge at the door ahead, and wait for Gideon to blow the door open. Take out the foes inside, along with a straggler in the next room.

OBJECTIVE

 D GATHER INTEL ON MANTICORE

Cloaked, move down the hall as two men in hazmat suits pass by. Get behind them, and dispatch each one with a melee attack.

Cut left through the lab and up the steps. Once the door is open, take down the lone enemy inside. Step up to his computer, and begin the upload.

OBJECTIVE

 E NEUTRALIZE THE MANTICORE SUPPLY

"BE ADVISED. WE'VE GOT ENEMY PAX SWARMING THE TARGET." —*Kingpin*

Wait at the exit while the situation is assessed. Once the doors open up, enemies attack from a hallway on the other side of the processing room. They spill into the room and attempt to flank your team from the right.

Spend a little time fighting the enemies in front of your position, and then move right down the hall to clear out the other rooms.

At the next hallway, a sensor scans the area above the far doorway as more soldiers set up nearby.

SENSORS

The rest of the facility is equipped with sensors that scramble your Exo Suit when one spots you. They hang on the walls and emit a blue beam. If you come in contact with it, you lose your abilities for a short time. You can take down sensors with weapon fire, so knock them off the wall whenever you see one.

Farther ahead is an open area with hallways around the perimeter that overlook the lower floor. You can shoot enemies around the perimeter through the windows. Cautiously fight your way through the right or left side.

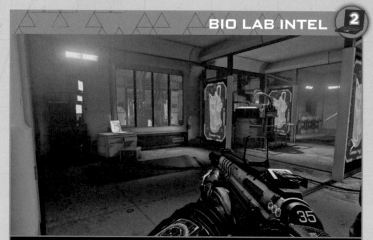

BIO LAB INTEL **2**

When you reach the open area, move right, and enter the Main Compound Synthesis Lab on the right side. Just inside, the second Intel sits on a cabinet against the left wall.

USE YOUR ABILITIES

The facility is littered with enemy soldiers and can become very dangerous if you are not careful. Be sure to use your Exo abilities to survive the onslaught. The Exo Shield, Overdrive, and Cloak can all save you from death if you use them wisely.

At the next cross hallway, take some time to pick off the enemies and sensors in the next open area—both on the same floor and on the ground level.

A group of enemies is holed up in the Final Outpost Stations. Fight your way through the room, and descend to the first floor. There, you find the Manticore supplies. Plant an FRB on the canisters where indicated. Follow the squad into the next room, and detonate the explosives.

OBJECTIVE

F LOCATE THE TANK

"PRIMARY LZ IS TOO HOT. SKIES FULL OF HOSTILES. WE'VE ESTABLISHED LZ-BLACK THREE KLICKS TO THE SOUTHEAST." —*Kingpin*

Plans are changed, and now you must reach a hovertank and fight your way to the new extraction point.

Follow the team outside, where you are met with strong resistance. There are three lanes that that lead to the hangar; we will take the left. Fight your way into the warehouse, watching out for the foes who hide behind cover and are positioned inside the far rooms.

As you exit the building, look on the roof ahead to spot a rocket launcher. Take out its operator first before you eliminate the others. As you approach the hangar, an AST emerges from inside.

OBJECTIVE

G DISABLE THE SCRAMBLER

After you've taken care of the AST, you are informed that a scrambler is keeping the team out of the building. Enter the white structure, and find a ladder in the middle. Climb to the roof, and plant a jammer on the equipment.

OBJECTIVE

H LOCATE THE TANK

As Knox attempts to get the door open, more hostiles enter the area. Defend his position from the attack until he gets it open. Follow the path until you find the tank inside the hangar.

BIO LAB INTEL 3

Before descending into the main room with the tank, break one of the windows of the Auto-Assisted Fabrication Room on the right side of the hallway, and climb inside. The final Intel sits on a desk against the left wall.

OBJECTIVE

1 ESCAPE THE FACILITY

Use the steps behind the tank to get inside. Now it is time to escape this compound and get to the extraction point.

HOVERTANK

The T-740 hovertank is well-equipped, featuring three types of weapons and a Trophy System. Use the Left Stick to guide the tank, and use the Right Stick to move the aiming reticle. Three of the face buttons select the weapon, while the Fire button uses them. The selected weapon is highlighted and blinks along the bottom of the HUD. Hold the Aim button to zoom in on your targets.

Here is a rundown on the hovertank's equipment:

›› Anti-Personnel Missiles (Use button).

These missiles are most effective against ground troops, as they guide themselves to their targets. They also work well against smaller vehicles.

›› Cannon (Switch Weapon button).

Switch to these powerful projectiles when faced with bigger vehicles. The heavier armored tanks require a couple shots to take down. These fire in a straight line, so be sure to steady the ride before firing.

›› EMP (Crouch button).

You can knock Warbirds and helicopters out of the air with the EMP gun. As soon as you see one enter the airspace, fire their way to get rid of them immediately.

›› Trophy System (Automatic).

This protects you from incoming projectiles, knocking them out of the air before they make contact. A meter on the left side of the HUD shows how much protection you have left. Once it runs out, all enemy shots will get through.

The path to exfil is fairly straightforward, with one split that rejoins just down the road. Use the appropriate weapons against the three types of enemies: soldiers, vehicles, and aircraft.

Do not rush into battles with the tanks, and back away if necessary to give yourself time to destroy them. However, you do want to be quick with your weapons, as you only have so much Trophy System before you are vulnerable to all attacks. Listen to your team as they call out incoming hostiles.

When you reach the LZ, sprint to the aircraft to complete the mission.

ACHIEVEMENT/TROPHY

RESTRICTED AIRSPACE

EMP 10 enemy aircraft out of the sky with the hovertank. As soon as you see a Warbird or helicopter, launch an EMP to knock them out of the sky.

ACHIEVEMENT/TROPHY

IRONS IN THE FIRE

You earn this Achievement/Trophy once you complete Bio Lab.

COLLAPSE

LOCATION San Francisco, California, USA | **DATE** June 15, 2060 — 0830 hrs | **MISSION DETAILS** Prevent an attack on the Golden Gate Bridge.

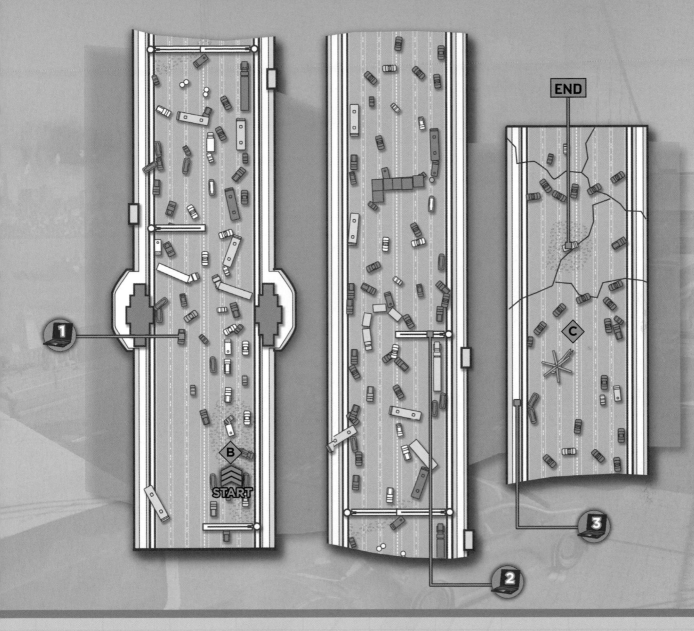

FACTION

SENTINEL TASK FORCE

SQUAD MEMBER

Gideon

MISSION OBJECTIVES

- Ⓐ Intercept the Van
- Ⓑ Regroup with Sentinel
- Ⓒ Open the Van

LOADOUT

PRIMARY

HBRa3

SECONDARY

MDL

EXO TYPE

Assault

VARIABLE GRENADES

LETHAL	TACTICAL
Smart	Threat
Contact	Flash
Frag	EMP

EXO ABILITIES

EXO TYPE
ASSAULT

- BOOST JUMP
- SONICS
- STIM

"I AM HERE TO SOLVE THE WORLD'S PROBLEMS, AND I BELIEVE THE WORLD'S PROBLEMS BEGIN WITH YOU." —*Gideon*

A INTERCEPT THE VAN

You start out driving an Pitbull toward the Golden Gate Bridge as Gideon spots a suspicious van speeding by.

Hold the Fire button to accelerate, and keep the van within sight. Just beyond the tunnel, avoid the out-of-control bus by cutting through the pylons on the right and following the muddy path back up to the highway.

Three enemy SUVs have entered the area. When one passes your vehicle, a reticle appears around it. Squeeze the Aim button to fire your rockets, blowing the car to smithereens. Keep the van in view as you take out the other two when they move past.

Next, you are knocked into the center of the highway. Move quickly into the left lanes to avoid a parked truck. Eventually, you are knocked into the railing, and your vehicle flips over.

OBJECTIVE

B REGROUP WITH SENTINEL

"CORMACK, OUR PITBULL'S OUT OF ACTION. PROCEEDING ON FOOT."

—Jonathan Irons

Now on foot, you still need to reach the van, but numerous enemy soldiers intend to impede your progress. Head down the bridge as hostiles hop onto the vehicles ahead. Pick the snipers off of the semis.

KNOW YOUR ENEMY

The enemies are still decked out in the black gear with Exoskeletons, while you fight alongside Sentinel forces wearing camo under their Exo Suits. Remember: your allies' names appear in blue when you ADS on them.

| ALLY | ENEMY |

COLLAPSE INTEL 1

Shortly after crashing the Pitbull, run down the middle of the bridge and spot the SUV that sits with its doors open, just left of the yellow line. You can find the first Intel on the passenger seat.

EXO ABILITY: SONICS

Your fight across the Golden Gate Bridge can get extremely tough, so use Sonics freely if you find yourself in trouble against a group of hostiles. Stagger them with this ability, and flee to cover. Also, note that some car doors have been left open and can serve as shields if needed.

Hop over the trucks that block the road, and fight back the enemy forces. Carefully make your way between the vehicles. Foes can pop up anywhere. Traffic signs above the highway offer a nice vantage point, though you are more vulnerable there.

The pedestrian paths along each side of the bridge are great for flanking the hostiles. Watch out, though, as the opposition will reciprocate. Be aware of everything around you, as enemies here even attack from behind.

As you progress down the bridge, drones take to the air. Be ready with an EMP Grenade.

COLLAPSE INTEL ②

After the traffic sign that spans across the entire road, a smaller sign lists times to certain destinations. Hop onto the small red maintenance room on the right side of the bridge, and then Boost Jump up to the sign. The second Intel sits on the other side.

COLLAPSE INTEL ③

On the left pedestrian sidewalk, almost to the helicopter, look for a small white towing car. Find the last Intel on its trailer.

C OPEN THE VAN

After passing the helicopter, approach the van, and walk around to the rear. Open it up to find out what is inside.

ACHIEVEMENT/TROPHY

GG

You earn this Achievement/Trophy once you complete Collapse.

ARMADA

LOCATION San Francisco, California, USA **DATE** June 15, 2060 — 0930 hrs **MISSION DETAILS** Race to secure the Arclight Weapon System.

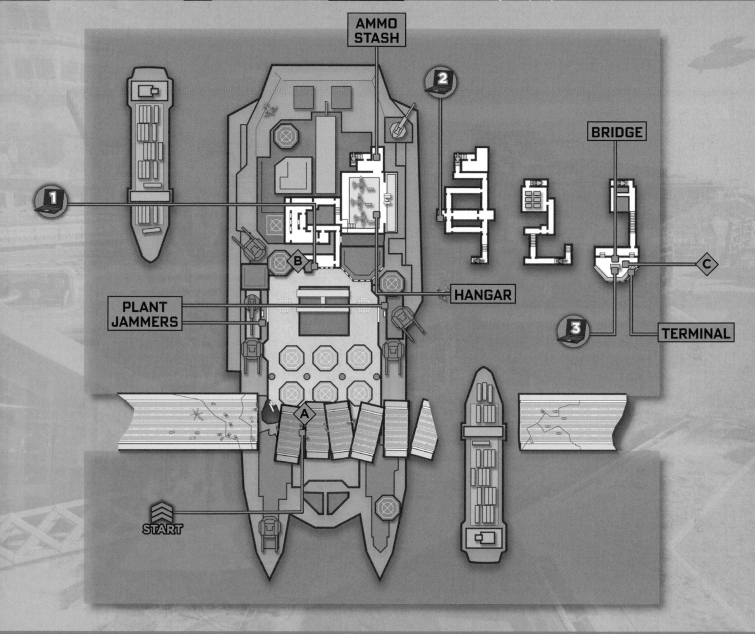

AMMO STASH

BRIDGE

HANGAR

PLANT JAMMERS

TERMINAL

START

FACTION

SENTINEL TASK FORCE

MISSION OBJECTIVES

Ⓐ Plant the Jammers on the Railguns

Ⓑ Reach the Bridge

Ⓒ Destroy the Cargo Ships

SQUAD MEMBERS

 Gideon

 Cormack

 Knox

LOADOUT

PRIMARY

HBRa3

SECONDARY

MDL

EXO TYPE

Assault

VARIABLE GRENADES

LETHAL		TACTICAL	
	Smart		Threat
	Contact		Flash
	Frag		EMP

EXO ABILITIES

EXO TYPE
ASSAULT

○ BOOST JUMP
○ SONICS
○ STIM

OBJECTIVE

A PLANT THE JAMMERS ON THE RAILGUNS

"THEY'RE GOING TO TRY TO TAKE THE SHIP'S BRIDGE. LET'S MOVE." —*Cormack*

Follow your team up to the main deck, where Atlas forces have already swarmed the ship. Immediately start shooting at the enemies on the platform ahead.

KNOW YOUR ENEMY

The usual dark Atlas outfits are still present on the enemies, but you also fight against foes in red gear. Sentinel allies are in their typical camo under an exoskeleton. Infantrymen in fatigues accompany your squad.

Your first objective is to plant jammers on two railguns, with one located just to the left and another farther away on the right. Fight your way toward the objective marker, Boost Jump up to the platform, and plant a jammer on the wall.

As drones fly into the area, use an EMP Grenade to get rid of them. Two hostiles guard the second railgun. Take them out, and plant the second jammer.

OBJECTIVE

B REACH THE BRIDGE

With the railguns jammed, head toward the objective marker, and meet up with your squad inside the ship.

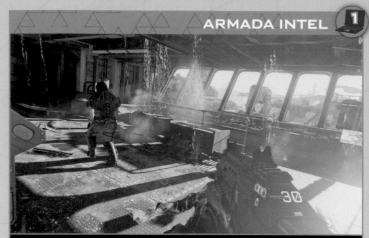

> After joining your crew, move around to the right until you reach a console against the windows. The first Intel is located on the right side.

Cut through the navigation room, reload at the ammo stash, and wait for Cormack to get the door open. Follow him through the halls until you reach a room that is pitch black. Press Right on the D-pad to turn on night vision.

Enter the left door, and step up to the opening on the right. Enemies with their own night vision search the next room. Take them out from there before moving inside. Continue behind Cormack as he exits the room, turning off night vision as you move through the corridor. This hallway leads to the hangar.

Hangar Fight

ENTER
AST AND MORE TROOPS
EXIT

Hostiles are dropped in ahead. Kill them as you move farther into the hangar.

ACHIEVEMENT/TROPHY

MAN OVERBOARD!

Melee an enemy so he flies off the side of the ship. Enter the hangar, and move over to the far-right corner. Fight the hostiles until one gets close to the edge. Simply use a melee attack to knock him overboard. If the AST shows up before you obtain this Achievement/Trophy, restart the checkpoint, and try again.

Hostiles are dropped in throughout the area. Pick off a few of them before you move down the steps. Take cover behind the forklift as you continue to kill the foes.

After you eliminate most of the initial set of enemies, an AST and more forces enter the area, so be ready with your EMP Grenades. Keep moving as you fight the hostiles, keeping cover between you and them as much as possible. The Sonics ability comes in handy if you get surrounded.

When you toss an explosive, make sure the targeted enemy isn't grappling with a friendly. Taking out an ally causes a reset to the beginning of the hangar.

Jumping onto the big pile of crates offers a good vantage point, and the AST will not chase you there. Stay alert for incoming grenades, tossing them back or hopping down to avoid taking damage. You are vulnerable from most sides at this location, so you may need to spend some time sniping some of the soldiers before focusing on the AST.

Once you clear out the hangar, exit through the new opening, and reload your weapons at the ammo stash. Once the door is open, follow the allies up the steps and across the catwalk.

ARMADA INTEL 2

After the hangar fight, follow the first catwalk into the right doorway. Enter the first room on the right to find the second Intel.

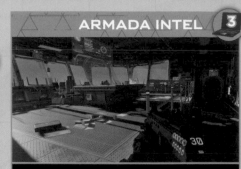

ARMADA INTEL 3

When you reach the bridge, grab the Intel off the strategy table on the right before accessing the terminal.

OBJECTIVE
C DESTROY THE CARGO SHIPS

"THOSE CARGO SHIPS ARE TEARING UP THE FLEET. WE JUST LOST ANOTHER BOAT." —*Kingpin*

Return to your team, and stay behind Cormack until he reaches another dark room. Switch on night vision, as enemies fire from the far side of the room and a catwalk above.

Spend some time in the stairwell as you fight the hostiles, backing down the steps to recover health when necessary. When it's safe to enter the room, step inside and move from one side to the other, taking out the enemies who fight from the far side. Use the computer equipment as cover.

Fight your way through the far doorway, and ascend to the upper walkway. Watch out, as there may be a soldier or two left behind. Take them out if necessary before you sprint up the steps on the right to reach the bridge.

"I NEED YOU TO TARGET FOR ME, MITCHELL. GET ON THAT TERMINAL."
—*Cormack*

Approach the terminal next to Cormack, and use it to take control of one of the ship's guns. The Aim and Fire buttons operate the left and right cannons, respectively. Send a few shots into the ship to sink it, and then do the same to the second one after switching views. You can also shoot the Warbirds out of the air, but the cargo ships are your primary targets.

ACHIEVEMENT/TROPHY

WRATH OF ATLAS
You earn this Achievement/Trophy once you complete Armada.

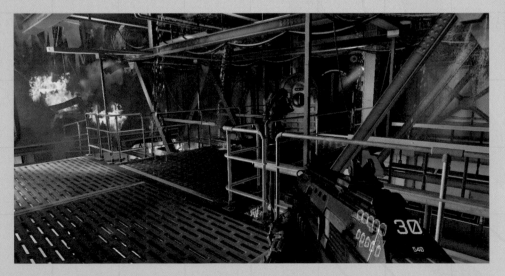

THROTTLE

LOCATION New Baghdad, Iraq | **DATE** January 8, 2061 — 1000 hrs | **MISSION DETAILS** Fly into New Baghdad and capture the leader of the opposition.

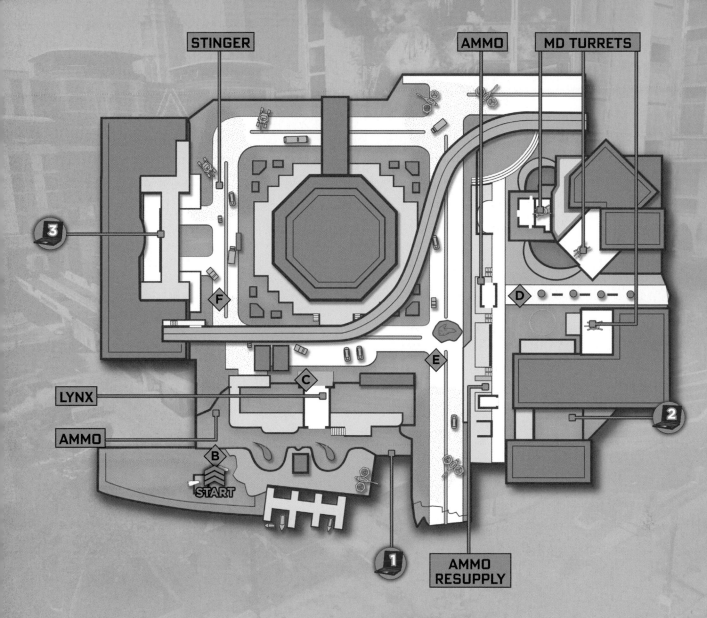

STINGER

AMMO

MD TURRETS

LYNX

AMMO

AMMO RESUPPLY

START

FACTION

SENTINEL TASK FORCE

SQUAD MEMBERS

Gideon

Ilona

Knox

MISSION OBJECTIVES

- Ⓐ Reach New Baghdad
- Ⓑ Follow Gideon
- Ⓒ Destroy the MD Turrets
- Ⓓ Regroup with Sentinel
- Ⓔ Eliminate the AST Units
- Ⓕ Destroy the Tank with the Stinger

LOADOUT

PRIMARY

ASM1 Hybrid Sight

SECONDARY

EM1 Red Dot Sight

EXO TYPE

Assault

VARIABLE GRENADES

LETHAL
Smart
Contact
Frag

EXO ABILITIES

EXO TYPE
ASSAULT
- BOOST JUMP
- SONICS
- GRAPPLE

"WE ALL KNEW WHAT HAD TO BE DONE. THIS WAS THE BEGINNING OF THE END... FOR ONE OF US." —*Mitchell*

A REACH NEW BAGHDAD

To reach New Baghdad, you must pilot a fighter jet through the canyons. Hostiles attempt to deter your progress with troops on the ground, on bridges, and flying alongside. Take out as many of the opposition as possible as you fly through the narrow passage.

FIGHTER JET CONTROLS

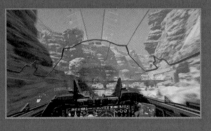

The Left Stick steers the aircraft. You can activate afterburners with the Jump button, but be sure you have enough room ahead, or you could plow into the side of the canyon. Crouch initiates the air brake, allowing for tight turns and quick avoidance maneuvers. Press the Aim button to fire the machine guns, using the yellow reticle to line up the enemy. The plane's weapon system automatically locks on to targets in the middle of your HUD, as indicated by a red outline. Squeeze the Fire button to release a missile, which homes in on a target.

If you prefer your flight pitch controls to be inverted, you can enable this in the Options menu.

Watch out for falling bridges, arches, and buttes. Use the air brake, and steer away from the falling debris. At the hydroelectric dam, lock on to the key points, and fire your missiles to bring it down.

Slow down to get behind trailing enemy aircraft, and light them up as they pass.

FLYING ACE

Shoot down 10 foes with machine guns. Line up the reticle with enemy aircraft, and squeeze the Aim button to bring them down. Avoid using missiles on enemy planes until you earn this accomplishment.

B FOLLOW GIDEON

"WE'RE TRYING TO ADVANCE, BUT THOSE MD TURRETS ARE TEARING APART OUR AIR SUPPORT." —*Ilona*

After crashing down in New Baghdad, follow Gideon to the left, using your Grapple ability to quickly reach higher ledges.

THROTTLE INTEL ① 1

Before following your squad through the building on the left, run down to the end of the boardwalk. Find the first Intel on a bench, just before the Atlas wall.

C DESTROY THE MD TURRETS (x3)

Cut through the building to join the battle. Three MD Turrets have set up on the balconies to the right in order to repel air strikes. Your first objective is to destroy them. You do not have to completely obliterate the gun, as long as you remove the gunner.

You have several options for how to proceed. You can use the Lynx sniper rifle at the entrance to reduce the turrets' numbers before moving in. You can take a direct approach by jumping

down to the street and fighting your way to the turrets. A third option is to use your Grapple to reach the guns quickly.

KNOW YOUR ENEMY

By now, you should be familiar with Atlas' dark gear. Sentinel forces are decked out in brown or the usual camouflage. Numerous soldiers fight on both sides of this battle, so be wary of whom you are firing at.

ALLY | ENEMY

Turrets Fight

MD TURRETS

LYNX
ENTER

This fight can quickly become overwhelming. Soldiers litter the street and the balconies around the turrets. You can skip much of the chaos on the street by grappling over to the tracks, where only a couple enemies get in your way as you run toward the objective.

A Warbird flies between you and the turrets. When you get the chance, grapple up to it to take out one of the enemies inside. Quickly shoot the pilot, and bail out the other side.

From here, you can grapple up to one of the MD Turrets. You can take them out in any order, though there are advantages to taking one before the other. Grapple up to the far-right balcony and then up to the roof to reach the first turret.

There are four ways to take out the turrets:

» **From standing next to a turret.**
Hold the Use button when next to a turret to jump on top and automatically rip the gunner out.

» **From on top of a turret.**
Hop on top of a turret, look at the hatch, and press the Melee button to pull the foe out.

» **Grapple directly to a turret.**
If you can get an angle to grapple directly to a turret, you automatically open the hatch and grab the pilot.

» **Destroy from afar.**
You can also just destroy the gun, though it is unusable at that point. Use another turret to target it, or use your own weapons to take it down.

If a turret is overtaken, you control the weapon until you exit. Hold the Fire button to shoot the cannon. Hold the Lethal Grenade button to lock on to your target, and then release the button to fire the missiles. Two aircraft show up each time you enter a turret, so shoot them down.

At this point, you can move on to the other two turrets and overtake them, or simply use the first one to destroy them from afar.

D REGROUP WITH SENTINEL

Your objective changes to regrouping with the rest of Sentinel once you have destroyed the turrets. However, ASTs soon show up below, and they are much easier to take out with an MD Turret. Exit the gun, wait for someone to mention the ASTs, and then get back inside.

E ELIMINATE THE AST UNITS

Target the red-outlined enemies below, and take them out with the cannon and missiles. Once you run out of targets, hop down and join the fight on the streets of New Baghdad.

THROTTLE INTEL 2

After destroying the three MD Turrets, hop down to the lowest level, and run to the left. The second Intel sits on a table on the rooftop between two taller buildings, right at the edge of the map. Be careful on the street below, as you will leave the area and have to restart if you continue that way.

Fight your way down the street, using the various levels to avoid packs of enemies. ASTs are present all the way down the street, so be ready with an EMP Grenade if needed.

GRAPPLE KILL AN AST

If you can get behind an AST, a grapple icon appears on the operator's back. Use the device to pull the pilot out and slam him into the ground—a very satisfying way to eliminate him.

The streets remain extremely hectic the rest of the way through the mission. Stay on your toes, and use everything you have to defeat the hostiles. The Boost Jump and Grapple abilities allow you to quickly retreat from danger.

AMMO STASH

There are ammo dumps all over the streets, so if you need a refill, seek one out. However, it isn't too hard to find another gun. Refer to the map for their locations.

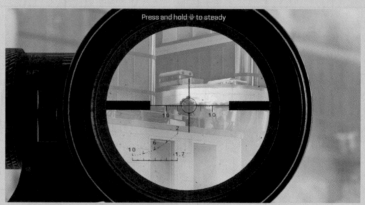

Press and hold to steady

If you left the Lynx sniper rifle before, grab it and start thinning out the opposition on the next street. From the bus stop shelter, you can get a bead on another AST that patrols the raised walkway on the left side of the street.

F DESTROY THE TANK WITH THE STINGER

Tanks show up at the end of the street, but a Stinger rocket launcher has been spotted nearby. As usual, it is up to you to get it and destroy the tank. Hop onto the left walkway, and clear out some of the hostiles on the street. Then, run over to the gun that leans against a crate just before the tanks.

ACHIEVEMENT/TROPHY

MANTICORE UNLEASHED
You earn this Achievement/Trophy once you complete Throttle.

THROTTLE INTEL 3

While on the raised walkway on the left side of the street, grab the last Intel that rests on a bench about halfway across.

CAPTURED

LOCATION Unknown Location   **DATE** January 8, 2061 — 1430 hrs   **MISSION DETAILS** Escape from the prison camp.

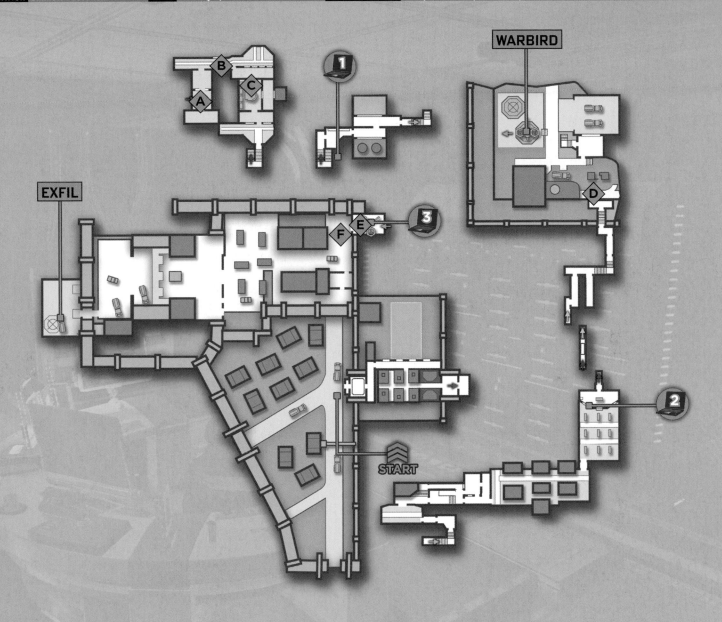

WARBIRD

EXFIL

START

FACTION

SENTINEL TASK FORCE

SQUAD MEMBERS

Gideon

Cormack

Ilona

MISSION OBJECTIVES

- Ⓐ Escape the Facility
- Ⓑ Follow Gideon
- Ⓒ Activate the Elevator
- Ⓓ Reach the Warbird
- Ⓔ Enter the AST
- Ⓕ Regroup with Ilona

LOADOUT

PRIMARY
None

EXO TYPE
None

VARIABLE GRENADES
None

EXO ABILITIES
Overdrive (after equipping Exo Suit)

"STAY ALERT. ANY DETAIL COULD MAKE THE DIFFERENCE." —*Gideon*

Go where you are instructed. The guards will knock you around if you veer from the path, take too long, or even look back. If you fool around too much, you will die.

OBJECTIVE

A ESCAPE THE FACILITY

After being freed from your restraints, follow Gideon to the far door.

OBJECTIVE

B FOLLOW GIDEON

Move down the hall, and stop at the Network Access Room. Once Gideon has taken care of the operator inside, grab the foe's Exo Suit and handgun.

NO RELOAD

Your left arm has been destroyed and cannot be used during this mission. Therefore, you can fire a gun, but there is no reloading it. Pick up weapons off dead hostiles when needed.

OBJECTIVE

C ACTIVATE THE ELEVATOR

Move over to the computer, and access it to activate the elevator. Two guards enter from the right. Quickly pick up your handgun, and take one out.

KNOW YOUR ENEMY

Atlas hostiles are equipped in their dark gear with exoskeletons, while Gideon wears his gear from the Throttle mission.

ALLY   ENEMY

HEAVY-HANDED

Go through 20 gun drops in one-armed combat. Each time you find another dropped weapon, pick it up. Before long, you will earn this accomplishment.

As you proceed through the facility, keep an eye out for hostiles, taking cover at a doorway to recover health when needed. After climbing to the second floor, do not shoot the scientists who surrender in the next room. They get in your way quite a bit during this mission, so stay alert.

CAPTURED INTEL 1

Soon after gaining the Exo Suit and climbing to the second floor, look for the Network Access Room. Step inside, and collect an Intel that sits on a cabinet to the right.

Step to the side of the next doorway; once it is open, enemies start shooting.

Stay behind Gideon as he runs back downstairs. More guards and scientists are gathered around the prosthetics area. Pick up new weapons frequently to avoid running out of ammunition at a bad time.

Inside Materials Storage, enemies hide around every corner, so move cautiously. Retreat if you sustain injury, and collect new weapons often.

Exit through the far door and follow Gideon into the autopsy room. When you reach the closed-off glass room, help him open the door.

CAPTURED INTEL 2

After forcing your way into the glass autopsy room, collect an Intel that sits on a cabinet to the left.

Gideon opens a chute in the back of the room. Hop inside to escape the guards who are in pursuit.

Drop between the containers, and help Gideon push one out of the way. Once underneath the platform, crawl over to your partner. Follow the walkway around to the right, down the stairs, and to the exit.

OBJECTIVE

D REACH THE WARBIRD

"I'VE SECURED A VEHICLE FOR EXFIL. RV AT THE NORTH WALL." —Ilona

Once outside, enemies swarm the area. Fight your way to the metal platform in the far-left corner, selecting a new weapon from the dead bodies when low on ammo.

Cut through the building, follow Gideon over the rail, and sprint to the Warbird.

CAPTURED INTEL ③

After the Warbird crashes but before you enter the AST, turn around and collect the third Intel.

OBJECTIVE E ENTER THE AST

Step up to the downed AST, toss the pilot aside, and climb inside.

OBJECTIVE F REGROUP WITH ILONA

With the power of the AST suit, walk through the crumbling wall ahead.

CONTROLLING THE AST SUIT

Moving in the AST suit and aiming are controlled just as always, with the Left Stick and Right Stick, respectively. Push the Left Stick in to move faster. Three shoulder buttons fire the weapons. Refer to the HUD to see when each is ready. The AST highlights enemies in yellow for better visibility.

Here is a rundown of the AST weapon system:

» GAU-3/A Gatling gun (Press Fire button).

This high-powered machine gun works very well against soldiers, drones, and light-armored vehicles. A meter in the lower-right corner of the HUD increases as you hold down the button. If you hold it until the meter reaches the top, the gun overheats and can't be used for a short while.

» Mk 4 Rockets (Press Lethal Grenade button).

These rockets are very powerful, but they are unguided and require about a five-second cooldown time before you can use them again. Use these against the slow, well-armored enemies.

» AT-6 Anti-Tank Guided Missiles (Press Tactical Grenade button).

The missiles are not as powerful as the rockets, but they are guided and lock on to multiple targets. Hold down the Tactical Grenade button while targeting up to eight enemies—signified by red diamonds. Release the button to fire the missiles. These also require a five-second cooldown.

Fight your way through the enemy forces, and plow through the gate at the other end to enter a warehouse.

AST Warehouse Fight

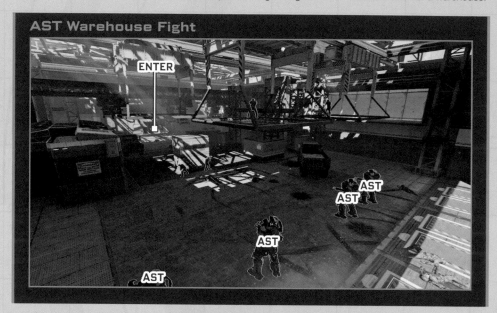

ENTER

Numerous soldiers occupy the building. As you push inside, a group of ASTs shows up. Backpedal as you light them up with your missiles and rockets. Move into the left corner to protect yourself from part of the ASTs; they won't all attack at once.

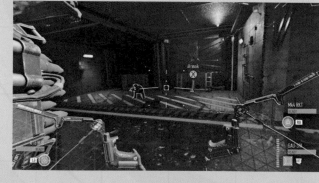

A big group of drones enters the outdoor area, along with two vehicles full of soldiers. Use your missiles and Gatling gun to eliminate the foes. Walk over to the exit, smash the lock, and rapidly tap the Use button until you both have escaped the prison.

ACHIEVEMENT/TROPHY

THE WHEAT FROM THE CHAFF
You earn this Achievement/Trophy once you complete Captured.

TERMINUS

LOCATION New Baghdad, Iraq　　**DATE** January 8, 2061 — 1900 hrs　　**MISSION DETAILS** Assault the opposition command center.

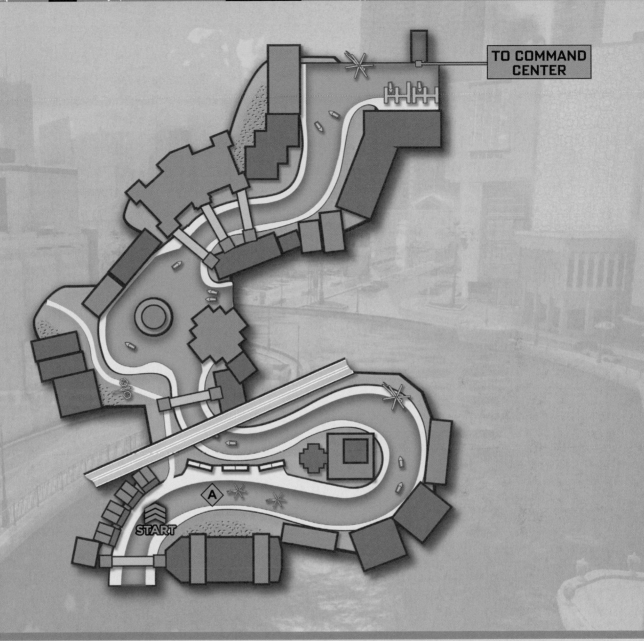

TO COMMAND CENTER

A

START

FACTION

SENTINEL TASK FORCE

SQUAD MEMBER

Gideon

MISSION OBJECTIVES

ⒶReach the Atlas Command Center

ⒷStop the Manticore Launch

ⒸEscape the Command Center

ⒹStop Your Target

LOADOUT

PRIMARY

None

EXO TYPE

AST

VARIABLE GRENADES

None

EXO ABILITIES

EXO TYPE
A.S.T.
○ CHAIN GUN
○ MICRO ROCKETS
○ S.W.A.R.M. MISSILES

"IT'S THREE OF US AGAINST AN ARMY. IT'S SUICIDE." —Ilona

OBJECTIVE

A REACH THE ATLAS COMMAND CENTER

Drones carry you and Gideon (both wearing AST suits) along the New Baghdad canal. As enemy boats, vehicles, and soldiers show up, light them up with your AST weapons, controlled just as they were at the end of the previous mission.

When prompted, detach from the drone to be dropped into the water. Walk along the bottom of the canal, and enter through a hole in the wall. Follow Gideon up a staircase to reach the command center.

OBJECTIVE

B STOP THE MANTICORE LAUNCH

Just inside, enemy forces start attacking. Mow them down with your guided missiles and Gatling gun.

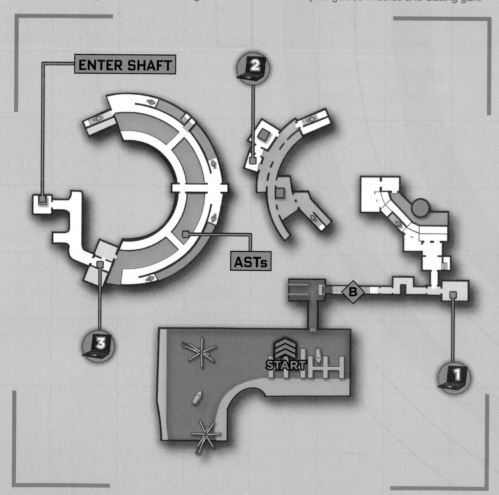

ENTER SHAFT

2

ASTs

3

START

B

1

KNOW YOUR ENEMY

Throughout the mission, you fight alongside your partner in AST suits. As you move through the facility, you face Atlas troops and enemy ASTs. The ASTs look identical, but you can tell them apart by their targeting outline. Your ally is outlined in blue, whereas hostiles have a thin, yellow line around them.

ALLY

ENEMY

TERMINUS INTEL 1

At the first hallway, where you first fight enemy soldiers, run to the other end and enter Maintenance Bay 2. The first Intel rests on a table against the right wall.

Follow Gideon into the silo as hostiles attempt to keep you out. As long as you don't let yourself get surrounded, you can dispatch these foes easily with your powerful weapons.

WATCH YOUR SIX

Try to clear out each area before moving on. Occasionally, though, an enemy gets behind your location. Pay attention to the blood smears that show the direction from which you're being attacked, and quickly eliminate hostiles who confront you from behind.

Continue behind your teammate as he descends down a level.

TERMINUS INTEL 2

After taking the steps down to the 7th floor, turn left and enter Server Control. Another Intel sits on the table, behind a stack of equipment.

Clear out the attacking hostiles as you take another staircase down, followed by a ramp. Watch out for rocket launchers and incoming grenades, as these can cause some serious damage if they hit their target.

Silo AST Fight

"ASTS AHEAD. TARGET THEM FIRST." —*Gideon*

When it appears that you have reached a dead end, the wall lowers as four ASTs join the fight on the other side. Use your rockets on them whenever available, and take them out before targeting the rest.

With the hostiles taken care of, follow Gideon through the door and into the vehicle access area.

Follow the path to the end, and locate a hatch in the floor to the left. Approach the nearest piston, and once Gideon is in position, grab it. Rapidly tap the Use button to pull it off and hop down the shaft.

Holding the Aim button sticks out your left leg to slow your descent, while the Fire button does the same with your right leg. If you do not slow down enough, you will die at the bottom. Hold both buttons the entire time until you safely reach the exhaust vent.

Walk behind your partner until you reach the rocket. Fire all of your weapons at its thrusters until you destroy it.

TERMINUS INTEL 3

Just before entering the vehicle access area, move into the security station on the left. The final Intel sits on a desk inside. This is the final Intel. If you have been collecting them all to this point, you earn the Ferrum Absconsum Achievement/Trophy.

 OBJECTIVE

C ESCAPE THE COMMAND CENTER

When you gain control of your handgun, fire at the guards at the end of the hall. Six enemies total enter the area.

 OBJECTIVE

D STOP YOUR TARGET

When prompted to do so, rapidly tap the Use button until you are released from your Exo. Sprint up the steps, and run after your target. Keep the Left Stick pressed in the entire time, and make sure you react to each obstacle quickly. Otherwise, you will lose the objective.

Slide under the closing gate, and immediately melee the guard as he drops in front of you. From there, follow the onscreen prompts as soon as they appear to complete the campaign.

ACHIEVEMENT/TROPHY

COMPLETED CAMPAIGN

By completing the campaign, you earn an Achievement/Trophy based on the difficulty setting:

A New Era	Earned the first time you complete the campaign.
Hard Hitter	Earned by completing the campaign on Hardened.
SP Prestige	Earned by completing the campaign on Veteran.

ACHIEVEMENTS/TROPHIES

COMPLETE THE CAMPAIGN

Completing both the single-player levels and the entire campaign earns the following awards. Finish the game on Veteran to get them all in one playthrough.

Achievement/Trophy	Description	Gamer Points	Trophy Type
SEOUL MATES	Complete "Induction."	25	Bronze
WELCOME TO ATLAS	Complete "Atlas."	25	Bronze
LIFE IN THE FAST LANE	Complete "Traffic."	25	Bronze
RADIOACTIVE	Complete "Fission."	20	Bronze
MOTOR CITY	Complete "Aftermath."	25	Bronze
BORN TO DIE	Complete "Manhunt."	20	Bronze
BETRAYAL	Complete "Utopia."	30	Bronze
CRATES ON A PLANE	Complete "Sentinel."	30	Bronze
THE DESTROYER RETURNS	Complete "Crash."	30	Bronze
IRONS IN THE FIRE	Complete "Bio Lab."	30	Bronze
GG	Complete "Collapse."	30	Bronze
WRATH OF ATLAS	Complete "Armada."	30	Bronze
MANTICORE UNLEASHED	Complete "Throttle."	30	Bronze

Achievement/Trophy	Description	Gamer Points	Trophy Type
THE WHEAT FROM THE CHAFF	Complete "Captured."	30	Bronze
A NEW ERA	Complete the campaign on any difficulty.	30	Silver
HARD HITTER	Complete the campaign on Hardened difficulty.	50	Silver
SP PRESTIGE	Complete the campaign on Veteran difficulty.	75	Gold

CAMPAIGN LEVEL-SPECIFIC AWARDS

All but two of the single-player levels have an extra Achievement/Trophy or two that you earn by completing specific tasks. Refer to the campaign walkthrough section of this guide for details on how to complete each of these.

Achievement/Trophy	Description	Gamer Points	Trophy Type
NOT ON MY WATCH	Prevent the walking tank from being destroyed by the Drone Swarm in "Induction."	10	Bronze
DEADEYE	Score "excellent" in the shooting range in "Atlas."	10	Bronze
GRENADIER	Score "excellent" in the grenade range in "Atlas."	10	Bronze
LOOK BOTH WAYS	Kill all the KVA in the traffic section without damaging a civilian vehicle in "Traffic."	10	Bronze
FIRE AND FORGET	Kill 10 enemies with the Mobile Turret missiles in "Fission."	10	Bronze
WHEELMAN	Finish the hoverbike sequence without hitting any walls or obstacles and taking no damage in "Aftermath."	10	Bronze
SITTING DUCKS	Kill 3 enemies with one shot of the Sniper Drone in "Manhunt."	10	Bronze
PARTY CRASHER	Kill 20 enemies with the Grappling Hook in "Sentinel."	10	Bronze
RESTRICTED AIRSPACE	EMP 10 enemy aircraft out of the sky with the hovertank in "Bio Lab."	10	Bronze

Achievement/Trophy	Description	Gamer Points	Trophy Type
MAN OVERBOARD!	Melee an enemy so they fly off the side of the ship in "Armada."	10	Bronze
FLYING ACE	Shoot down 10 enemies with machine guns in "Throttle."	10	Bronze
HEAVY-HANDED	Go through 20 gun drops in one-armed combat in "Captured."	10	Bronze

OTHER CAMPAIGN ACHIEVEMENTS/TROPHIES

You earn these accomplishments by completing specific actions anywhere in the single-player campaign. Note that some are limited to a specific mission since they require a particular piece of equipment.

Achievement/Trophy	Description	Gamer Points	Trophy Type
CARMA	Kill an enemy by throwing a car door at them.	10	Bronze
NEVER SAW IT COMING	Boost Jump, dash forward, then air stomp on an enemy. With an adversary directly ahead, perform a Boost Jump, dodge straight ahead, and then press the Crouch button to perform the air stomp. Give yourself plenty of distance to complete this maneuver.	15	Bronze
ESCAPE ARTIST	Avoid 20 grenades by dodging with your Exo.	20	Silver
LOUD ENOUGH FOR YOU?	Kill 10 enemies or drones while affected by a sonic blast. Achieve this on "Fission," "Crash," "Collapse," "Armada," or "Throttle," as these are the levels where Sonics are equipped. Use this ability whenever available to rack up the 10 kills quickly.	15	Bronze
MAXIMUM OVERDRIVE	Kill 50 enemies while using Overdrive. Overdrive is equipped in eight of the campaign levels, so you should have plenty of time to get the necessary kills. Use Overdrive whenever available against big groups of foes. Quickly take down as many as you can before your battery is depleted. You can always replay the levels to work toward the 50 kills.	20	Silver
GENIUS	Kill four enemies with a single Smart Grenade. There are many chances to get this one, but a good opportunity is during "Fission," inside the reactor room. Not long after you enter, 4 hostiles fight from a platform just to the left. Toss a Smart Grenade their way to collect this award.	10	Bronze
THREAT DETECTED	Paint 10 enemies with a single Threat Grenade. There are several occasions where at least 10 foes are present, such as in the "Throttle" level.	15	Bronze
FLY SWATTER	Knock 25 drones out of the sky with EMP Grenades. This number accrues collectively through the campaign, so take these pests down with your EMP Grenades as soon as you see them.	15	Bronze

Achievement/Trophy	Description	Gamer Points	Trophy Type
WHERE ARE YOU GOING?	Stop an AST with an EMP Grenade. Simply toss an EMP Grenade at an AST to cause it to stop in its tracks. Your first chance is in the "Utopia" mission when you face the AST at the docks.	10	Bronze
RIOT CONTROL	Kill 20 enemies while linked to the Mobile Cover Drone. In "Fission," link up with one of the drones in the first street. Lower the shield, and take out 20 hostiles as you move down the road.	10	Bronze
HISTORY IN THE MAKING	Collect over half of the Intel. As you play through the campaign, collect every Intel. You will earn this after grabbing the second one in the "Sentinel" level.	15	Bronze
FERRUM ABSCONSUM	Collect all the Intel. There are 45 Intel in all, three in each level.	30	Silver
ADVANCED SOLDIER	Spend your first Exo upgrade point. Complete the challenges to gain upgrade points, and then spend them on Exo upgrades after completing a level.	5	Bronze
SECOND SKIN	Spend 10 Exo upgrade points.	10	Bronze
WE HAVE THE TECHNOLOGY	Spend 20 Exo upgrade points.	25	Silver
POWER CHANGES EVERYTHING	Completely upgrade your Exo. This requires 33 upgrade points. Use your grenades and go for headshots whenever possible, since they go toward two of the Exo challenges.	50	Gold

EXO SURVIVAL

You earn the following awards by playing a lot of Exo Survival mode. Flipping a map twice for Flip Flop is the toughest to complete, as you must get through 50 total waves to get it. However, note that you can complete it on any difficulty. Exo Survivor can be completed on the Bonus Survival wave after unlocking the last tier map.

Achievement/Trophy	Description	Gamer Points	Trophy Type
EXO SURVIVAL VETERAN	Play 50 Exo Survival Matches.	10	Bronze
CLASS WARFARE	Play 30 minutes with each class online in Exo Survival.	10	Bronze
EXO FLIP	"Flip" a map. Complete Wave 25 to start back at Wave 1 with tougher enemies.	10	Bronze
FLIP FLOP	Flip a map twice. Reach Wave 25 twice in one game of Exo Survival.	30	Bronze
EXO SURVIVOR	Successfully complete the Exo Survival Bonus Wave.	10	Bronze

MULTIPLAYER COVERAGE

Welcome to the *Call of Duty®: Advanced Warfare* Multiplayer guide. In the following chapters, you can explore every aspect of combat in the future. We begin with an overview of the game's basic concepts. We then dive into the biggest change of all, the Exo Suit. Subsequent chapters tackle the most important aspects of the Multiplayer experience in much greater detail. If you're fairly new to *Call of Duty®* or just want to brush up, we recommend that you start with the Multiplayer Intro & Basics chapter that starts on the next page. If you're a seasoned player looking for in-depth stats and analysis, refer to the topic-specific chapters that follow. Read on to learn that power does, in fact, change everything.

MULTIPLAYER INTRO & BASICS

Welcome to *Call of Duty®: Advanced Warfare* Multiplayer.

Not too far in the future, private military corporations wage proxy wars for nations and sophisticated technology has changed the battlefields, but nothing has changed the need for skilled soldiers and trained operators.

In *Call of Duty®: Advanced Warfare* Multiplayer, you take the role of one such elite operator, utilizing all the arms and armaments of the future, waging war for either the Atlas or Sentinel forces.

WHAT'S NEW

EXO SUITS

Refer to the Exo Skeleton chapter on page 106 for more details.

Every player in Multiplayer is armored with an exoskeleton that grants superhuman strength and comes equipped with a set of boosters that allow rapid movement and map traversal. The Exo Suit grants you the ability to Boost Jump, as well as Boost Dodge on the ground, dash in the air, and Boost Slide on the ground.

You can chain together Exo movement abilities in any order. For example, you can jump off of a ledge, dash in mid-air, jump a second time, and then dash a second time. This rapid  movement has massive implications for combat in *Call of Duty®: Advanced Warfare*. Therefore, it is of utmost importance that you begin practicing these movements the minute you get your feet wet in a Multiplayer match. The best players will master this new style of movement.

There are other changes, as well. What were once Tactical and Lethal Grenades are now Exo abilities and Exo Launcher Grenades. Your Exo Suit grants you abilities that give you a wide range of tactical combat options. Exo Launcher Grenades are more traditional explosive weapons, while non-Lethal Grenades provide tactical advantages and can be detonated in mid-air. You cannot manually detonate the Variable Grenade, which gives you four types of Tactical Grenades: Stun, EMP, Threat, and Smoke.

SUPPLY DROPS See page 114 for more info on Supply Drops.

New to the *Call of Duty*® series is the concept of loot! Now, you can earn unique, special versions of weapons after a Multiplayer match. You can also acquire new cosmetic options to equip your soldier in Multiplayer matches.

You can earn some Supply Drop items by completing certain challenges, but the majority are simply awarded as you play Multiplayer matches. There are three tiers of Supply Drop loot: Enlisted, Professional, and Elite. Each tier increases in rarity.

Note that while there are variant weapons (with unique skins, and some with unique abilities), they are not strictly "better" weapons. Instead, they have slight attribute changes—typically a penalty in some stats and bonuses in others.

You're still free to use the weapons you prefer and thrive in competitive matches, but now you have the added excitement of earning unique loot after every match...

REINFORCEMENTS

A subset of Supply Drop loot, Reinforcements are special one-shot care packages that award you Perks or Scorestreaks during a fight. They aren't permanent bonuses, but they can give you a nice early edge in a match!

DIRECTED-ENERGY WEAPONS

The Weapons chapter on page 118 covers all weapon types.

One consequence of the near-future combat envisioned in *Call of Duty*®*: Advanced Warfare* is the deployment of directed-energy weapons (DEWs) to the battlefield—or, as a layperson might say, laser rifles! DEWs have the benefit of not requiring ammo. They cannot run their battery dry, but they can overheat. However, you can manually vent heat by "reloading."

VIRTUAL FIRING RANGE (VFR)

See page 117 for more on the VFR.

A great addition to the Multiplayer lobby, you can now instantly jump into a firing range between matches. Want to quickly test out a new weapon or an attachment combination? Hop in the VFR, and take some shots.

CO-OP SCORESTREAKS

The Scorestreaks chapter starts on page 156.

In addition to the return of Scorestreaks (instead of straight Killstreaks), there are some Scorestreaks that you can use in a co-op fashion. Certain streaks allow a teammate to "join" you in the active Scorestreak, often acting as a second gunner or target spotter. This is a great way for skilled players to let their newbie buddies experience powerful Scorestreaks, and then lay a two-person smackdown on the enemy team.

CUSTOM SCORESTREAKS

The Scorestreaks chapter starts on page 156.

If all the customization options in *Call of Duty®* weren't enough for you already, it is now possible to mod your Scorestreaks via Modules. Every Scorestreak has multiple Modules that you can attach, up to three at a time. The cost is a direct increase in the score needed to earn the streak, but the benefit allows you to customize specific offensive, defensive, and tactical streaks to different game modes and your preferred style of play.

PICK 13

For more on Pick 13, turn to page 116.

An expansion of the Pick 10 system used in *Call of Duty®: Black Ops II*, Pick 13 adds the three Scorestreak slots to the mix as selectable options. You do *not* have to take all three streaks; you can take one, two, three, or none at all if you want. And there's even a Wildcard to gain a *fourth* streak slot! If you remove all streaks from a build, you gain three extra points that you can put toward other weaponry, perks, or gear.

FAST RELOADING

For reload charts on each weapon class, see the Weapons chapter on page 118.

You can quickly reload any weapon except single-fire weapons (such as the RW1 and MORS) and energy weapons by performing a mag dump. Double tap the Reload button to have your operator discard the current magazine and reload a fresh mag more quickly. The tradeoff? You lose the remaining ammo in the mag you dropped. Try to reload quickly too often, and you may find yourself scavenging for a new weapon on the battlefield.

CREATE AN OPERATOR

See page 115 for more on Create an Operator

You can heavily customize your soldier, as there are dozens and dozens of available pieces of gear and custom Exo paint jobs to flaunt your style. You can earn such customizations from Supply Drops, challenges, Exo Survival, or special promotions. All are cosmetic, so wear what you like!

INFINITE SPRINT

The Exo Skeleton chapter starts on page 106. For more info on Perks, turn to page 150.

The mobility offered by the Exo Suit is your primary means of rapid traversal in *Call of Duty®: Advanced Warfare*. To keep ground movement relevant, you don't need a Perk to sprint endlessly; you can always move quickly while on the ground. The Lightweight Perk allows you to move faster.

MAP DESIGN

Detailed Multiplayer maps start on page 196.

The maps in *Call of Duty®: Advanced Warfare* have been built specifically with Exo Suit movement in mind. Maps feature clean lines of fire, wide open spaces for Exo Suit movement, and many rooftops and vertical pieces of cover that you can jump on or over.

You may find that there is a lack of "traditional" cover compared to what you're used to finding in a *Call of Duty®* Multiplayer map. However, after a few matches, you will begin looking at the maps differently. Very large bulky objects nearby become "active" cover when you can Boost Dodge behind them to escape a firefight. Hugging walls as you're moving on the ground allows you to evade and ambush adversaries in elevated positions above you.

GAMEPLAY MODES

See page 172 for details on every game mode.

Uplink is a new teamplay-focused objective mode, Hardpoint returns, and Momentum makes a return from far in the *Call of Duty®* past. What are you waiting for? Get in there, and check out the new goods!

MULTIPLAYER BASICS

Multiplayer in *Call of Duty®: Advanced Warfare* is very straightforward on a basic level: pick your gear, get out there, and fight your opponents with your chosen weapon and loadout. But the options available for you to customize your soldier and Exo Suit are very broad and deep, indeed.

This section is meant to give you a quick overview of the various aspects of customizing your operator, as well as a basic guide to combat in Multiplayer matches. Ultimately, developing your skill in Multiplayer simply comes down to practice (and lots of it!). This guide will arm you with the knowledge you need to equip yourself wisely and tackle combat situations intelligently, but the rest comes down to your own skill.

CREATE AN OPERATOR

For more info on Create an Operator, refer to page 115.

In Multiplayer, you start in the class system. While you cannot customize your class loadouts for the first few levels, you quickly unlock the ability to fully modify your loadout with a dizzying

number of options. Learning how to combine the huge range of weapons, Perks, Exo kit, Wildcards, and Scorestreaks is vital to your success in *Call of Duty®: Advanced Warfare*. Later chapters in this guide cover each aspect of customizing your classes in much greater detail, but this section is meant as a primer to get you started.

PICK 13 BASIC LOADOUT

Your class consists of many different configurable options:

>> One primary weapon, with up to two attachments

>> One secondary weapon, with up to one attachment

>> Up to three Perks

>> One Exo ability

>> One Exo Launcher Grenade

>> Three Scorestreak slots

>> Three Wildcard slots

Each item on that list costs one of your Pick 13 points. A basic loadout consists of a primary weapon with two attachments, a secondary weapon, three Perks, an Exo ability, a grenade, and three Scorestreaks. However, you can deviate wildly from the basic loadout. Want six Perks? Go for it. Three attachments on your primary, and no secondary? Sure! Four Scorestreaks, loaded weapons and abilities, no Perks? Okay!

Because there are so many possible options, it is very important to understand the value of each point. Is a grenade worth losing a permanent Perk or Scorestreak for? Be aware of how combining options creates a more powerful class when built well (especially, say, if you have Perks and Wildcards that support a powerful objective sieging grenade build).

Early on, when you're learning in Multiplayer, experiment with builds, using whatever looks appealing to you. As you become more experienced and more interested in creating focused builds for specific modes or playstyles, come back here and examine the advice on all the parts of the Pick 13 system to help inform your creation of powerful, focused classes.

WILDCARDS

Wildcards are a special option that allows you to "break the rules" of the basic Pick 13 system, opening up additional slots for weapons, Perks, equipment, and Scorestreaks. You can use Wildcards to unlock a third primary attachment, a second secondary attachment, up to three additional Perk slots, and one additional Scorestreak slot.

Wildcards can also allow you to take a third grenade, a second Exo ability, or two primary weapons instead of a primary and a secondary. Each Wildcard costs a point, and the item occupying the newly opened slot also costs a point. Although you definitely pay for the additional customization power, Wildcards are the key to making powerful, focused builds.

WEAPON SELECTION

The Weapons chapter on page 118 covers all weapon types. The Attachments chapter starts on page 146.

The basics of choosing a weapon are fairly simple: pick a weapon that suits both your favored engagement distance and the most common engagement distances on the map and mode you're playing. If it's all close quarters combat (CQC), bring a shotgun or SMG; if it's more long-range fighting, take a sniper or Heavy Weapon. Assault rifles can work well in most situations, though they aren't quite as good as the specialists up close or far away.

Keep in mind that Exo movement has affected the weapon balance. For example, Heavy Weapons are traditionally slow-moving, cumbersome weapons. They still are, in terms of handling. However, with Exo movement and the open map design, it is now much easier to zip around a map and put heavy, long-range firepower where you need it, when you need it. Similarly, shotguns and SMGs are even nastier at short ranges than they usually are. Boost Dodging allows you to hip fire, dodge, and resume hipfiring, throwing off your opponents' aim and keeping a steady stream of fire headed in their direction.

WEAPON CUSTOMIZATION

The Weapons chapter on page 118 covers all weapon types. The Attachments chapter starts on page 146.

You can modify weapons with attachments, including items like basic sights, grips to reduce recoil or improve handling, modified magazines, and many other options. Attachments let you personalize your weapons, improve their strengths, and soften their weaknesses.

Attachment choices are almost as personal as weapon selection. You should use what feels best to you, especially when it comes to sights. However, many attachments have very specific effects that you must fully understand to get the most benefit from them. See the Weapons and Attachments sections of the guide for more details on the specifics of how they interact, and use the information to improve your modified weaponry.

A favorite weapon with the correct mods for the game mode and the playstyle you prefer is the first step in customizing your build to perform well.

SUPPLY DROP WEAPONRY AND ATTACHMENTS

Some special Supply Drop weapons have fixed attachments that you cannot remove. This can interfere with your ability to modify the weapon (for example, if it comes with a barrel or sight mod that you would prefer to replace). However, the benefit is that the attachment is "free" as far as your Pick 13 points go. You still lose the attachment slot, but if the attachment is one you want anyway, you can use the extra point elsewhere in your build!

This is one of the very few areas where a Supply Drop weapon can be "better" than a normal weapon, though even in this case, you're trading flexibility on your weapon for more flexibility in your build.

SCORESTREAKS

The Scorestreaks chapter starts on page 156.

Scorestreaks are powerful combat support items awarded for earning enough score without dying (hence the name). These range from low-key (but still vitally important) options like the UAV for radar sweeps all the way up to the awesomely devastating Paladin Droneship, a heavily armed and armored orbiting drone that rains down death from above.

You can take anywhere from one to three streaks normally, each costing one point. If you really want to pile on the streaks, it is possible to take a fourth streak by spending a Wildcard point. Earning Scorestreak rewards requires that you play smart, mixing aggression and objective play with caution and retreat to stay alive in unfavorable situations. You can earn low-end rewards (and Support-modded streaks) with a few quick objective plays, but mid- to high-tier streaks require some effort.

It's important to pick streaks that support your playstyle and the game mode you are playing, and make a point of sticking to streaks that are achievable at your skill level. Taking high-end Scorestreaks if you can't hit them consistently consumes points that could be helping you win gunfights. As you improve in Multiplayer, you can gradually edge your streaks (and modified streaks) toward the high end with more frequent success.

You may find that you simply prefer to cut down to very few Scorestreaks and run with more Perks or equipment; there's nothing wrong with that. If you feel you're more effective with extra Perk muscle or gear, use those instead of Scorestreaks.

SCORESTREAK MODULES

New to *Call of Duty®: Advanced Warfare*, it is now possible to modify your Scorestreaks. Each of the streaks in the game has a range of Modules, and you can attach up to three to any of your selected streaks. Adding Modules raises the score cost of the streak, so you must balance their added power or utility against the increase in score required to earn them.

SUPPORT STREAKS

One particularly important mod known as the "Support" mod only appears on four of the streaks. This mod allows points earned toward the streak to persist through death, allowing you to always earn the streaks as long as you're playing reasonably aggressively or playing the objective frequently.

The Support mod does increase the cost of the streaks significantly, so you pay for the ease of earning them with fewer potentially earned per match. Still, Support is often a good tradeoff to provide you and your team with guaranteed streak benefits.

As there are four Support-capable streaks, you can run a build with the Streaker Wildcard and run all four Support streaks in a single build for the cost of five points.

OPERATOR

For more info on Create an Operator, refer to page 115.

Customizing your operator is purely cosmetic—gear yourself out however you see fit! There are a great many pieces of new gear for your operator that you can earn via Supply Drop. The longer you play, the more you earn. There is also a very special, very shiny set of gear for true weapons masters, unlocked by completing many weapon challenges…

GAME MODES

See page 172 for details on every game mode.

Game modes are the heart of the *Call of Duty®: Advanced Warfare* Multiplayer experience. From the organized chaos of a Team Deathmatch to the heavily objective-focused Uplink or Momentum, or the classic Domination and competitive Hardpoint, there are modes for every mood and every style of player.

Multiplayer playlists are divided up into different game modes (or combinations of modes), so choose to tackle whatever suits your preferences the best. Clan Wars encourage you to tackle a variety of game modes with your clanmates. Do so, and reap rewards like new customization options and new gear.

PRIVATE AND BOTS

It is possible to play private matches with just you and your friends. This is a great way to experiment with custom game modes, as you can tinker with all of the game settings in private matches. It's also an excellent place to learn the maps. Additionally, if you're particularly nervous about tackling other players online, bots have you covered. You can fight against AI opponents on any map or game mode as you see fit.

COMBAT

Face your rivals in Multiplayer matches on diverse battlegrounds in many different modes of play. Use this advice, train, fight, and grow stronger.

WEAPON USAGE

The Weapons chapter on page 118 discusses all weapon types in detail.

Basic weapon usage in *Call of Duty®: Advanced Warfare* is quite simple. Using it well in every situation while under fire and using your Exo movement to its fullest is another matter. The next section provides some basic tips for handling your weapon in Multiplayer.

AIMING—ADS

Aim Down Sights (ADS) is simply the act of aiming your weapon. Hipfiring a weapon is very inaccurate past close range, so your standard engagement action should be pulling up your sights as you open fire.

You cannot Boost Dodge while aiming, so keep in mind that you need to drop ADS to quickly dodge to the side. Alternately, you can jump out of your aim and quickly air dash behind cover.

While aiming and firing, you fight the recoil forces of your weapon. These vary significantly depending on the weapon in question and which attachments you are using on it.

Over time, you can develop a feel for the specific recoil pattern of each weapon in the game, as they all handle differently. Remember that when firing fully automatic weapons, if you hold the trigger down, you're going to be fighting the full force of the weapons recoil. At long distances, fire in short bursts to maintain accuracy. At very long distances, you may need to tap in single or double shots.

SLOW MOVEMENT

Entering ADS slows your movement speed, and it also prevents the use of Boost Dodge. However, remember that you can ADS while in mid-air. Indeed, you'll need to do so often once you're taking full advantage of your Exo Suit movement.

HIP FIRE

The opposite of a controlled, aimed burst, hip fire is the very definition of spray and pray. That said, it is possible to use hip fire effectively. Shotguns and SMGs are built for close-range hip fire, and hipfiring allows you to retain full movement speed while strafing.

You cannot Boost Dodge while firing, but it is faster to stop shooting from hip fire very briefly, dodge, and then resume firing than it is to cancel an ADS and resume ADS. In that situation, hip fire gives you a mobility edge, as well.

With the proper gun and attachment, you can hip fire out to a surprising distance, but keep in mind that it is less reliable than going ADS. You also tend to burn a lot of ammo, so bring attachments or Perks to extend your supply.

ACCURACY

To see recoil plots for each weapon class, see the Weapons chapter on page 118.

Accuracy is a function of the weapon you're using, whether you're in ADS or hipfiring, or if you're crouched or prone. Taking damage, jumping, and hipfiring all cause a loss of accuracy.

Going ADS, crouching, or going prone all improve accuracy, as does firing in bursts with full auto weapons. Keep in mind that with the speed and height of movement provided by the Exo Suits, trying to crouch behind cover or go prone for an extended period of time is a very bad idea.

SWAY

Sway is simply the natural motion of the weapon you are holding while in ADS. This gentle bobbing usually isn't a factor in accuracy unless you are aiming at a very distant target, but it is a factor, so keep it in mind.

For sniper rifles specifically, sway is a bigger issue. When you enter a full sniper scope, your view bobs significantly, and you must steady the scope by holding the Sprint button. Sniper rifles with the Iron Sights attachment don't have to be steadied, but other weapons using the Thermal Sight do.

RELOADING

See the Weapons chapter on page 118 for reload charts covering each weapon class.

Reloading seems straightforward, but there are a surprising number of nuances. To begin with, every weapon in the game has several different reload times.

» **Empty** reload, when the weapon is fully empty, requires both changing the magazine and pulling the charging handle. This is the longest and slowest reload.

» **Normal** reload is the time it takes to reload a partially expended magazine.

» **Ammo Add Time** is the time it takes for the reloaded ammo to become "active"— this is faster than the full reload animation. While it varies by weapon, this generally occurs the instant your soldier inserts a fresh mag into the weapon. As soon as you see ammo on the UI refresh, your weapon is reloaded.

» **Speed Reloading** is triggered by double-tapping the Reload button. Doing this causes you to throw away the current magazine and reload more quickly. You lose any remaining ammunition that was in the mag, but you get a faster reload in exchange.

The added ammo is also the key to a faster method of reloading without speed reloading. By cancelling the remaining animation of the reload, either by sprinting or quickly double-tapping the Weapon Switch button, you can have a readied weapon with full ammo without finishing the entire animation.

Generally, in Multiplayer matches, you should always be either reload cancelling by sprinting (even a single step works) or by speed reloading if you are at all threatened in a combat situation. Learn to recognize situations where you need to speed reload, and get in the habit of reload cancelling by sprinting all the time. You want your weapon up and ready as quickly as possible.

WEAPON SWITCHING

Like reloading, switching weapons is a natural and obvious action in combat. However, it's important to know that the speed at which you switch weapons is not always the same. The Fast Hands Perk can greatly speed your switch times, and switching to or from heavy, slow weapons is much slower than switching to or from light, nimble weapons like SMGs or pistols.

Switching to a pistol is extremely fast, so switching and firing when you run dry on your primary is a useful technique. Even with speed reloads, it's faster to switch and finish a damaged opponent than it is to reload.

Keep in mind that Exo movement can give you the evasion you need to complete a reload, but dodging is no guarantee of survival. Spend some time practicing the quick switch and finish—you may find that a backup pistol suits your playstyle.

MELEE

Your Exo allows you to perform powerful, lethal punches at short range. Keep in mind that melee distance is extremely short and has very little automatic tracking. You must be right on top of your target, and missing a melee strike is an almost guaranteed death if your opponent is aware of you.

Use melee attacks when you run straight into an enemy, or if you happen to sneak up on an opponent. Otherwise, hipfiring paired with quick evasion is generally a much safer tactic at close range.

BOOST SLAM

By holding the Crouch button while in mid-air, you can use your Exo Suit to perform a Boost Slam, slamming into the ground with potentially lethal force. If you directly hit an enemy, you can one-shot kill them. If you land very close, you may stagger them slightly, particularly if you take the Overcharged Perk, which provides a bonus to Boost Slams.

HEALTH AND DAMAGE

Player health is internally set to 100, with most weapons doing enough damage to kill in around four shots. However, the exact number depends on the weapon in question, the range at which you engage, and if you score any headshots. After taking non-lethal damage, you regenerate fully after a few seconds.

HIT MARKERS

When you score a damaging hit on any player, your crosshair flashes red, and you hear an audio cue. When you land a headshot, your crosshair flashes in a double hatch pattern. Use hit markers from grenades to locate enemies inside rooms or behind cover, or use penetrating wall shots to sniff out enemies with your weapon.

FLINCH

Getting damaged causes your view to jerk and slows your movement slightly. You can slightly mitigate this effect with the Toughness Perk, but flinch is another reason that landing the first shot is always best. Flinch also makes hip fire effective at the correct distance because you can maintain a stream of fire that throws your opponents' aim off while you continue moving at full speed.

BASIC MOVEMENT

Movement has always been equally important as (or perhaps even more important than) aiming in *Call of Duty®*. This is now truer than ever with the addition of Exo Suit movement. Moving through maps smoothly and safely is a vital skill to master. You must learn which routes enemies take in each gameplay mode, which areas are most exposed, and how you can move from place to place as quickly as possible.

SPRINTING

Sprinting allows you to move quickly while on the ground. You can sprint indefinitely, but just be aware that you are easier to hear while running. You also have your gun down, and it takes longer to bring it up again. Sprinting around corners into areas where you suspect enemy presence is a bad idea. Without the proper Perk, you cannot reload while sprinting.

The Lightweight Stock attachment helps to speed your weapon's recovery from a sprint. Lighter weapons in general (such as pistols and SMGs) recover from a sprint more quickly.

CROUCH AND PRONE

Crouching and going prone both help stabilize your aim and lower your profile, letting you hide behind low cover to reload and avoid enemy fire. Be aware that with the vertical lines of sight offered by Exo Suit movement, it is not safe to crouch or go prone for a long period of time in any one location.

MANTLING

Mantling is simply pulling yourself over low cover or onto a ledge. There is a very handy setting in the Control Options menu that lets you auto-mantle any ledge if you are falling toward it. That is, if you're coming down in the air from a Boost Jump or Air Dash, you can let auto-mantle automatically pull you onto a rooftop or ledge. You can disable this option if you prefer to mantle manually by tapping the Jump button. Just be aware that this makes it a bit slower and harder to quickly move vertically through the maps.

EXO MOVEMENT

To delve into the Exo Suit in greater detail, including all aspects of Exo movement, check out the Exo Skeleton chapter on page 106.

Your Exo Suit grants you amazing maneuverability, so it is vital that you learn to use it and use it well.

SLIDING

Perform a Boost Slide by sprinting on the ground and holding the Crouch button. A Boost Slide propels you forward across the ground quickly and changes your profile, potentially causing long-range enemies to miss you. This is very useful for sliding into cover or for sliding around a corner and surprising an enemy who was aiming at head height.

DODGING

Dodge from side to side or backwards by pressing in the Sprint button while moving sideways or backward. You can also dash while in the air, and this includes dashing forward. Beware of dashing shotgun users who can close distances incredibly quickly by jumping and Boost Dashing forward. Dodging is an extremely useful move, but keep in mind that you can't dodge while firing or in ADS.

BOOST JUMP

You can perform a Boost Jump simply by pressing the Jump button a second time while in the air. You can do a second jump at any time in the air, whether you jumped yourself, or fell off a ledge, or just finished an Air Dash.

COMBINED MOVEMENT

Jumps, Boost Jumps, Boost Dodges, aerial dashes, slides, and slams can all be freely chained together. A critical skill you must master is combining Boost Jumps and Air Dashes. You can jump, dash, jump again, and dash again, or jump twice and dash.

Those two movement combinations are your most frequently used Exo Suit movement combos for covering ground rapidly, so master them.

It is also very useful to perform single dodges on the ground, or quick jump dashes in any direction. Moving laterally can get you behind cover, moving forward can get you in range with a short-range weapon, and moving backward can help you escape from someone with a shotgun.

MOVE!

It can't be overstated how important it is to master the combination of Exo Suit movement abilities. Start using them early and often. Initially, it may feel awkward, but with practice, you can soon be zipping around the maps and scoring aerial kills.

MOVEMENT SPEEDS

Heavier weapons slow your movement. Although Exo movement can help mitigate some of this speed loss, you are still more sluggish when moving with a Heavy Weapon than you are with an SMG. This is particularly important to remember when fighting in CQC, or while using mobile hip fire. Stick to lighter weapons if close-range mobility is key to your build or your playstyle.

If you're using a heavy primary, carrying a lightweight secondary lets you move more quickly by switching to it. Just be careful to have your primary ready when you approach suspected enemy territory.

COVER

Cover has always been important in *Call of Duty*®, and the nature of cover has changed in *Call of Duty*®: *Advanced Warfare*. Seek out very large, thick objects like buildings and huge obstructions to use as cover. Their importance is equal to or greater than smaller obstacles that you can aim over.

SITUATIONAL AWARENESS

Situational awareness is one of the most powerful skills you can master in Multiplayer. It is learned through practice and observation until it becomes second nature, but the very best players have an almost inhuman ability to track and monitor enemy positions during and outside of combat. Pay attention to all of the cues that the game gives you to monitor your adversaries' positions.

By using Exo movement, you can quickly get behind heavy cover, dodging out of line of sight of nearby (or distant) enemies and completely shutting down their ability to hit you. While it has always been possible to move behind hard cover in past *Call of Duty*® titles, it has never been as fast or easy as it is with Exo movement.

In this game, you must learn to think about the maps differently. Look for areas where you can fight in the open or on a rooftop, and then quickly drop from the roof. Find thick cover to Boost Dodge behind if the situation turns sour. Smaller cover still exists, and it remains quite useful. However, when your enemies can round a corner 20 feet in the air aiming down at you, you need to reevaluate what is a safe defensive position!

SIGHT, SOUND, AND UI

Spotting enemies, bullet tracers, grenades, Scorestreak usage, movement—all can alert you to an enemy presence. Also, hearing an adversary in any way can alert you to their position. The sound of footsteps, a reload, a grenade, a Scorestreak, or gunfire all can warn you of nearby foes.

ROOFTOP FLANKING

In the past, entering rooms and rounding corners were two of the most dangerous actions you could take in a Multiplayer match. Now, Exo Suit movement has added a new wrinkle, with three dimensional "corners" that can be crossed.

When you are on a rooftop or another elevated position, enemies directly below you hugging the walls beneath you are difficult or impossible to spot. If they Boost Jump up to your roof, there's a very good chance they'll surprise you or hit you from the flank or rear. Keep this in mind on both offense and defense. Rooftop locations are power positions for covering terrain and opening lines of sight, but they are exposed to sudden attack by enemies from below.

When you know an enemy is camping a certain elevated position, look for a route that takes you beneath their position and hugs the walls near them. Odds are, you won't be spotted, and when you leap up, you can terminate the target quickly.

Your HUD can also help alert you to nearby enemies: with the mini-map, with the death markers of your teammates, with objective indicators changing, or by scoring hit markers with grenades or through walls with penetrating bullets.

Even the position of your teammates can alert you to the likely position of your foes. After all, except in rare situations, enemies are not located where your teammates are, and that narrows the possibilities significantly. Pay attention to map flow and player positions at all times.

USING THE KILLCAM

If you die at the hands of another player, you can watch the killcam to see what happened. Keep in mind that, due to the realities of Internet latency, killcams are never 100% accurate from your perspective. What you saw and what they saw are going to differ slightly—don't sweat the specifics. If you lost a gunfight, pay attention to what they were using, where they attacked you from, and (potentially) what their loadout was.

If you're a new player, watching the killcams of top players on the enemy team can help you to learn Exo Suit movement techniques, hiding spots, and solid builds that you can explore yourself.

THE MINI-MAP

The mini-map is extremely important, and learning to read it at a glance and figure out friendly and enemy positions is vital. The Peripherals Perk greatly extends the range of your mini-map, allowing you to spot enemies at a greater distance. This comes at the cost of some shorter range fidelity when trying to pinpoint a very near opponent.

Whenever an enemy fires an unsilenced weapon or uses their Exo Suit movement abilities without a Blast Suppressor Perk equipped, they appear on the mini-map.

Friendly players always show on the mini-map, and they show when they're firing, as well.

The UAV Scorestreak is vital for radar intelligence. While active, it constantly sweeps and updates your mini-map with all enemy positions. Depending on the upgrades, the mini-map can also indicate which direction adversaries are facing, and even outline them in the world.

Learn to read your mini-map frequently. The presence or absence of friendly players in an area, combined with the location of objectives and your own familiarity with map routes, can warn you of enemy presence even if they aren't showing up on the mini-map.

Players firing weapons show up as a bright dot, but players using Exo Suit movement only appear as a brief "ping" on the mini-map. Players can move extremely rapidly with Exo movement. It's important to understand that seeing an enemy in one position even two seconds ago does not mean that they will still be there when you arrive. Use caution when approaching a known enemy location. It's very likely they have relocated, and depending on how you approach the area, you can expose yourself to significant danger.

USING EXPLOSIVES

For more details on grenades, turn to page 5.

The various grenade types available to your Exo Launcher allow you to bombard enemies with lethal Frag or Semtex Grenades, or disorient and detect them with a variety of Tactical Grenade options. Causing any explosion to go off near an enemy causes severe flinching. Such explosions actually drop adversaries out of ADS.

This makes Tactical Grenades a particularly helpful option for beginning a siege on a known enemy position. Just be aware that it's usually a better idea to let a teammate make the charge immediately when the grenade detonates. This lets your teammates hit at the very instant.

Note that non-lethal Tactical Grenade options (excepting the Variable Grenade) can be detonated in mid-air manually. This allows you to nail players using Exo Suit movement. Lethal Grenade options or the Variable Grenade options are better used in interior areas, or near objectives where enemies are forced to stay on the ground and nearby.

USING EXO ABILITIES

Refer to page 108 for much more detail on Exo Abilities.

Exo abilities are powered by a one-shot battery, and activating the ability begins draining the battery immediately. The duration depends on the ability in question and how long you activate it, but you can generally get a few seconds or a few activations out of any Exo ability. There are a range of Exo abilities suitable for a variety of combat situations. See the Exo Suit section of the guide for more details.

The Overcharged Perk gives you a bit more battery life from your Exo abilities, and the Tactician Wildcard lets you take a second Exo ability in place of your Exo Launcher slots.

FIGHTING SCORESTREAKS

For detailed analysis of all Scorestreaks, turn to page 156.

Scorestreaks are powerful, but the majority of them are vulnerable to secondary launchers. The Stinger M7 and the MAAWS can both lock on to any of the Scorestreaks with a battlefield presence (though you can't lock on to an Orbital UAV). The MAHEM can be fired unguided at slower-moving or stationary streaks (say, an emplaced Sentry Turret).

There are also some Perks that can hide you from the AI targeting of Scorestreaks. If you find that dealing with certain streaks is particularly frustrating, always keep a build with Perk protection and an Exo Launcher around so you can switch classes and destroy them.

In practice, this means that you need the fewest bullets to down a target up close, and the most at a long distance. In general, weapons suitable for long-range combat have less falloff. This includes weapons like precision assault rifles, Heavy Weapons, and sniper rifles. Pistols and SMGs fall off much more rapidly, making them a poor choice for eliminating enemies at long range.

PENETRATION

Any bullet can potentially fire through thin cover, with heavier weapons having better penetration capability from their bullets. Penetrating cover is a great way to score hits and sometimes kills if you know an enemy is behind it. You can use a detection streak, ability, or grenade, or simply learn where players are likely to hide out, especially near objectives. Scoring penetration kills tends to use a wasteful amount of ammunition, so bring attachments or Perks to mitigate the ammo usage.

MECHANICS

There's a fair amount going on under the hood of the game whenever you pull the trigger, so here's a bit of insight into some factors that can affect you in combat.

DAMAGE FALLOFF

The majority of weapons in *Call of Duty®: Advanced Warfare* cause a flat damage amount, but that amount falls off over distance. At close ranges, you deal maximum damage, and at very long ranges, you deal a minimum damage. Between the two, damage generally falls from the max to the min in a smooth manner.

EXO SKELETON

The Exo Suit is a game-changing piece of equipment. Empowering you with superior strength and mobility, you can move through the battlefield like never before. Your Exo is your best friend in combat. Master its usage and thrive, or fail to take advantage of its power and fall to other players who do.

EXO SUIT MOVEMENT

Exo movement is vital to mastering *Call of Duty®: Advanced Warfare*. If you want to succeed in Multiplayer, you must learn to use Exo movement and use it well. Don't worry too much if you feel a bit awkward and uncomfortable with it at first. After a few days of practice, it begins to feel more natural, and after a week or two, you can fly through maps with incredible speed and instinctively dodge incoming fire. Learn the timing, the ranges, and the heights of your jumps and dodges. Get used to shooting at players in the air, and to shooting at players while in the air yourself.

EXO MOVEMENT STEALTH

Be careful with Exo movement: any time you execute a dodge, dash, or Boost Jump, you appear as a short-lived radial ping on the mini-map. You also are visible to anyone using the Exo Ping ability.

The Blast Suppressor Perk conceals your exhaust, hiding your ping on the mini-map. This is a very useful upgrade if you often fight near the enemy team and use Exo movement constantly (which you should be doing anyway).

Because you can move so rapidly with the Exo Suit, it's not a problem to briefly appear on the mini-map. Remember, everyone else on your team is likely lighting it up with blips, as well. However, try to stay near your teammates. If you are on your own, make sure you aren't where your last ping appeared when the enemy comes looking for you.

BOOST JUMP

Double-tap the Jump button to activate your thrusters and double jump.

The most basic of all Exo movements, Boost Jumps allow you to gain additional height and distance, letting you bound across rooftops, stand on top of cover, gain an elevated firing position, spot enemies behind low cover, jump behind cover, and quickly evade nearby adversaries.

Double jumping is important, and as it can be freely mixed with Boost Dashes and Slams, it is the key to all combined Exo movement. Practice Boost Jumping extensively. Learn the heights, when to extend a jump fully and when to cut it short, how to mix dashes in mid-air to evade incoming fire or control your movement carefully, and how to traverse levels with it quickly.

BOOST DODGE

Dodge on the ground by pressing the Sprint button and any direction except forward.

Pressing left, right, or back and the Sprint button causes you to perform a Boost Dodge. Dodging gives you a sudden burst of lateral or reverse speed, perfect for evading an enemy in CQC or getting some space from a shotgun rusher. Remember that you cannot perform a Boost Dodge while ADS or hipfiring. You must either dodge before you begin shooting, or momentarily pause to evade.

Use dodging to avoid incoming fire, sidestep explosives, quickly get behind cover, or evade a rushing opponent.

BOOST DASH

Dodge in the air.

Dashing allows you to quickly shift your momentum in mid-air, performing a dash in any direction (including forward). Note that you don't have to Boost Jump to Boost Dash. You can perform a single jump and then dash; in fact, this is one of the best ways to close distance while remaining on the ground.

Jump forward and dash forward with a shotgun or an SMG to get into close range extremely quickly. Jumping and dashing sideways or backwards can also throw off an opponent's aim, giving you a bit of extra distance on your dodging maneuver.

DODGE AND DASH COOLDOWN

Dodges (and dashes, when in the air) have a short cooldown period that prevents you from repeatedly using them. However, your dodge refreshes quickly enough that you can jump off a ledge, dash, jump a second time, and then dash a second time. This is the key to traversing levels incredibly quickly, as well as breaking up your arc of travel in mid-air while foes are targeting you at long range.

You can also combine Boost Dashes with Boost Jumps freely, and it is possible to dash if you end up in the air by any means, not just jumping. For example, if you drop off a ledge (or fall accidentally), you can still dash.

BOOST SLAM

Hold the Crouch button while in mid-air, and perform a melee smash from the air.

Boost Slams are a sort of aerial melee attack, and like melee strikes, they are instantly fatal if you directly connect with an opponent. The Overcharged Perk adds a concussive wave around your impact, staggering and damaging nearby enemies even if you don't land a direct hit.

Boost Slams have one other very important use: they speed your descent from the air. When you're Boost Jumping frequently, you make an easy arcing target in the air if you don't break up your movement. By mixing in Boost Dashes and the Boost Slam, you can cause your path of movement to shift wildly and quickly, throwing off enemies.

Experiment with Boost Slams. They can be tricky to use as an offensive weapon, but they enhance your mobility in a useful defensive manner, allowing you to get behind cover or out of the air more rapidly than falling.

BOOST SLIDE

Hold the Crouch button while sprinting to perform a slide.

Boost Slides let you close distance and break up your target silhouette at the same time. While they are particularly effective when you're using the Gung-Ho Perk with a shotgun (or an SMG, to a lesser extent), Boost Slides are also very useful for breaking up your profile when moving between cover. Enemies at range aiming for your upper body may miss completely if you go into a slide toward cover.

EXO ABILITIES

Exo Abilities grant you a range of special powers, from defensive to informational. These abilities can give you an edge in an engagement, often just enough of one to score one or more guaranteed kills.

Exo Abilities are powered by a limited battery that drains while the ability is used. Once depleted, you cannot recharge the battery. The Overcharged Perk enhances battery life, and the Fast Hands Perk allows you to activate abilities more quickly. Both are important for a build making heavy use of abilities (especially a build running the Tactician Wildcard to use two Exo Abilities simultaneously).

Some Exo Abilities can be spotted at a distance. For example, the Overclock ability puts a yellow glow on the Exo Suit, while the Stim ability has a green glow. In the case of Stim in particular, this can warn you if your target will take a few extra bullets to down.

TACTICAL GEAR

For veteran *Call of Duty®* players, Exo Abilities are very similar to the "Tactical" equipment slot, though they have their own unique quirks.

EXO SHIELD

Quickly deploy a portable shield attached to your arm.

The Exo Shield blocks all frontal shots, can be used to melee an enemy (two hits to kill), and doesn't block your feet unless you are crouched. You can even use the Exo Shield in mid-air.

Deploying the shield is much faster with the Fast Hands Perk, to the point that it is a viable snap defense against being surprised by an enemy at the wrong range for your weapon. You can also use the Exo Shield to gain a few seconds on an objective, which can often be just long enough to secure it.

You can extend the Exo Shield and retract it; you don't have to burn the entire battery with one use. In fact, if you're careful, you can block a few enemies before it expires.

EXO OVERCLOCK

Gain a temporary speed boost.

Overclock offers boosted movement speed. Unlike other Exo Abilities, it does not have an activation animation. This is critical because it means that you can trigger it when you need it most, and you don't have to drop your weapon to do so. For builds focused on speed or objective running, Overclock is extremely useful.

EXO MUTE DEVICE

Silence your footsteps.

The Mute Device actually does a bit more than silencing your footsteps: it also dampens all sound around you, making it easier to hear enemy sounds. If you activate the Mute Device before moving into hostile terrain and you have a good audio setup, you can often detect enemies before they're aware of your presence.

This ability pairs well with a stealth build, though be aware that you can only use it for a short time. It is best used when you need to sneak a flag in CTF, or if you want to ambush campers or defenders who won't hear you coming. Mute Device is also highly map-dependent. If you're making heavy use of Exo movement, the sound dampening won't benefit you quite as much, given your increased visibility.

EXO STIM

Temporarily generate health beyond normal levels.

Stim gives you bonus health for a short time, which is all you need to triumph in a heads-up firefight against another player. Stim is also extremely useful on builds with many defensive Perks and gear. It amplifies the effect of Perks like Flak Jacket, or the utility of the Heavy Shield. Finally, it is also helpful for claiming or running objectives. The extra health can save your life from that one last bullet, potentially letting you secure an objective.

EXO CLOAK

Visually conceal yourself for a short duration.

Cloak does exactly what it says, masking your appearance with optical camouflage. Keep in mind that while you are transparent, you aren't actually invisible, so enemies can and will spot you moving. However, in dark areas or particularly bright areas with poor contrast, an opponent may not spot you until it is too late.

Firing your weapon decloaks you. This makes the Cloak a very strong ability for weapons with good one-shot kill potential. Lurking in buildings with a shotgun or staying out in the open with a sniper rifle can let you score easy kills on enemies who never even see you.

EXO HOVER

Hover in place for a short duration.

Hover lets you float in place or move slowly while in the air. You can use this to gain otherwise impossible lines of sight by utilizing Exo movement to get into the air, freezing yourself in place, and taking a shot.

Hover can also be used to interrupt your aerial movement in a surprising manner. If an enemy is tracking your movement and they expect you to continue an arc, but you suddenly stop mid-leap, it can throw off their aim. Just don't rely on this to save your life if an adversary has the drop on you; at best, they'll miss a few bullets. Be careful when using Hover, as you make quite an easy target floating in mid-air.

EXO PING

Show enemy Exo movement and weapons fire in your HUD.

Enemies who fire their weapons or use Exo boost movement appear on your HUD just as if a Threat Grenade had hit them. This makes Ping a very powerful informational ability. Activate it right before you approach known enemy territory. With a little bit of luck, an adversary will fire their weapon or use their Exo movement, lighting them up and making them an easy target. You can even use Ping to nail targets through walls if you have a weapon with sufficient penetration power and don't mind burning a bit of ammo.

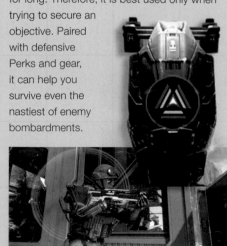

EXO TROPHY SYSTEM

Destroy up to two incoming enemy projectiles.

An important ability in objective modes where you fully expect incoming explosives, the Trophy System is otherwise less useful for general combat. Because the battery only lasts a short time, you can't maintain the defensive benefits for long. Therefore, it is best used only when trying to secure an objective. Paired with defensive Perks and gear, it can help you survive even the nastiest of enemy bombardments.

EXO LAUNCHER

Your "grenade" is actually a launcher mounted on your Exo Suit that you can use to deploy a wide range of munitions, from lethal explosives to tactical tools. You can manually detonate most non-Lethal Grenades in mid-air. This is extremely important for tagging other players using Exo movement with Stun or EMP Grenades.

You can normally take up to two grenades (for one point each), but the Bombardier Wildcard allows you to replace your Exo Ability slot with one additional grenade. This must be a different type of grenade than the one you choose for your normal grenade slot. Sorry, but you can't carry three Semtex or Frags!

FRAG

Cookable Frag Grenades.

The classic Frag Grenade is a flexible and useful explosive. Because you can "cook" the grenade by holding the Grenade button before releasing it, you can detonate Frags in mid-air. With practice, you can learn the heights that different times get you, and nailing adversaries in mid-air becomes a real possibility.

Employ cooking to ensure that your grenade detonates in the air when you throw it into rooms, objectives, or windows, and you can score guaranteed kills. If you do not cook your Frags, they can be picked up and thrown back. The Flak Jacket Perk also lets you pick up Frags and throw them with their full fuse time, no matter how little time was left when you picked one up.

While cooking a grenade, your crosshair pulses once each second. The grenade detonates after 3.5s, so don't hold it for more than three pulses!

STUN GRENADE
Blinds, disorients, and slows enemies. Can be manually detonated.

A powerful Tactical Grenade, the Stun Grenade staggers and blinds enemies hit by it. The blinding effect is strongest if the enemy catches the blast from the front. However, even if you don't blind a target, any foes who are hit are knocked out of ADS, and their movement is slowed.

A close hit can freeze an enemy in place, letting you use Exo movement to attack them from the side or rear for a free kill. Because the stagger effect is short-lived, Stun Grenades are extremely powerful if timed so that your teammates hit an area at the same time the grenade detonates. It's harder for you to launch and detonate the grenade, and then immediately get into range to take advantage of it.

Stun Grenades are also useful when retreating. You can blind and slow an opponent's pursuit long enough to escape safely with some quick Exo movement.

VARIABLE GRENADE
Cycles through Stun, EMP, Threat, and Smoke Grenades. Cannot be manually detonated.

The Variable Grenade allows you to use Stun, EMP, Threat, and Smoke Grenades, but as a tradeoff, you cannot detonate them manually. It also takes time to switch between the different grenade types, and doing so in combat can easily get you killed. Consequently, it's extremely important to have the proper grenade for the job selected ahead of time.

Because you can't air detonate Stun or EMP Grenades, both are best used against areas you know enemies are defending, typically objective areas. EMPs are also useful for dealing with various equipment on the ground. Threat and Smoke Grenades are much easier to use, as the lack of manual detonation isn't much of a problem.

The Variable Grenade is very flexible but can be difficult to use. Keep its limitations in mind, and use the best grenade for a particular situation to reap the most benefit from it.

SEMTEX
Timed sticky explosives.

A sticky explosive, Semtex sticks to any player or surface it hits, then detonates after a fixed fuse time. Semtex is generally a bit easier to use than Frag Grenades, as it's a more "fire and forget" sort of explosive. However, you lose the fine control of a perfectly cooked Frag throw.

Semtex is great for quick tosses into objective areas or known enemy positions. If you score a stick on an adversary, it's a guaranteed kill. Semtex has an identical blast radius to Frags, so whichever one you use comes down to personal preference.

TRACKING DRONE
A piece of equipment that tracks and highlights enemy players.

The Tracking Drone deploys an autonomous AI drone that seeks out nearby players and highlights them with a tracking light. This paints them with both a threat signature on your HUD and a directional arrow on the mini-map.

The drone has a short throwing distance, but once activated, it floats and automatically seeks out nearby enemies. This makes the Tracking Drone a very powerful piece of kit for entering a building or objective area safely. You can deploy it ahead of you to scout the way. Just be careful, as the drone cannot track or tag players who are using the Blind Eye Perk.

You can shoot and destroy an enemy drone, but understand that doing so is likely to give away your position to the player who deployed it nearby just as surely as getting tagged by it. Still, avoiding the threat highlight and mini-map signature is usually worthwhile.

THREAT GRENADE

Temporarily shows enemies through the walls. Can be manually detonated.

The Threat Grenade causes a large "explosion" that scans the area for any hostiles and highlights them in red on your HUD. This highlight effect can be seen through walls, allowing you to use Threat Grenades to spot enemies inside buildings or on the other side of cover. Threat Grenades can be nullified by the Cold-Blooded Perk. If you're in an area where you suspect an enemy presence, don't assume that a lack of targets appearing means that a room is empty. The highlight doesn't last long. Use it to get a rapid survey of enemy positions, make a decision on how to attack (or where to run), and engage quickly.

EMP GRENADE

Disable enemy equipment and Exo movements. Can be manually detonated.

The EMP Grenade shuts down enemy Exo movement and the ability to activate Scorestreaks. It does not disable the Exo Launcher or Exo Abilities. However, because it shuts down Exo movement, it can give you a powerful advantage in a fight, especially if you manage to tag multiple enemies. EMP Grenades are also a one-shot answer to any form of hostile ground equipment, from Remote Turrets to Recon Drones or Explosive Drones.

SMOKE GRENADE

Temporarily create a smoke screen. Can be manually detonated.

A very powerful tool for creating visual cover, Smoke Grenades can make securing an otherwise extremely difficult objective almost trivial. You can also use them to cover an assault or a retreat, but keep in mind that with the new vertical lines of sight opened up by Exo movement, they aren't perfect visual blocking in the open. Smoke Grenades work best in an area with at least some blocking cover, and always indoors. The Thermal Sight can see enemies through smoke, though the Target Enhancer cannot.

EXPLOSIVE DRONE

A proximity-triggered drone that tracks enemies and explodes when near them.

A sticky explosive, you can attach the Explosive Drone to any surface and leave it as a nasty surprise for hostiles. The drone activates when an enemy comes within range, then flies toward them rapidly and detonates. It is possible to evade the drone with quick Exo movement, but if you place it carefully, doing so is difficult or impossible. Use the Explosive Drone to block off approach routes, guard your back, protect an objective, or cut off an escape route.

SPIKE DRONE

A lethal thrown drone that returns on command.

A sort of throwing weapon, the Spike Drone is instantly fatal if you can land a direct hit on an enemy. It has the best launcher range of any "grenade," and you can return the Spike Drone to your Exo Launcher by pressing the Grenade button again after it is deployed. Note that calling the drone back can cause it to kill players. If you plant the Spike Drone in a door or narrow hall, you can even use it as a trap, pulling the drone to you when an enemy runs through and potentially killing them instantly.

SUPPLY DROPS

For additional customization, *Call of Duty®: Advanced Warfare*'s all new loot system called Supply Drop lets you unlock new items based on time played. Supply Drops give you the chance to acquire Weapon Loot, Character Gear, and Reinforcements that let you further customize your operator to fit your unique playing style. These rewards also come in three rarity classes: Enlisted, Professional, and Elite.

You can acquire three different items from the supply drops:

>> **Weapon Loot**

>> **Character Gear**

>> **Reinforcements:**

- EXP Boost

- Orbital Care Package
  (must be used in your next match)

- Rapid Supply
  (decreases time until next supply drop)

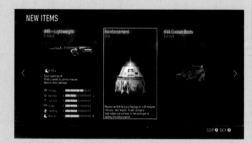

Supply Drop **Weapons** are customized variants of the base weapons in *Call of Duty®: Advanced Warfare*. You can find new weapons with custom skins, custom models, stat modifications, and even a few that have special fixed attachments.

EARNING SUPPLY DROPS

There's no trick to earning more supply drops; they only drop as you continue to play the game.

Gear is used in the Create an Operator system. It allows you to customize your character with many, *many* visual options. Gear doesn't affect your power in a match in any way, but it does let you flaunt your style!

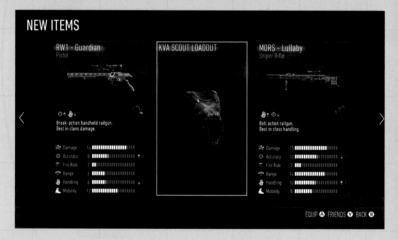

Reinforcements are one-shot special bonuses that give you an early yet temporary edge in a match. You can acquire Scorestreaks or even Perks, which are useful for coming out strong as a battle begins.

EXP Boosts simply give you an edge in earning experience for a short time. You can burn these to speed your leveling.

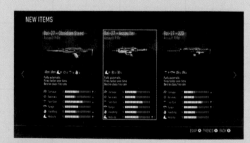

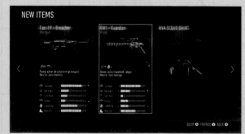

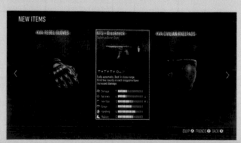

CREATE AN OPERATOR

Create an Operator is an entirely new character customization system built from the ground up. It allows a new level of freedom to precisely fine-tune your operator down to the very last detail, letting you create your character exactly the way you want.

EARNING GEAR

There are two main ways to unlock gear: through the Supply Drops and through completing challenges. Similar to weapons, each piece of gear has a rarity of Enlisted (common), Professional (uncommon), and Elite (rare). The frequency of these drops depends on the rarity. The rarer a piece is, the less likely it is to drop. Completing various challenges throughout SP and MP will unlock themed gear associated with those challenges.

Any new gear you earn through the Supply Drop system goes into your gear storage, and you can freely swap around gear to customize your character as you see fit.

CUSTOMIZATION

You can earn and store a wide variety of gear for your operator, everything from hats and glasses to completely customized Exo suits.

CREATE A CLASS

The Create a Class system in *Call of Duty®: Advanced Warfare* is broad and deep. With a host of options to customize your Class loadouts, you can tune each of your Classes to suit your specific preferences and your favorite game modes.

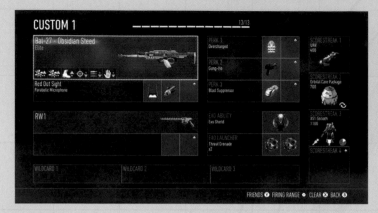

PICK 13

Topics related to building a Class: See page 92 for additional comments on Pick 13. For details on Weapons, see page 118. For Attachment info, go to page 146. Perks start on page 150. See Scorestreak details on page 156. The Exo Skeleton chapter starts on page 106.

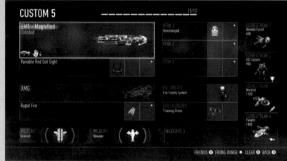

The Pick 13 system allows you to *completely* customize your operator, adding or removing weapons, attachments, Perks, Scorestreaks, and Exo equipment (both grenades and Abilities) as you see fit.

You can also use special 'Wildcards' that allow you to bend the rules, taking a fourth Scorestreak, a third grenade, a second primary weapon, or other unusual options.

Any item that you take with the Pick 13 system—whether a weapon, an attachment, a Perk, or anything else—takes up one of your points. Likewise, you can free up points by removing equipment.

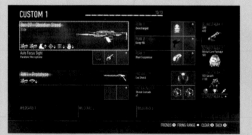

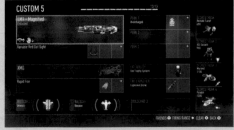

Pick 13 is highly flexible; if you want to run a Class with no Perks (or six Perks), you can do so.

Because fully customizing your Class is a very deep topic, you can explore the various chapters covering each part of the Pick 13 system in detail: Weapons, Attachments, the Exosuit, Perks, and Scorestreaks.

VIRTUAL FIRING RANGE

In the lobby of *any* Multiplayer match, you can instantly jump into the Virtual Firing Range.

This firing range allows you to quickly test any weapon combination you want. Try out different attachments to get a feel for handling, recoil, sights, and so on.

Inside the Virtual Firing Range, you can step into several different firing lanes. Each one creates a different target array, instantly creating unique terrain, cover, and targets against which you can test your weapons.

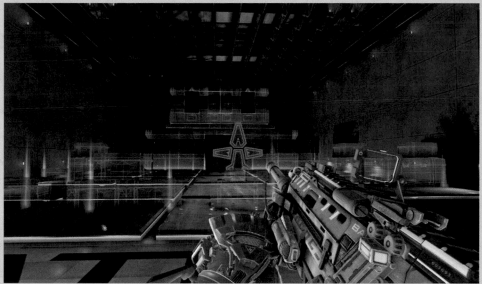

Some of the targets even move as though they have Exo Suits, jumping and bounding around in your view. Pay particular attention to these targets; hitting airborne, fast moving targets is a vital skill to learn!

The Virtual Firing Range is extremely useful for experimenting with weapon setups between matches, and you can even practice Exo movement while you're inside it.

MULTIPLAYER WEAPONS

Choosing the correct weapon for the job at hand is a big part of doing well in Multiplayer. Taking a sniper rifle into a map with a lot of fighting in close quarters around objectives isn't going to do you any favors. Trying to use an SMG on Overwatch defending an objective area from long-range attackers won't work, either.

Use the correct weapon for a particular situation, and you will thrive in Multiplayer. Improving your aim and reaction time comes with practice, but selecting the proper weaponry before a match begins gives you an edge before the first round is fired. Remember that when you construct a build with a weapon, your Perks and equipment should support your intended usage. Whether you plan on fighting in CQC, at long range, or playing an all-rounder role, it's important to focus your build.

UNIQUE WEAPONRY

Call of Duty®: Advanced Warfare has a host of weapons, and within each weapon class, almost every gun in the game has at least one unique trait. Beyond the statistical differences that define the baseline behavior of a weapon, you can find many interesting traits in this game's arsenal.

There are weapons that shoot slower or faster over time, fire four- or five-round bursts, print ammunition, fire beams of directed energy, stabilize as they fire, or display many other traits. While some of these traits have a small impact on the performance of a weapon, others define a gun's personality.

Examine the entire arsenal at your disposal: explore, experiment, and find your favorites. Use this chapter to guide your exploration and help you narrow down your choices between your favorite weapons.

WEAPON CHARTS AND RECOIL PLOTS

Where applicable, each weapon class in the game has been given a series of charts and recoil plots in this chapter to help you get a feel for the characteristics of each weapon. The following are explanations of some of the terms and concepts that appear in this chapter's charts.

AMMO CHARTS

MAG is the magazine size, STARTING is your initial ammunition load, and MAX is the most you can possibly carry, typically from using the Scavenger Perk.

RATE OF FIRE

The Rate of Fire chart simply shows the rates of fire for each weapon in rounds per minute (RPM), as well as any modifications from the Rapid Fire attachment, if the weapon can use it.

RELOAD TIMES

Reloading has an ADD time for when the ammo enters the magazine and you can sprint or weapon switch to cancel the remaining animation.

RELOAD is the normal reload time, if you still have some ammunition in the chamber.

EMPTY is the reload time on an empty magazine, when you must pull the charging handle, rack the slide, etc. The additional animation causes empty reloads to be a bit slower for most weapons.

Remember that you can cancel both Reload and Empty animations. The only exception is if you're using the Fast Hands Perk, which allows you to reload while sprinting. This has the side effect of preventing you from using sprints to cancel reload animations. You can, however, still double-tap the Weapon Switch button to cancel the remaining animation.

Where appropriate, Dual Mag attachment and Speed Reload times are shown.

SHOTS TO KILL (STK)

This is a simple measure of how many bullets it takes to kill a target at a given range (assuming a torso hit). You can use these charts to get a comparative feel for how different weapons with different attachments stack up, as Suppressor and Advanced Rifling are both shown. Suppressor reduces effective range, while Advanced Rifling increases it.

Headshots deal bonus damage, and as a general rule of thumb, scoring a headshot shaves one shot off the number of shots needed to down a target. When you score a headshot, your crosshairs flash in a double hatch pattern.

Note that the shotguns show pellets to kill, which isn't the same as shots. You can potentially kill a target in a single shot with a shotgun, but the greater the distance, the more likely one or more pellet will miss. This increases the number of pellets (and eventually, the number of shots) it takes to kill a target.

Sniper rifles depend on damage multipliers to kill in one shot, generally for scoring hits to the upper body (typically, the chest, neck, and head). Headshots are generally lethal, with the stronger snipers capable of kill shots anywhere in the upper torso.

Weapons with low shots to kill are more damaging, but keep in mind that they are often balanced with lower rates of fire, greater recoil, slower handling, slower reloads, and so on. Use the Shots to Kill tables to get a rough idea of the effective range of each weapon.

RECOIL PLOTS

The recoil plots in this chapter are a simulation of thousands of rounds fired, designed to give you an idea of the direction and intensity of a weapon's recoil forces. Keep in mind that good trigger control can help mitigate the effects of a weapon with heavy recoil. In general, though, a weapon with low recoil or straight vertical recoil is easier to handle.

PRIMARY WEAPONS

Primary weapons are your main weapons in *Call of Duty®: Advanced Warfare*, and their effective ranges largely define them. Using the proper weapon for the engagement ranges you expect on any given map is extremely important.

Keep in mind that Exo movement has shaken up some of the traditional *Call of Duty®* weapon roles. Exo movement speed can compensate for the sluggishness of Heavy Weapons, or emphasize the close-range power of SMGs and shotguns. Assault rifles remain potent general-purpose weapons, and sniper rifles gain the highly relevant and useful ability to one-shot kill targets out of mid-air.

ASSAULT RIFLES

As workhorse tools of war, the assault rifles of the future are versatile and powerful.

Intended Role: Flexible all-purpose combat
Ideal Range: Close-medium to medium-long
CQC and Hip Fire Potential: Moderate to low
Precision and Long Distance Potential: Moderate to high

Assault Rifles can perform well in a variety of combat scenarios. While they do not excel at extremely close- or long-range combat, they are ideal for mixed engagements where you transition between medium-range sightlines. Depending on the rifle you select and the attachments you use, ARs can function effectively at shorter or longer distances than usual, giving you some flexibility to adapt your chosen weapon to the map and mode you are playing.

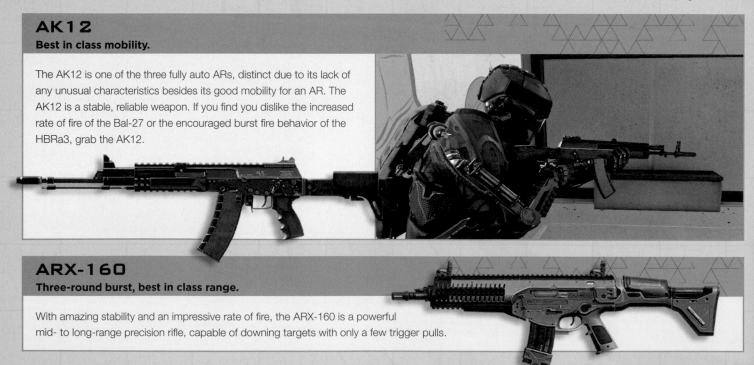

AK12

Best in class mobility.

The AK12 is one of the three fully auto ARs, distinct due to its lack of any unusual characteristics besides its good mobility for an AR. The AK12 is a stable, reliable weapon. If you find you dislike the increased rate of fire of the Bal-27 or the encouraged burst fire behavior of the HBRa3, grab the AK12.

ARX-160

Three-round burst, best in class range.

With amazing stability and an impressive rate of fire, the ARX-160 is a powerful mid- to long-range precision rifle, capable of downing targets with only a few trigger pulls.

BAL-27
Fires faster over time. Best in class fire rate.

The second full-auto AR, the Bal-27 increases its rate of fire as you hold the trigger. This means that your time to kill decreases the longer you fire, and if you happen to catch a second (or even third) target after spraying a first, they drop extremely quickly.

Extended Mags or Scavenger upgrades are recommended due to the ammo consumption for firing full auto in extended bursts. If you stick to short bursts, you can use the Bal-27 reasonably effectively on targets at a distance, keeping the rate of fire low to help control recoil.

HBRA3
First three rounds of a burst fire faster. Best in class handling.

A balance between the bullet-spitting Bal-27 and the reliable AK12, the HBRa3 fires the first three bullets more quickly each time you hold down the trigger. If you do fire in short bursts to take advantage of this higher rate of fire, you can down distant targets more quickly. At shorter distances, the burst speed-up simply improves your time to kill very slightly, though you pay for this at a medium distance where the initial burst can bump your aim around a bit.

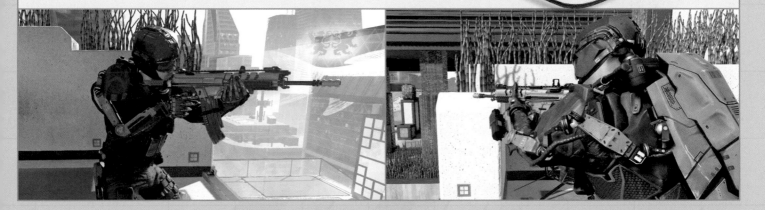

IMR
Four-round burst. Prints rounds to ammo reserve. Best in class damage.

The IMR is unique among non-energy weapons because you do not need to worry about backup ammo: it has an ability to print more ammunition! The IMR also fires in four-round bursts, making it preferable to use outside short range, where you can drill a target with multiple bursts to drop them.

MK14

Best in class accuracy. Semi-automatic.

The only semi-automatic rifle, the MK14 is a highly accurate weapon, but it demands exceptional aim and trigger control to land multiple hits on very mobile targets. Downing another player using rapid Exo movement is very difficult.

Look for lines of sight that are more along the lines of a sniper lane of fire; you want enough time to land all the hits needed to down a target. Avoid short-range engagements when possible, or bring a secondary that can provide you with some close-range punch.

ASSAULT RIFLE CHARTS

ASSAULT RIFLE AMMO STATS

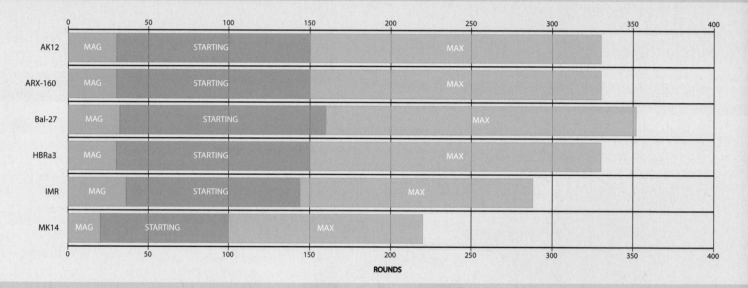

ASSAULT RIFLE RATE OF FIRE

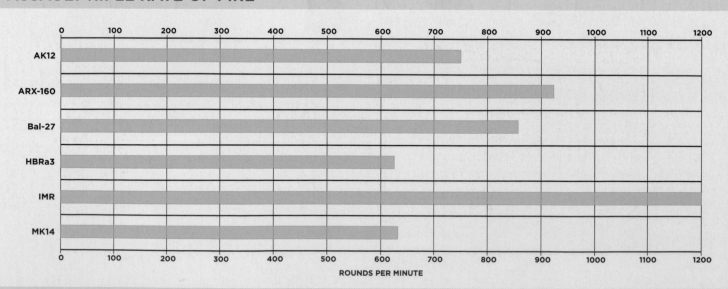

ASSAULT RIFLE RELOAD TIMES

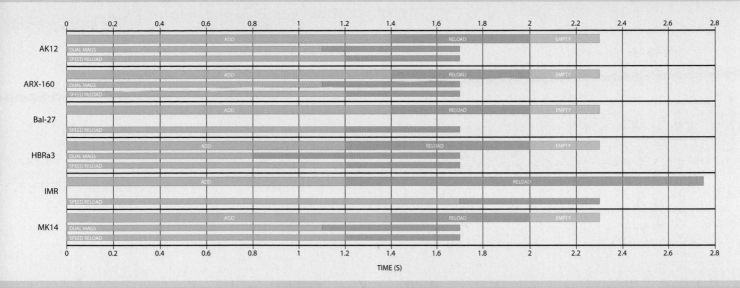

ASSAULT RIFLE SHOTS TO KILL (STK)

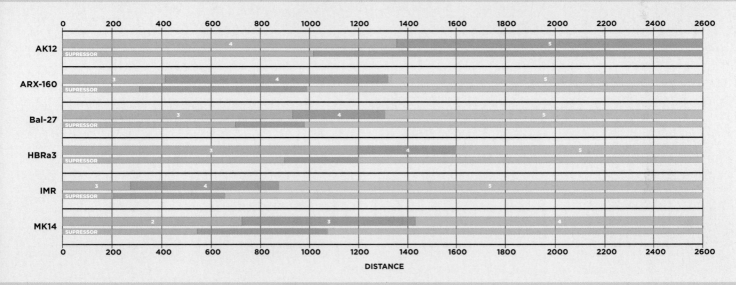

ASSAULT RIFLE RECOIL PLOTS

AK12

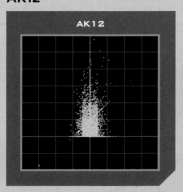

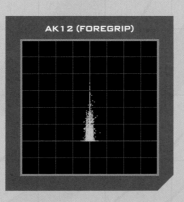

ARX-160

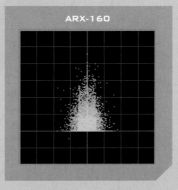

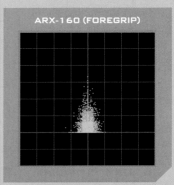

BAL-27

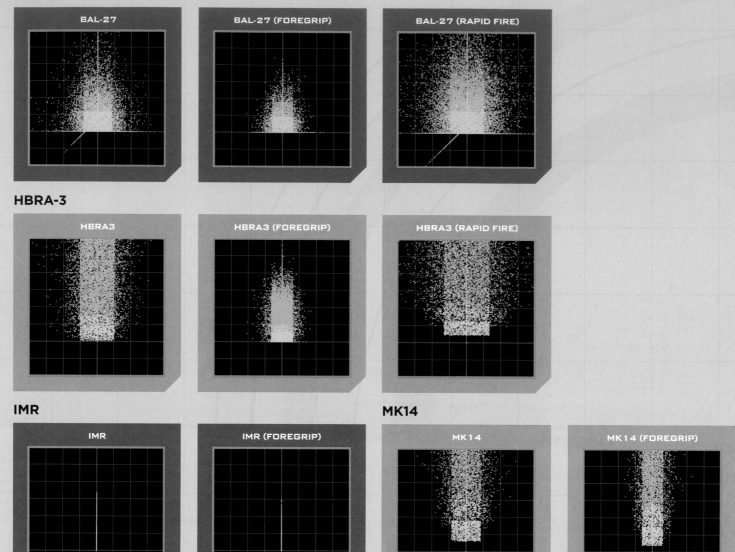

HBRA-3

IMR

MK14

SUBMACHINE GUNS

Compact weapons for the fast-moving operator, SMGs allow rapid battlefield mobility and provide superior close-range firepower.

Intended Role: Close-quarters combat

Ideal Range: Close to medium

CQC and Hip Fire Potential: High

Precision and Long Distance Potential: Moderate to low

SMGs are purpose built for close-range combat. With high rates of fire and good mobility and handling characteristics, they are ideal for taking the fight to the enemy. SMGs have excellent hip fire accuracy, making them easy to use in close quarters.

With the added mobility granted by Exo movement, SMGs can get into close range frighteningly quickly. In CQC, they can use Exo Boost Dodges very effectively when combined with hip fire. Some SMGs are stable enough to use out to a medium distance, though their damage drops off quite quickly compared to ARs. Avoid getting into too many long-range engagements. If you find yourself fighting in ADS at medium distances more often than you are up close, you may find you prefer an AR instead.

KF5

First five rounds in magazine have increased damage. Best in class range.

The KF5 is a flexible all-around SMG, with the added bonus that its first five rounds deal increased damage. This means that when on a fresh mag, you have an edge against the first opponent you encounter (as long as your shots are on target). While you do get a damage boost on your first five rounds, don't reload so frequently that you get into trouble when fighting in CQC! If there are more enemies nearby, handle them first.

Speed reloads and Dual Mags benefit the KF5, for obvious reasons.

MP11

Best in class mobility.

When you need to get to a target quickly, this is the weapon to take.

Pair the MP11 with Exo Overclock and Lightweight, use your Exo movement well, and you can zip across any map at high speed. This is perfect for an objective-focused build. It is also a good choice if positioning is important to you…you can use the speed advantage to get into key lines of sight early in a match (very useful in S&D and S&R).

ASM1

Reduces fire rate and increases accuracy over time. Best in class damage.

An unusual weapon, the ASM1 is almost a cut-down AR, with high damage for an SMG and good accuracy. It is an effective weapon at close or medium range.

SN6

First three rounds of a burst fire faster. Best in class accuracy.

Burst-firing the SN6 allows you to benefit from the sped up rate of fire for distant targets. When up close, though, stay on the trigger; save the burst fire for targets at a distance.

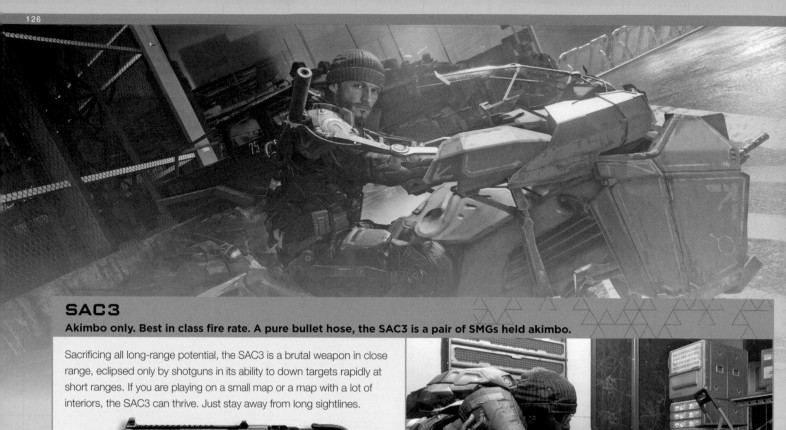

SAC3

Akimbo only. Best in class fire rate. A pure bullet hose, the SAC3 is a pair of SMGs held akimbo.

Sacrificing all long-range potential, the SAC3 is a brutal weapon in close range, eclipsed only by shotguns in its ability to down targets rapidly at short ranges. If you are playing on a small map or a map with a lot of interiors, the SAC3 can thrive. Just stay away from long sightlines.

AMR9

Allows underbarrel attachments. Best in class handling.

The only SMG that can use underbarrel attachments, it is otherwise an all-around SMG with no other unusual quirks.

SUBMACHINE GUN CHARTS
SUBMACHINE GUN AMMO STATS

SUBMACHINE GUN RATE OF FIRE

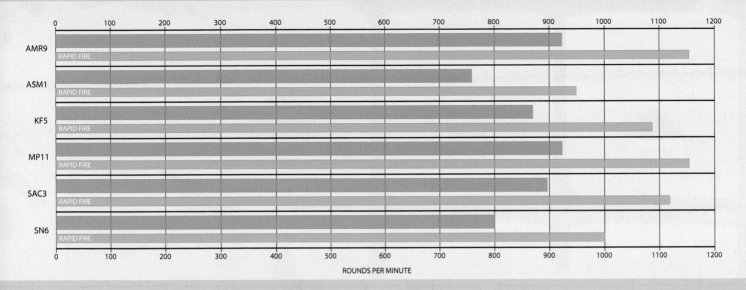

ROUNDS PER MINUTE

SUBMACHINE GUN RELOAD TIMES

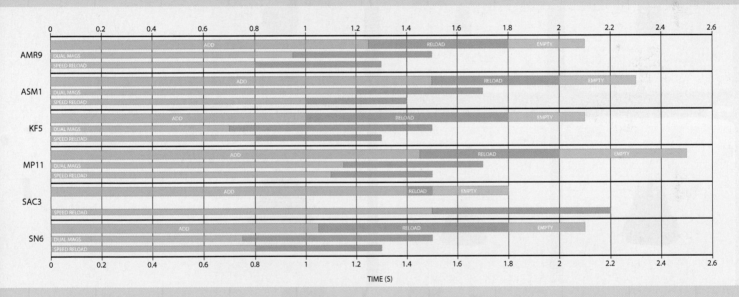

TIME (S)

SUBMACHINE GUN SHOTS TO KILL (STK)

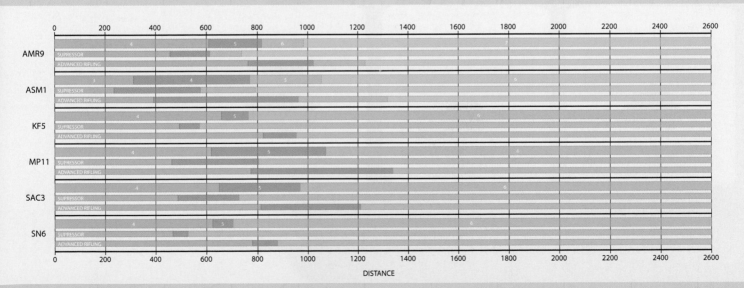

DISTANCE

SUBMACHINE GUN RECOIL PLOTS

AMR9

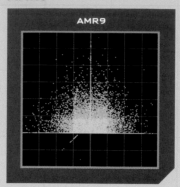

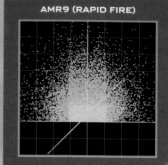

ASM 1

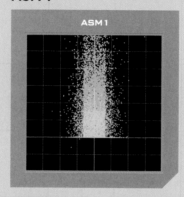

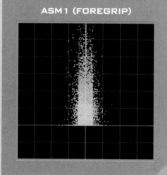

KF5

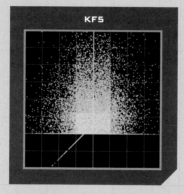

MP11

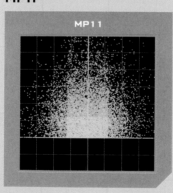

SAC3

| SAC3 | SAC3 (RAPID FIRE) |

SN6

| SN6 | SN6 (FOREGRIP) | SN6 (RAPID FIRE) |

SNIPER RIFLES

Powerful precision weapons capable of one-shot kills, sniper rifles dominate long-range combat.

Intended Role: Flexible all-purpose combat
Ideal Range: Close-medium to medium-long
CQC and Hip Fire Potential: Moderate to low
Precision and Long Distance Potential: Moderate to high

Sniper rifles are designed to fight at a distance, with powerful scopes that require steadying to aim and fire accurately.

Snipers have sluggish handling characteristics and poor hip fire, making them a bad choice up close. But at medium to long range, they can lock down a sightline, preventing enemies with shorter-range weaponry from retaliating. A sniper rifle with the Ironsights attachment can function at shorter ranges. Just keep in mind that the Ironsights attachment demands pinpoint accuracy so that you don't fall to rapid-fire weapons up close.

LYNX
Semi-automatic. Best in class range.

The Lynx is a quick-firing sniper that is best used for tagging enemies with two swift body shots. If you prefer weapons like the MK14, you may find the Lynx to behave like its longer-range cousin.

MORS

Bolt-action railgun. Best in class handling.

Next to the Atlas 20mm, the MORS is the most reliable sniper for one-shot kills. However, the MORS reloads one round after every shot, so it is at its best when your accuracy is extremely high. Missing a shot is punishing.

NA-45

Semi-automatic two-round fire system. Primer (first round) explodes when the Catalyst (second round) hits nearby.

The NA-45, a very unusual weapon all around, fires a Primer round that impacts and sticks. Then, the Catalyst round must land nearby to cause the Primer to detonate. This has some very unusual applications. As a pure sniper, there are better options, but as a makeshift long-range explosive weapon, the NA-45 has no equivalent in the game; the closest you can find is a grenade launcher.

It is even possible to use the NA-45 while in mid-air with Exo movement, firing both rounds in quick succession at a target on the ground. If you're fast enough, the detonation can take out your opponent without even having to hit them.

You can also use the NA-45 to flush out adversaries who are hiding behind cover, doorways, and windows. Simply detonate the Primer near them on the ground, wall, or ceiling.

ATLAS 20MM

Semi-automatic. Shoulder mounted, with no hip fire. Best in class damage.

The most reliable sniper for one-shot kills, the Atlas is a massive 20mm shoulder-mounted cannon. You cannot fire it from the hip, period. In exchange, you get very reliable kill shots, and the Atlas is at its best when you can keep your distance and settle in to ADS.

SNIPER RIFLE CHARTS
SNIPER RIFLE AMMO STATS

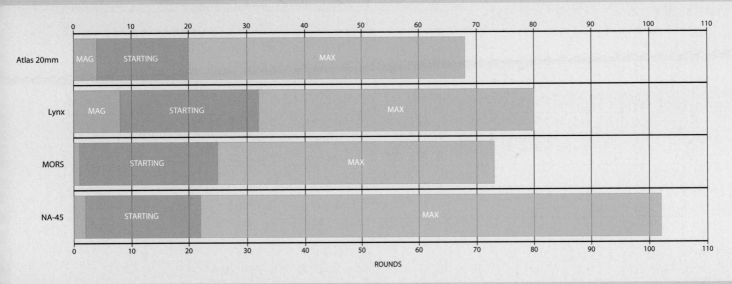

SNIPER RIFLE RATE OF FIRE

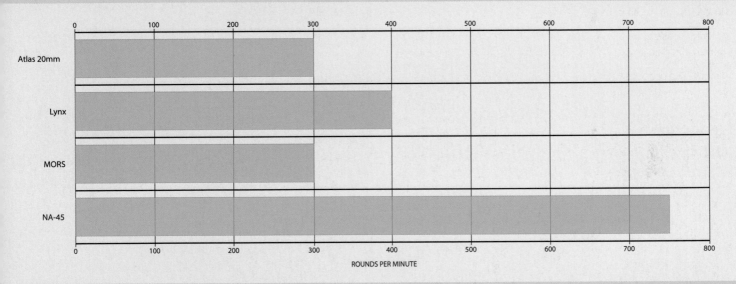

SNIPER RIFLE RELOAD TIMES

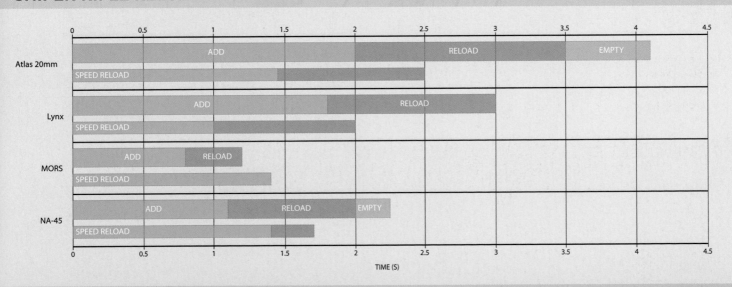

SNIPER RIFLE SHOTS TO KILL (STK)

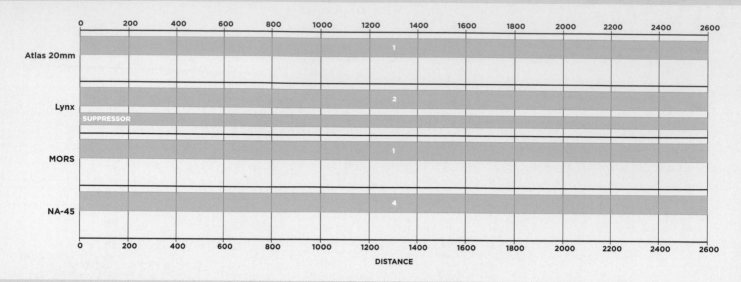

DISTANCE

SNIPER RIFLE RECOIL PLOTS

ATLAS 20MM

LYNX

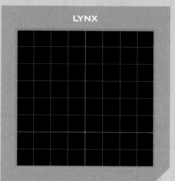

MORS

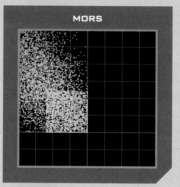

NA-45

SHOTGUNS

Brute force close-quarters weapons, built for stopping power above all else.

Intended Role: Extreme short-range combat
Ideal Range: Short
CQC and Hip Fire Potential: High
Precision and Long Distance Potential: Nonexistent

Shotguns are your room-clearing, close-range powerhouse weapons. Even more than SMGs, shotguns are made for extremely close-range combat. While they are unreliable or completely ineffective at a distance, up close, they can kill in one shot and clear a room or an objective of enemies in seconds.

Exo movement has added significant power to shotguns by enhancing your mobility tremendously. Exo movement allows you to close distance very quickly and either avoid long-range lanes of fire entirely or move through them swiftly. Remember that while you cannot do a forward dodge on the ground, you can jump forward and do a Boost Dash forward. This combined move can close the gap to land a guaranteed one-shot kill, and it is particularly effective in tight spaces. Don't try this against a fully aware target in a wide open area!

TAC-19
Pump-action directed-energy weapon. Best in class mobility.

A powerful "shotgun" that blasts your enemies apart with a controlled shockwave, the Tac-19 excels at performing one-shot kills, but fades rapidly at a distance.

S-12
Fully automatic. Best in class fire rate.

Capable of throwing a wall of lead, the S-12 can down multiple targets in close proximity to one another extremely quickly. However, it pays for this rate of fire with the least consistent one-shot kills of the shotgun class, so you need those extra shots to score a kill.

BULLDOG
Semi-automatic. Best in class damage.

A balance between the Tac-19 and the S-12, the Bulldog fires more rapidly than the Tac-19 and deals more damage than the S-12. If you find that the delay between shots on the Tac-19 causes you problems, but you want more consistent one-shot kills than the S-12, give the Bulldog a shot.

SHOTGUN CHARTS
SHOTGUN AMMO STATS

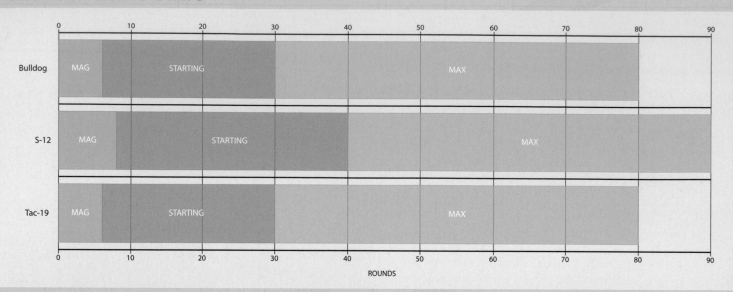

SHOTGUN RATE OF FIRE

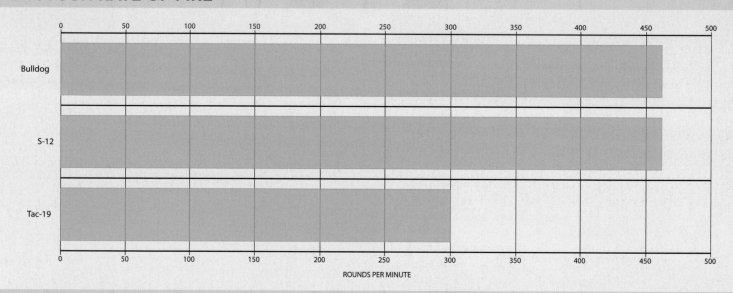

SHOTGUN RELOAD TIMES

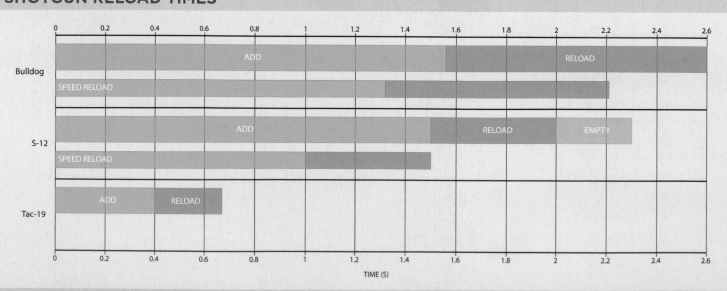

SHOTGUN SHOTS TO KILL (STK)

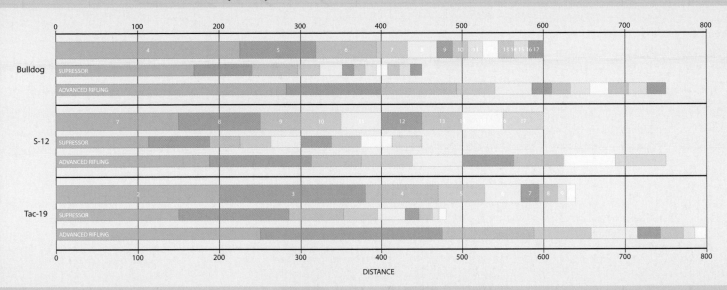

DISTANCE

SHOTGUN RECOIL PLOTS

BULLDOG

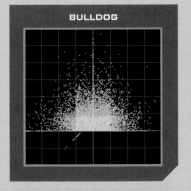

BULLDOG

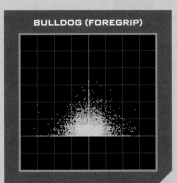

BULLDOG (FOREGRIP)

S-12

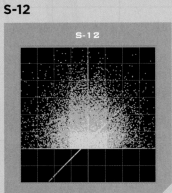

S-12

S-12 (FOREGRIP)

TAC-19

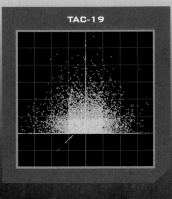

TAC-19

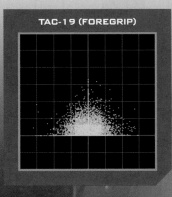

TAC-19 (FOREGRIP)

HEAVY WEAPONS

Powerful specialized weaponry, heavy weapons serve a variety of roles on the battlefield.

Intended Role: Long-range suppression, infrequent reloads
Ideal Range: Medium to long
CQC and Hip Fire Potential: Low
Precision and Long Distance Potential: Moderate to high

Heavy Weapons include directed-energy weapons, light machine guns, and the XMG heavy machine guns (HMGs). All three types have remarkably deep ammunition reserves (potentially infinite in the case of the energy weapons), though their uses diverge beyond that similarity.

Heavy Weapons serve as powerful range suppression weapons. They have similar damage to ARs, with good penetration but deeper magazines, allowing you to keep firing at distant targets long after an AR must reload. You can also abuse the penetration and magazine sizes by making use of Threat Grenades and other equipment and streaks that reveal your adversaries' positions, and then shooting them directly through thin walls.

Directed-energy weapons have the benefit of potentially never needing to reload, and they also never run out of ammunition. Heat can be manually vented as a "reload," but they do naturally cool off over time. The two energy weapons in this category, the EM1 and the EPM3, are a continuous-fire beam weapon and a pulse-fire beam weapon similar to the MK14 in functionality, respectively. Both weapons have the notable disadvantage of being very visible on the battlefield, especially the EM1. Don't try to use them in a stealth setup, as the bright energy beams attract a lot of attention.

Finally, the XMG heavy machine guns are twin HMGs that would normally be impossible for a soldier to carry. Luckily, the strength of your Exo Suit lets you hold one in each hand.

EM1

Constant beam of directed energy. No ammunition, but can overheat. Best in class damage.

Firing a continuous beam of energy, the EM1 has extremely accurate hip fire, allowing you to fire and keep the beam on target even while moving at full speed. It takes good steady contact on a target to take them down, so you must be accurate even against an opponent who is using evasive Exo movement if you hope to keep up with other weapons.

Firing the EM1 builds up heat. Although you can manually vent heat as a "reload," it is not necessary to do so if you're careful with the trigger. The Heat Sink attachment is a wise choice for this weapon, giving you extended fire time without worrying about overheating.

PYTAEK

Fully automatic. Reduces recoil over time. Best in class accuracy.

The Pytaek has the unique trait of stabilizing over time as you fire it. And not just stabilizing… it becomes rock solid if you fire enough rounds continuously. This encourages wasteful ammo usage, but it is amazingly powerful for mowing down multiple targets at range with ease. Once stabilized, you can track targets through the air without trouble. Bring the Scavenger Perk if you intend to take full advantage of the Pytaek's accuracy bonus.

XMG
Fully automatic heavy machine guns. Akimbo only. Increased fire rate and accuracy in lockdown mode.

The XMGs are even more sluggish and inaccurate than the Heavy Weapons, but they have the special ability to enter "lockdown mode." Doing so causes you to literally lock yourself in place while deploying the XMGs fully. This improves their accuracy and (most critically) massively increases their damage. XMGs in lockdown are one of the most lethal weapons in the game, but the tradeoff is a total loss of mobility. In most situations, you need to use lockdown in advance of enemy contact, lining up a lane of fire and opening up on any foes who show themselves.

You can also take advantage of lockdown when defending an objective area. Set up camp in one location, and then change positions after downing an enemy so they're always looking in the wrong place for you whenever they try to come for the objective. If you try to use lockdown in the middle of a firefight, you're all but guaranteed to get killed before you can even fully enter lockdown. Consider bringing a secondary for fighting on the move, as the XMGs are not nearly as potent outside of lockdown.

EPM3
Semi-automatic directed energy. No ammunition, but can overheat. Best in class range.

A variant of the EM1, the EPM3 fires its energy in short, sharp bursts, similar to a semi-automatic rifle like the MK14. The EPM3 has a sluggish ADS time, but you need the additional accuracy to land multiple hits on a target, and you need those multiple hits to score a kill. Using the EPM3 against highly mobile and aerial targets can be difficult in the field. It is easier to use if you're already in cover or guarding a lane before you sight your opponent.

AMELI
Fully automatic. Best in class fire rate.

A straightforward Heavy Weapon without any unusual traits, the Ameli has somewhat more controlled recoil than the Pytaek, though its recoil tends to go the other direction the longer you fire. (That is, it becomes out of control, rather than more in control.) Used carefully, you can still employ the Ameli to cordon off an area from the enemy team, but exercise greater trigger control. Unlike the Pytaek, you don't want to be holding it down on full auto for extended periods of time.

HEAVY WEAPON CHARTS
HEAVY WEAPON AMMO STATS

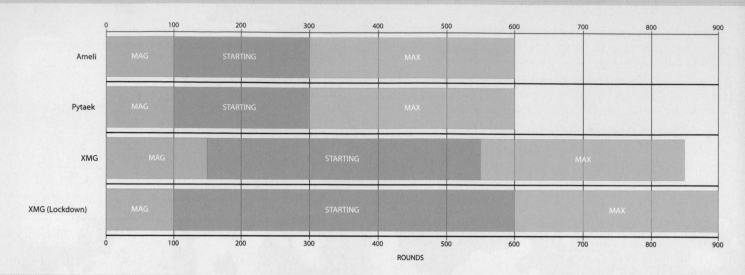

HEAVY WEAPON RATE OF FIRE

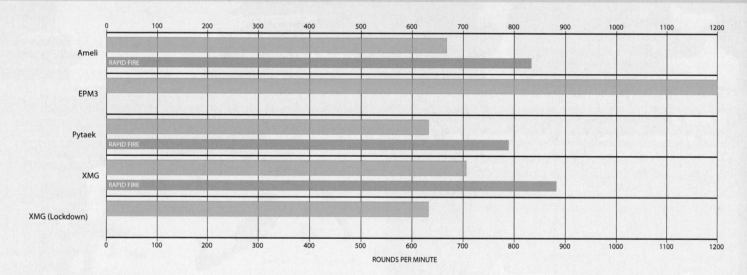

HEAVY WEAPON RELOAD TIMES

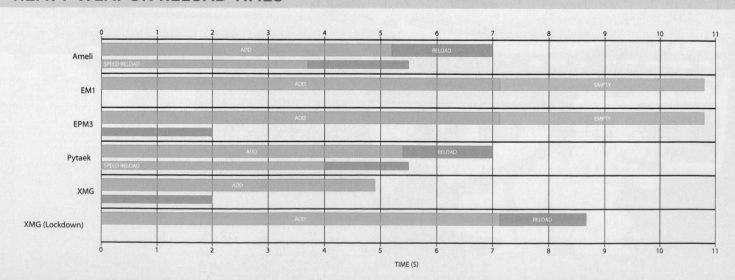

HEAVY WEAPON SHOTS TO KILL (STK)

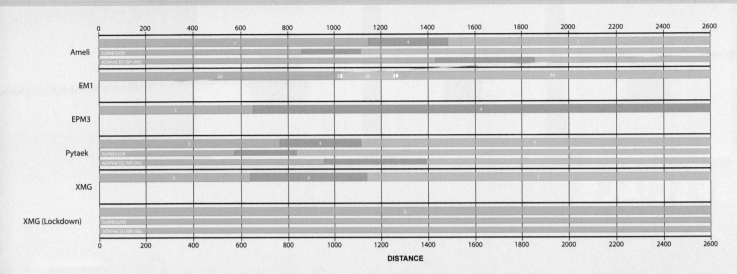

HEAVY WEAPON RECOIL PLOTS

AMELI

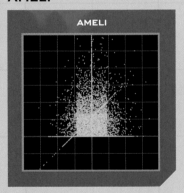
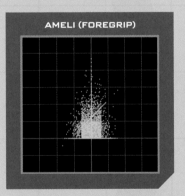
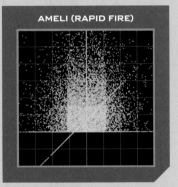

EPM3

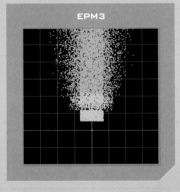
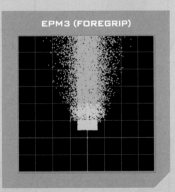

PYTAEK

XMG

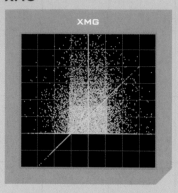

XMG

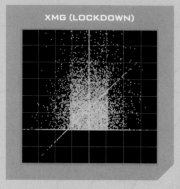

XMG (LOCKDOWN)

XMG (RAPID FIRE)

SPECIALS

Specialized combat equipment.

Intended Role: Objective defense or Siege

The Heavy Shield and MDL give you one defensive and one offensive option, both suitable for objective game modes.

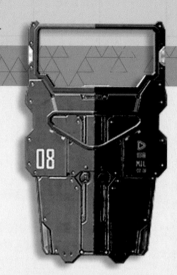

HEAVY SHIELD

A deployable shield.

The Heavy Shield is a powerful defensive tool, extremely useful for seizing contested objectives in Momentum, Domination, and Hardpoint. The shield protects you from all frontal gunfire, and if you crouch, it also covers your feet. You can also plant the shield in place, creating instant cover anywhere on the map. This can be extremely useful in areas with sparse cover, and it can also help you set up an ambush for known incoming enemy players.

The Heavy Shield has three unique attachments: Fast Melee, Fast Plant, and Shock Plant. Fast Melee speeds up shield bashes, which take two hits to kill with, unlike normal melee swings. Fast Plant lets you deploy the shield at double speed, making it a more viable option mid-engagement. Finally, Shock Plant causes the shield plant to emit a stunning wave of energy that disrupts any foes nearby who are hit by the wave.

A build loaded up with defensive Perks and abilities capped with a Heavy Shield can secure objective points that would normally be extremely difficult without it. If you enjoy playing objectives heavily, make a build focusing on the Heavy Shield…you earn quite a few assist points for distracting enemies with the shield!

MDL
Semi-automatic. Launches time-detonated grenades.

A grenade launcher, the MDL gives you a primary explosive weapon. The grenades that the MDL fires are time-detonated, not proximity. You must get them into the correct area to deal damage, and they are nearly impossible to use against aerial targets.

Use the MDL to siege objectives where enemies must wait, particularly Domination, Momentum, and Hardpoint areas. The MDL can also be effective at flushing out or killing campers occupying small rooms or windows. Fling a few grenades in to get them moving.

SECONDARY WEAPONS

Backup pistols, launchers to handle Scorestreaks, and the Crossbow all fit in this category. Taking a secondary is not mandatory, but for certain situations, they are very useful.

PISTOLS

Fast-switching backup weapons, pistols can save your life if your primary runs dry.

Intended Role: Backup weapon
Ideal Range: Close to close-medium
CQC and Hip Fire Potential: Moderate
Precision and Long Distance Potential: Low

Pistols have excellent handling characteristics, making them quick to switch to and from, and quick to ADS. This makes them ideal backup weapons for close-range combat when you are using a primary like a sniper rifle, the MK14 or EPM3, or even an AR or SMG if you simply want a weapon that you can fast swap to if you run out of ammo mid-fight.

ATLAS 45
Semi-automatic. Best in class handling.

Capable of a two-shot kill only at extremely short range, the Atlas is nevertheless one of the smoothest pistols in its class. Easy to handle, it isn't difficult to score multiple shots on target at short ranges with this weapon. If you fast-switch on a damaged target, you can easily down them.

If you intend to rely on the Atlas 45 as your main weapon up close, when using a long-range primary, you may want to use them akimbo to get more lead on your adversaries quickly.

RW 1
Break-action handheld railgun. Best in class damage.

Capable of one-shot kills, the RW1 is a lethal backup weapon if you are accurate. Miss, and you're stuck reloading the RW1 after a single shot. The RW1 rewards accuracy and harshly punishes missed shots, so experiment with it to see if your aim is up to the task.

MP443 GRACH
Two-round burst. Best in class range.

Firing in two-round bursts, the Grach can potentially kill in two shots, though it takes three or more bullets to down a target. Other than the burst fire, the Grach is fairly similar to the Atlas 45; experiment with both to see which you prefer.

PDW
Fully automatic machine pistol. Best in class fire rate.

A backup mini-SMG, this machine pistol gives you a fully automatic backup weapon, and it does not need akimbo or a quick trigger finger to down a target quickly. Keep in mind that while the PDW is fully automatic, it has harsh recoil and significant damage falloff, so it can't compete with SMGs at range. Stick to using it as a short-range emergency tool, and it will treat you right.

PISTOL CHARTS
PISTOL AMMO STATS

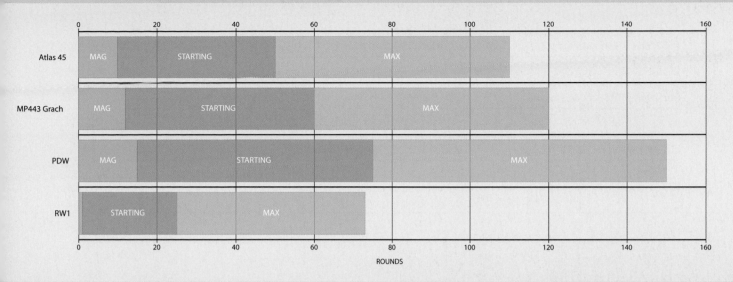

PISTOL RATE OF FIRE

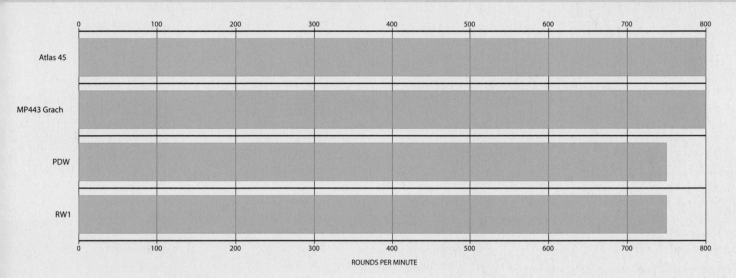

PISTOL RELOAD TIMES

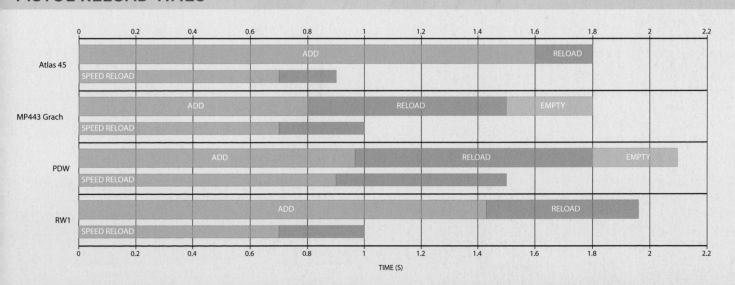

PISTOL SHOTS TO KILL (STK)

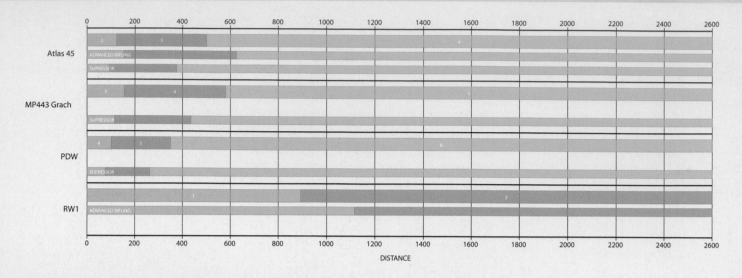

PISTOL RECOIL PLOTS

ATLAS 45

ATLAS 45

MP443 GRACH

MP443 GRACH

PDW

PDW (RAPID FIRE)

RW1

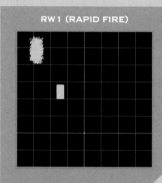

RW1 (RAPID FIRE)

LAUNCHERS

Powerful explosive weapons, capable of locking and destroying Scorestreaks.

Intended Role:

Scorestreak destruction, objective siege

Ideal Range: Medium

CQC and Hip Fire Potential: Low

Precision and Long Distance Potential: Low

Launchers have several important roles, particularly when paired with defensive Perks. When used with Perks that conceal you from AI Scorestreaks, you can destroy hostile streaks safely, with little danger of being targeted (sometimes even by player-controlled streaks).

Launchers can also be used with grenades and other explosives alongside the Danger Close Perk to create a powerful explosive offense that you can direct against enemy objectives and defensive positions.

STINGER M7

Vehicle or enemy lock-on missiles.

The Stinger is your anti-air launcher of choice, and it can also lock on to your opponents because of their Exo Suits! The Stinger takes a moment to lock, and flares can divert its shots. Therefore, it may take you more than one shot to down more expensive aerial streaks.

MAAWS
Laser-guided missile.

A compromise between the full lock of the Stinger and the unguided MAHEM, the MAAWS lets you fire a guided missile that you can direct toward a streak or an opponent. The guidance is particularly useful for targeting the missile precisely into a window, hall, door, or other narrow space where you know there is an enemy presence.

MAHEM
Unguided. Fires a projectile of molten metal.

With no guidance system, the MAHEM is highly destructive, but you must aim carefully to deliver its payload. A poor choice against most Scorestreaks (except the Goliath), the MAHEM is generally better used against foes in confined spaces or on objectives, though you can use it against a Remote Turret reasonably effectively. A single shot from a MAHEM can also wipe out the XS1 Goliath if it isn't using the Trophy System, so keep that in mind as a possible counter.

SPECIALS

CROSSBOW
Bolt-action crossbow. Fires explosive bolts.

An entirely unique weapon, the Crossbow fires explosive bolts that stick to their target. Instantly fatal if they stick and detonate, the Crossbow demands extreme accuracy and compensation for its travel time and arc of flight. If you are using a very short-ranged primary, a Crossbow can also act as a slightly longer-range backup weapon, though it is a demanding one to use well!

COMBAT KNIFE

This is your only remaining weapon if you remove both your primary and your secondary. The Combat Knife isn't a weapon you normally choose. Rather, it is something you acquire if you remove your primary and secondary weapons. It's generally a good idea to secure a dropped weapon from a teammate or enemy as quickly as possible…

SUPPLY DROP WEAPONS

Besides all of the base versions, there are special versions of every weapon in the game, coming as **Enlisted**, **Professional**, or **Elite** (in increasing order of rarity). You can earn Supply Drop weaponry from completing challenges, or most often, simply by participating in Multiplayer matches. Clan Wars and special promotions are another potential source of drops.

Supply Drop weapons aren't necessarily any better than the base version. They usually trade off one stat for another, but they sometimes have unique attachment quirks. All of them have cool paint jobs, and many have custom models. Strut your stuff on the battlefield.

ATTACHMENTS

Customize your arsenal to create your perfect weapon. Attachments allow you to modify your weapons in many ways. You can add sights to enhance target acquisition, grips to improve handling, and other specialized attachments to boost your performance in different areas.

In general, you should take attachments that make a weapon feel good to you. However, there are certain attachments that have very noticeable, very strong effects on combat, and the correct attachments on the proper weapon can win gunfights. Experiment and explore. Remember that certain Supply Drop weapons may have fixed attachments, extra allowed attachments, or even blocked attachments!

The following section lists all attachments alphabetically and provides advice for using them effectively. Remember, each attachment takes one point in your Class, but you can gain a third attachment on your primary weapon or a second attachment on your secondary weapon with the Primary and Secondary Gunfighter Wildcards.

MIXING ATTACHMENTS

Mixing and matching attachments is generally straightforward, but here are a few tips:

Sights are all mutually exclusive.

The Parabolic Mic, Laser Sight, and Tracker all share the same slot.

Advanced Rifling and Suppressor are mutually exclusive.

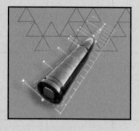

ACOG SCOPE

Enhanced zoom.

A basic sight that has an enhanced level of zoom compared to the Red Dot Sight, this is a good choice primarily for highly accurate weapons. You need to stay at long range to take full advantage of this sight. If you're fighting at medium or close range with the ACOG, you're going to be at a disadvantage against faster sights with a better field of view up close. Fight from long range, and pick off SMG and shotgun users who can't attack you effectively. You should have an advantage against most AR users, as well.

Note that on snipers, ACOG sights have a significant amount of sway built in. They're great for snapshots at medium range, but at longer range, you may experience difficulty landing shots with precision.

ADVANCED RIFLING

Increased range.

A simple and powerful modification, this attachment improves the distance at which your weapon deals full damage before it begins to suffer damage falloff. This is a vital attachment for shotguns and very useful for the majority of SMGs, unless you plan to play only at a short range.

It's difficult to know exactly how much Advanced Rifling benefits you during a match, but from time to time, it's going to cut the number of shots to kill a target by one. This benefit can win you the fight against an evenly matched opponent. In the case of shotguns, it extends the range at which you can reliably one-shot kill, making this a vital attachment for them.

AKIMBO

Hip fire two weapons.

Only available on pistols (the SAC3 SMGs are always akimbo), the Akimbo attachment allows you to dual fist your pistols. This trades off the ability to ADS for improved lethality up close.

Given that pistols are primarily useful as backup weapons at short range if you run out of ammo on your primary, Akimbo is a good attachment for ensuring that you land the last few shots you need to kill an already damaged target. As a backup weapon for sniper rifles, Heavy Weapons, or marksman-style ARs, Akimbo pistols can also help give you a fighting chance against enemies rushing you at short range. They aren't a guarantee of a win against a dedicated close-combat weapon, but they give you better chances than hipfiring a sniper!

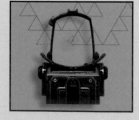

AUTO FOCUS SIGHT

Sight automatically zooms when aiming down the sights and not moving.

This multi-purpose sight normally functions very similarly to a basic Red Dot. However, if you remain stationary for a moment, the sight automatically zooms in.

This sight is useful for weapons that can function effectively at a distance with good trigger control, but the restriction on remaining stationary is dangerous. You must be positioned exactly where you want to be before you zoom in with the auto focus. If you move even a step, the sight zooms out, and this can spoil your aim. Try to use the zoom when you are behind good cover or in a dark area, so you don't have to immediately worry about taking fire from every enemy who enters your line of sight. If you can score the first hits (or finish your target), you're making good use of the auto focus ability.

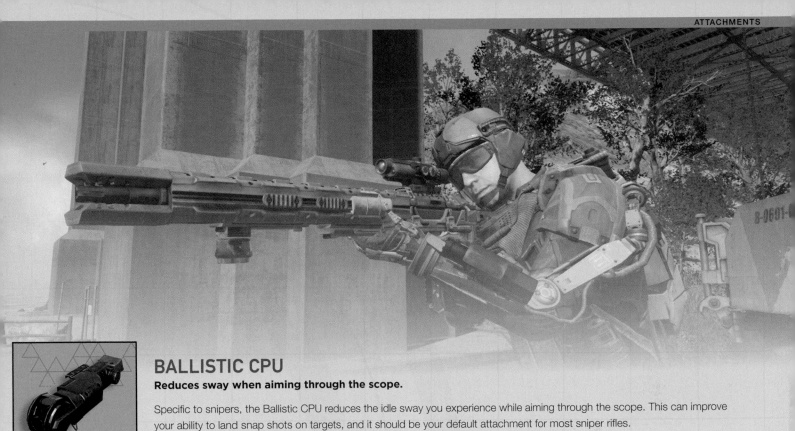

BALLISTIC CPU

Reduces sway when aiming through the scope.

Specific to snipers, the Ballistic CPU reduces the idle sway you experience while aiming through the scope. This can improve your ability to land snap shots on targets, and it should be your default attachment for most sniper rifles.

DUAL MAGAZINE

Faster reload, and stops loss of magazine ammo on every other speed reload.

A useful attachment, Dual Magazine grants you both faster reloads and saves ammo in your magazines every other speed reload. Faster reloads are most important in CQC. If you're fighting at close range or in close proximity to enemies frequently, you need faster reloads to survive multiple targets in quick succession. If you tend to fight at medium range or longer, quick reloads are less vital, and you can generally skip this attachment in favor of other options.

FOREGRIP

Vertical foregrip for reduced recoil.

The Foregrip has a simple and useful function: it slightly reduces the recoil of your weapon. This is more useful when you're fighting at a distance. While up close, you tend to rely more on hip fire, and automatic fire is still fairly accurate, even at a short distance.

Experiment with this attachment on weapons that have significant recoil. You may find it helps to make them a bit more manageable, though keep in mind that good trigger control can work just as well at long range.

GRENADE LAUNCHER

Underbarrel mounted grenade launcher.

This expendable Grenade Launcher nets you more explosive punch. On a Class focused toward explosives with the Bombardier Wildcard, the Danger Close Perk, and a secondary launcher, adding a Grenade Launcher can provide even more ability to bombard an objective area.

The Grenade Launcher doesn't have a massive blast radius, so you need to score a near-direct hit to get kills. However, if you can damage enemies near a key area while your teammates attack, you can make the fight very one-sided.

HEAT SINK

Extends firing time before overheating.

Exclusive to energy weapons, the Heat Sink allows you to fire longer before overheating or venting heat manually. This is a very useful attachment for both directed-energy weapons, so if you have the space for it in your Class, take it.

HYBRID SIGHT
4x magnifier with attached Red Dot Sight.

A very nice, flexible sight that gives you the benefits of two optics in one package. You need to remember to switch between the two sights before you enter a close- or long-range engagement area. You want the correct sight up before you start firing, not while you're trapped in an actively dangerous area.

IRONSIGHTS
Ironsights for sniper rifles.

This attachment removes the built-in high-magnification scope on your sniper rifle, replacing it with basic rail Ironsights. This gives you the ability to use your sniper rifle more effectively at close-medium to medium range, at the cost of long-range precision. The MORS is particularly well suited for this attachment, with its high lethality and a reasonably quick reload time for each powerful bullet.

LASER SIGHT
Increased hip fire accuracy.

A very useful attachment for SMGs, the Laser Sight can also be beneficial when used on full auto ARs. The Laser Sight tightens your hip fire spread significantly, making it more reliable to use at a distance. For some SMGs, this can let you spray down enemies at surprisingly long range without aiming. Because you move faster when you aren't ADS, this can give you a mobility edge, particularly when combined with Exo movement.

PARABOLIC MICROPHONE
Suppressed weapons fire appears on your mini-map.

A counter to the Suppressor, this attachment allows you to spot players using it on the mini-map, just as if their weapon were unsilenced. This attachment can either be very useful or completely useless; it depends entirely on what your opponents are using!

It is most consistently useful when playing defense in objective modes, a situation where you never want an enemy to blindside you. However, it is also a good choice in Search & Destroy and Search & Rescue, or in any match where you are up against organized players who are likely to use silenced weaponry.

QUICKDRAW GRIP
Aim down the sights faster.

A simple and useful attachment, the Quickdraw Grip is most useful in mid-range firefights where ADS is necessary and fractions of a second can win a fight. Quickdraw is also helpful when firing while using Exo movement. The faster you can get on target while in the air, the better.

When fighting at long range, bringing up your sights quickly is less important. Up close, you may be utilizing hip fire more frequently. However, at a medium distance, particularly in AR vs AR fights, Quickdraw can win the battle for you.

RAPID FIRE
Increased fire rate.

A strong but difficult to use attachment, Rapid Fire boosts your rate of fire at the cost of an extreme loss of accuracy. At short range, this can reduce your time to kill enemies, making you more reliably lethal and giving up the upper edge in CQC fights. Still, you pay for this edge with a severe increase in recoil. If you feather the trigger, you can still hit targets at medium distances, but be mindful of trying to hit enemies at mid-range, especially in the air.

RED DOT SIGHT
Precision sight.

The most basic of all sights, the Red Dot Sight has no particularly unusual characteristics. It simply provides a clean, clear view on your target. If you dislike Ironsights, but don't feel the need for a zooming optic, take a Red Dot. It is particularly useful at medium ranges where quick and accurate target acquisition is important, especially for landing hits on other players' heads when they are hiding behind partial cover.

STOCK

Move faster when aiming down the sights.

This is a very, very powerful attachment for mid and close-mid-range combat. Stock allows you to keep your movement speed while ADS. This means that you can move with your sights up, perfectly accurate, and still retain the ability to dodge incoming fire. In a mid-range firefight, this can be a decisive advantage (particularly when paired with the Toughness Perk). But even at shorter ranges, you can take advantage of the Stock by strafing around corners with your sights already up, or sneaking through rooms scanning doors and windows.

SUPPRESSOR

Invisible on enemy mini-maps when you are firing.

A critical attachment for stealth-based Classes, the Suppressor masks your weapons' fire from appearing on the mini-map, unless an enemy has the Parabolic Microphone attachment. Note that because your Exo movement causes you to briefly appear on the mini-map, a full stealth Class requires several Perks on top of the Suppressor to stay completely off enemy HUDs. The Suppressor also dampens your weapons' fire sound and suppresses muzzle flash slightly, giving you a clearer view on target.

TACTICAL KNIFE

Faster melee attack.

Specific to pistol-class weapons and cannot be taken with Akimbo, the Tactical Knife gives you a faster melee stab, with both a quick lunge and a rapid recovery. You give up some close-range firepower, but this attachment can make rounding corners in interior areas a bit safer. If you suddenly stumble across an enemy, you can swiftly and silently dispatch them with a fast melee stab.

TARGET ENHANCER

Advanced optic with built-in threat detection.

A sophisticated optical sight that highlights enemies without the Cold-Blooded Perk, the Target Enhancer is ideal for picking out adversaries behind cover or in dark areas. If you find you have trouble locating threats, use the Target Enhancer to aid your target acquisition.

THERMAL SIGHT

Magnified optic that shows heat signatures in warm colors.

The Thermal Sight is a zooming optic that requires steadying your aim, just like a sniper scope. The Thermal scope gives you infrared heat vision, allowing you to spot targets easily at a distance. The tradeoff is the steadying requirement, even on weapons other than sniper rifles.

You can use the Thermal Sight in combination with Smoke Grenades, as Thermal can pierce directly through the smoke. This can be surprisingly effective if used on key objective areas. Smoke the location to block enemy line of sight, and then shoot at any targets in or beyond the smoke to eliminate them.

TRACKER

Wounding an enemy causes them to show on your mini-map.

A nasty attachment for close to mid-range combat, the Tracker causes enemies to be highlighted on your HUD when you hit them with your bullets. Once tracked, you can pursue them anywhere; they can only avoid being tagged with the Low Profile Perk. This attachment ensures that if you wound a target at medium range, and they duck behind cover or evade with Exo movement, you can hunt them down and finish them off.

VARIABLE ZOOM SCOPE

A variable zoom scope with three levels of zoom.

A special sniper rifle scope that allows you to cycle through three levels of zoom, this is a very useful sight. It gives you a short-range magnification when you want to go for snapshots, and a longer-range zoom when you need precision fire at a distance. The flexibility is particularly useful on larger maps.

PERKS

Perks define your soldier's abilities on the battlefield. Perks enhance you, making you faster, tougher, stealthier, better equipped, and more dangerous. They are also entirely optional. If you prefer, you can take the points out of your Perks and invest them elsewhere in your build. But Perks are quite powerful, and most builds rely on a mutually supportive combination of Perks as the backbone of a build. Use the advice in this chapter to choose Perk setups. Take full advantage of them in combat, and you can thrive in Multiplayer.

PERK CATEGORIES

Perks are divided into three categories, though there's no difference in power; they're simply divided up to force you to make tough choices. You can take one Perk from each category, or if you're willing to spend points on Perk Wildcards, you can take up to two Perks from each category, for a maximum of six.

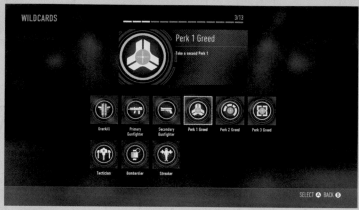

PERK 1

LIGHTWEIGHT
Move faster.

Simple and effective, Lightweight is very useful for CQC builds and objective builds for offensive classes. Lightweight gives you a mobility advantage, letting you reach key vantage points faster. It also helps very slightly in direct engagements, particularly when you are hipfiring at close range while moving and dodging.

Lightweight gives less of a benefit for weapons that are already slow. It's better to emphasize the speed of lightweight weapons than to try to boost a sluggish heavy weapon.

LOW PROFILE
Invisible to UAVs, tracking rounds, and Exo Ping.

A powerful stealth Perk, Low Profile's immunity to UAVs is the primary reason to take it. However, Exo Ping is a close second, and the invisibility to tracking rounds is a nice bonus.

Low Profile alone won't hide you from everything, but staying off radar is a strong benefit. If you prefer to operate alone, you need to be hard to find. Even when playing on defense (or playing defensively, period), concealing your position from attackers can give you a decisive edge in combat, especially if you constantly change your position after each engagement.

FLAK JACKET

Take less explosive damage. Cancel frag cooking with weapon switch. Reset fuse when throwing back frags.

A critical Perk for an objective-focused class, or any time you expect to face heavy explosive builds, Flak Jacket can keep you alive through a torrential barrage of enemy ordnance. Flak Jacket won't save you from multiple direct hits or powerful Scorestreak barrages, but it can absolutely save your life from a single thrown grenade on an objective. Even a few extra seconds is enough to claim an objective or win a match.

The frag-related benefits are fairly minor, as they're specific to one explosive in the game.

One last note about avoiding explosives: remember that the Lethal Grenades from the Exo Launcher cannot be manually detonated. The safest place to be when a grenade is nearby is in the air. Use your Exo movement to avoid explosives as much as possible, and let Flak Jacket save you from the ones you cannot avoid or must absorb to secure an objective.

OVERCHARGED

Increase Exo Ability battery life. Concuss nearby enemies with boost slams.

Most useful in builds with two Exo abilities taken, Overcharged gets you more mileage from your abilities. This is particularly useful for offensive builds where you rely on Overclock, Stim, or Ping, or defensive builds for Cloak, Shield, or Trophy System. Overcharged also has the secondary benefit of giving you a wider concussive effect to your aerial ground slams, staggering nearby enemies momentarily.

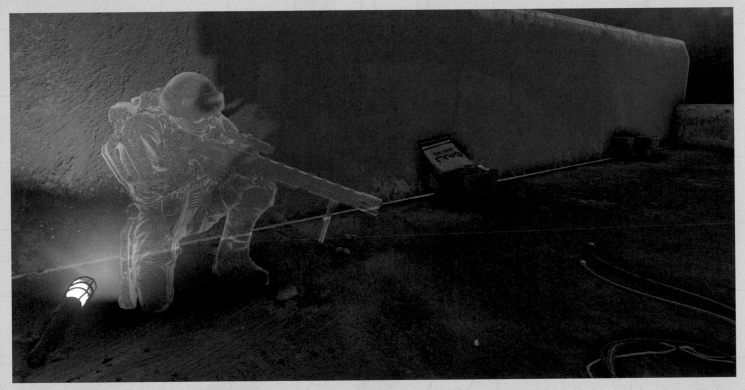

DANGER CLOSE

Do more explosive and Scorestreak damage.

This is a very powerful Perk for builds running three grenades, Exo Launchers, and offensive Scorestreaks. This is most effective in objective modes that tend to cause players to clump up in small areas, such as Momentum or Domination. Danger Close adds reliability to your explosives, almost always ensuring a kill against any player not using the Flak Jacket Perk.

PERK 2

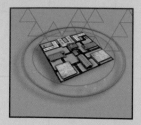

PERIPHERALS

Increase mini-map coverage. Take out enemies without displaying their death location.

Peripherals grants a massive increase in mini-map size, covering nearly the entire level on some maps. This can give you superior situational awareness, and it is especially helpful if you warn teammates of enemy positions with your enhanced range. One quirk: because Peripherals causes your mini-map to essentially "zoom out," you do lose some close-range fidelity on enemy positions. Still, this is rarely enough of a hindrance to give you cause to avoid this Perk.

Peripherals also has the side benefit of enhancing your stealth play slightly: it eliminates the death marker when you kill an adversary. On a completely stealthy build, this can help prevent the enemy team from detecting you. Just be aware that if you are playing against an organized team, they can still communicate their death over voice chat quite easily!

BLIND EYE

Undetectable by Tracking Drones, Explosive Drones, and all Scorestreaks except the UAV.

Here's another stealth Perk, but of a different variety. Rather than offering invisibility to most player-specific forms of detection, Blind Eye offers protection from autonomous AI detection. Roaming Tracking Drones, hidden Explosive Drones, and all hostile (and lethal) Scorestreaks become a minor problem.

You aren't entirely immune to them, though. An Explosive Drone can still detonate and kill you if you're nearby, even if you didn't trigger it. And the 105mm cannon on the Paladin doesn't care if you're invisible or not if you happen to be in its blast radius. But most of the time, Blind Eye serves you well to protect you from errant missiles, sentry guns, Warbirds, and drones of all shapes and sizes.

It's a good idea to have a build around with Blind Eye and an secondary launcher equipped specifically to destroy dangerous AI-controlled streaks.

COLD-BLOODED

Immune to Thermal, Target Enhancer, Threat Grenade, and enemy callouts. No name displayed or reticle color change when targeted.

A very strong stealth Perk, Cold-Blooded shields you from all manner of improved detection gear, prevents your position from being called out automatically by enemy soldiers, and hides your name from your opponents' crosshairs. All of these effects serve to make you more difficult to spot. While the overall impact of Cold-Blooded can be hard to feel, rest assured that it is saving your life more often than you might guess.

The split-second hesitation of an opponent when they spot you and don't see a red name can be enough time for you to win a firefight, and that ignores the other benefits of avoiding detection from gear or callouts.

GUNG-HO

Fire while sprinting and sliding.

An amazing Perk for CQC builds, shotguns and SMGs with Gung-Ho are extremely dangerous. Combined with aggressive Exo movement and some accuracy attachments, you can gain a decisive edge in short-range firefights. If you can start firing during a sprint while your opponent is still bringing their weapon to bear, you're going to win the shootout. Likewise, being able to fire while sliding is very nasty with shotguns.

Exo dodges and dashes are already powerful for evasion and gap closing. Being able to fire while sprinting adds more offensive punch to your loadout.

FAST HANDS

Reload while sprinting. Swap weapons, use Exo Abilities, and use Exo Launcher faster.

A very important Perk for equipment-focused builds, using Exo abilities and grenades becomes much safer and more effective with Fast Hands. The ability to switch weapons nearly instantly and reload while sprinting is also quite nice, and the two combined make Fast Hands a versatile Perk that can fit in several different builds.

Fast weapon switching is very useful if you like to scavenge weapons from fallen enemies or if you're using the Overkill Wildcard. It can also save your life if you run dry on primary ammo or if you're using a sluggish primary and need to quickly switch to a CQC secondary.

Fast Hands' ability to reload while sprinting can save you time, but it also removes the ability to perform reload cancels by sprinting. You can still perform speed reloads by tossing your mags, but this burns ammo more quickly. If you have ammo problems frequently, consider using Scavenger.

PERK 3

HARD WIRED

Immune to System Hack, EMP, Nano Swarms, Stun Grenades, and Scramblers. Scorestreaks remain vulnerable.

Hard Wired is an unusual Perk. It provides strong protection from several very dangerous and debilitating streaks and pieces of equipment, but it can also be a complete dud if your opponents aren't using that gear. If you play part of a match and find yourself getting smacked with EMP and Stun Grenades constantly, if Scrambler-equipped UAVs are always in the air, or if System Hack and Nano Swarm missiles are being used regularly, break out a build with Hard Wired.

TOUGHNESS

Flinch less when shot.

A vital Perk for mid-range firefights, Toughness reduces the visible flinch you suffer when you take damage. At mid to long range, having your view jerked by hits can cause you to lose a fight, and Toughness can keep your aim on target to score a win if your opponent does not have it, as well. Toughness has less of an impact on CQC combat, where flinch isn't nearly as much of a factor. If you prefer to fight at mid to long range frequently, take Toughness; it can help you win battles.

BLAST SUPPRESSOR

Invisible on mini-map when performing Exo moves.

The last of the major stealth Perks, Blast Suppressor hides your mini-map "ping" when you make use of Exo movement. It also suppresses the jump jets on your Exo armor, changing them to a barely visible exhaust. Given the frequency of Exo movement usage, Blast Suppressor can keep you off the mini-map very often. If you're running any sort of stealth build or you prefer to fight near enemy lines, take this Perk.

While Exo movement is so quick that you can often be far from your mini-map ping by the time an enemy comes to investigate, the ping can still get you into trouble if you're performing a lot of quick dodges and dashes during combat. Opponents coming to investigate the pings may stumble across you recovering from a fight with another adversary.

SCAVENGER

Start with extra magazines and resupply bullet ammo from fallen enemies.

Scavenger both awards you more bonus ammo to begin with and lets you loot ammo from any foes' bodies. Scavenger is a very important Perk for builds that make heavy use of speed reloads and for weapons with very high rates of fire or that are highly customized.

Scavenger is especially important if you are using a favorite customized weapon. If you run dry on ammo, you normally must swap out your weapon for whatever you can find on the battlefield, but Scavenger lets you use your preferred weapon with your chosen mods indefinitely.

The combat benefit of using speed reloads nearly as often as you like should not be overlooked, either. This can help you survive encounters with multiple enemies more frequently, again without being forced to switch to a looted weapon.

HARDLINE

Decrease Scorestreak cost by 100.

A seemingly minor Perk, Hardline is actually incredibly useful if you use it with cheap Scorestreaks. While knocking 100 points off a 1400-point Paladin doesn't improve your odds much, taking 100 points off a 400-point UAV absolutely does. The trick to Hardline is running it with a set of cheap, useful, carefully upgraded streaks. Do so, and you can earn them more consistently, benefitting yourself and your team significantly.

SCORESTREAKS

As specialized tools of war, Scorestreaks allow you to call in powerful battlefield support, ranging from reconnaissance to devastating gunships and orbital strikes. Earning Scorestreaks requires that you earn points in combat. Killing other players isn't the only way to earn points though: completing objectives in game modes such as Hardpoint, Capture the Flag, and Uplink will also score you points towards your Scorestreaks.

If you die before earning a streak, your points are reset, unless you are using one of the four Support-enabled streaks. These streaks can be modified to save your score between deaths at the cost of an increased score requirement to earn them.

You can normally equip up to three Scorestreaks, with each costing one of your Pick 13 points. However, if you select the Streaker Wildcard, you can equip four streaks.

STREAK MODULES

New to *Call of Duty®: Advanced Warfare* is the ability to customize your streaks. Much like attachments modifying weapons, modules allow you to customize your streaks with up to three attached modules. Each module increases the cost of the streak, but all of them add new functionality.

For example, you can upgrade the simple Aerial Recon Drone with a longer lifespan, EMP Grenades, and a Cloak. You could also upgrade the devastating Paladin gunship with a wingman seat for a teammate, laser guided rockets, and faster weapon reloading.

You can use as many or as few modules as you prefer, tailoring the modules you choose and their cost to the mode you are playing. If you expect to survive for a long time playing defense near an objective while racking up objective score bonuses, go for higher streaks. But if you know you are likely to die frequently (say, running the flag or the Satellite Drone in CTF or Uplink), running low streaks, support streaks, or no streaks is a better idea.

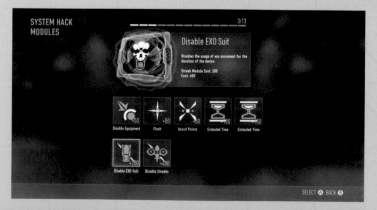

COMBATING SCORESTREAKS

Remember that secondary Launchers can destroy all airborne Scorestreaks except the XS1 Vulcan satellite Scorestreak, and that Perks can give you protection or invisibility from different Scorestreaks.

Always keep a class around that is loaded with defensive Perks and a secondary Launcher. If your team gets hit hard by powerful offensive streaks, you can spare the entire team a lot of pain by safely destroying the offending streak.

AERIAL RECON DRONE 350: SUPPORT CAPABLE

A SMALL, MANUALLY PILOTED, DRONE CAPABLE OF TAGGING ENEMIES.

You must manually guide this tiny drone, so for the 30 to 45 seconds it is active, be sure to conceal yourself in a safe location.

While controlling the Recon Drone, you can tag enemies to make them appear as threat signatures on your teammates' HUD. If you are careful about concealing the Recon Drone from enemy fire, you can tag a fair number of enemies for the life of the drone, and each tag as well as each assist from a tagged enemy killed earns you points.

CLOAK +50
Grants cloaking capability.

An inexpensive but marginal defensive upgrade, Cloak allows you to recloak the Recon Drone after "firing" a marker or an EMP Grenade. Keep in mind that the Cloak requires time to recharge. Given the limited lifespan of the Recon Drone, it is at best most useful for relocating from one position to another to focus on a new enemy cluster.

With upgrades, it is also possible to blind enemies and launch EMP Grenades to disorient enemies and destroy hostile equipment and some Scorestreaks.

The Recon Drone lasts for 30 seconds (or 45 with the time extension), allowing you to tag a target every three seconds (and EMP every six with the upgrade).

AR HUD +50
Adds augmented reality HUD for target acquisition.

The AR HUD highlights enemy players with a threat marker, allowing friendly players to spot them.

The Recon Drone gives you the ability to scout out enemy positions. This can be particularly useful in objective modes where you expect defenders or campers around key objective areas. It is less helpful in pure deathmatch modes, where the time you lose controlling the drone can result in fewer kills overall. The Recon Drone is particularly useful when you are in a party with friends and can verbally relay information about enemy positions. You don't need to tag a player to warn a teammate about their location when you're in a party.

FLASH MARKING +100
Marking enemies will also flash them.

One of the few offensive mods for the Recon Drone, Flash Marking causes your target marks to blind players. The mark "explodes" as a sort of flashbang, and if your enemies are facing it, it blinds them completely. Because of the fast refresh time on the mark, you can really torment a single player by keeping them blinded (very useful on defenders near objectives), or you can spread the love around to multiple targets.

EMP GRENADES +100
Fire EMP Grenades.

The second offensive upgrade, EMP Grenades gives you the very useful ability to shut down Exo Abilities on other players, as well as destroy other ground-based equipment. However, this is a pricy upgrade, particularly if you pair it with Flash Marking, so you may want to choose one or the other.

INCREASED LIFETIME +100
Increases the amount of time the Recon Drone can be used.

Adds +15 seconds to the lifespan of the Recon Drone, giving you more time to mark, flash, or EMP targets. As long as you can keep the drone alive for the full duration, you can usually come out ahead on points earned. Just be aware that you're out of the fight for a full 45 seconds with this upgrade. Don't use it if your presence is more urgently needed on offense or defense.

SUPPORT +400
Points earned towards this streak retain through death.

As the first of the four Support-capable streaks, this expensive upgrade gives you fewer potential Recon Drones over the course of a match, but you're guaranteed to earn them.

AERIAL ASSAULT DRONE 450

A SMALL, MANUALLY PILOTED, AERIAL DRONE WITH A HIGH EXPLOSIVE CHARGE THAT CAN BE DETONATED ON COMMAND.

A one-shot explosive suicide drone, the Aerial Assault Drone can be deployed and then launched and detonated at any target in line of sight. The detonation is fatal to nearby players, though the blast radius isn't extremely large. Aim for players clumped on objectives or near chokepoints, where they can't use Exo movement to evade the explosion.

With upgrades, you can improve the Assault Drone with machine guns or rockets, giving you a miniature assault platform. Be careful, though; these upgrades push the drone's cost well past its affordable 450 starting value up into the same territory occupied by the Warbird and other similar streaks.

The Assault Drone has a lifespan of 45 seconds, so it is possible to use it as a purely visual scouting aid. It is similar to the Recon Drone, though it lacks the marking capability. This is more useful in parties than playing solo.

AUGMENTED REALITY HUD +50

Adds augmented reality HUD for target acquisition.

This causes a targeting reticle to appear around hostiles. It is useful for picking out enemies in cover, though it is generally fairly easy to spot your opponents from the air.

CLOAK +50

Adds the ability for the drone to cloak.

Given that you uncloak when attacking, this is mostly useful if you don't plan on using the weapon upgrades and only want the Cloak to ensure that you get your explosive payload where you need it.

AI CONTROL +100

Adds the option for AI control of the drone.

For a slight cost increase, you can turn the Assault Drone into an autonomous weapon, either as a remote suicide bomb or a hovering mini-sentry with weapon upgrades. Keep in mind that the AI won't always target the exact enemies you want. While you can use it as a single target missile of sorts, don't use the AI Control streak if you want to guide the drone to a specific area or target.

HARDENED +100

Increases drone health but decreases movement speed.

A marginal benefit for the cost increase, this is only really worth considering if you plan on using the weapon upgrades. Keep in mind that even with the improved armor, dedicated hostiles can still take you out if you draw enough ire with your attacks.

MACHINE GUN +300

Adds a machine gun turret on the drone.

With no overheat, these machine guns are quite nice for picking off players, even those who are using Exo movement in the air. However, the cost increase is significant. Because you pay heavily for this upgrade, only use it if you can reliably score enough kills to make it worth the price.

ROCKETS +300

Adds a rocket launcher onto the drone.

Rockets grants you three rockets with a reload time. These powerful rockets can one-shot kill other players, but just as with the Machine Gun upgrade, you pay for their lethality.

UAV 400: SUPPORT CAPABLE

The UAV grants +10 support points per kill, and +15 with Extra Assist Points. One of the simplest streaks, the UAV is also one of the most powerful. No other streak gives your team as many benefits in such a cheap package.

Baseline, the UAV performs periodic radar sweeps of the battlefield every two seconds, revealing enemies with each sweep for 35 seconds, or 50 with the Extra Time upgrade added. You can upgrade the UAV with a variety of performance-enhancing modifications, but be wary of overloading your UAV with extra cost. In fact, one of its strengths is its power for a low cost.

You can improve your UAV's enemy detection, cause it to scramble the enemy team's radar, or modify it to become a support streak, maintaining score earned toward it through your own deaths.

When seeking to destroy UAVs, remember that all secondary Launchers cause highlight markers on UAVs to appear when scanning the sky, making them easy to target.

SPEED +50
Faster position updating to the mini-map.

A useful upgrade for the cost, Speed causes the UAV to sweep the map more frequently, giving you faster positional updates on enemies. Given the speed at which players can travel with Exo mobility, this streak is very helpful for tracking them.

EXTRA ASSIST POINTS +50
Grants user additional assist points for every active kill.

A very useful upgrade, the extra points from this are all but guaranteed. Whenever your teammates score kills with your UAV up, you get more points. Consider this a default upgrade unless you need to prioritize other upgrades.

EXTRA TIME +100
UAV lasts longer.

This helpful upgrade is useful for both the extra points you can earn and the extra radar coverage time.

SCRAMBLER +200
Obscure the enemy mini-map.

Though a bit expensive, this powerful upgrade shuts down the enemy radar, granting your team a huge information advantage. Despite the cost, it is well worth the extra points.

ENEMY DIRECTION +200
Adds facing arrow to mini-map.

For the benefits it gives, this is an expensive upgrade. Getting facing information about enemies is useful for flanking and ambushing your foes, but the cost is high, and you can often determine the direction an enemy is facing from the combat situation at hand.

THREAT DETECTION +300
Paints enemies with each sweep of the UAV.

An expensive and powerful upgrade, Threat Detection causes enemies to appear on your HUD as though they were struck with a Threat Grenade. This gives you a huge intelligence edge in combat, as you can locate adversaries hiding in buildings or on rooftops from below.

ORBITAL +300
Move UAV into orbit, where it cannot be shot down.

Another expensive upgrade, moving your UAV into orbit prevents it from being shot down, giving you guaranteed radar coverage. This module is only truly useful if you're up against an organized team that consistently shoots down your UAVs.

SUPPORT +300
Points earned towards this streak retain through death.

This second Support-enabled streak is a very useful one. While you can earn fewer UAVs over the course of a match, this is still extremely useful for aggressive builds, or if you are uncertain of your ability to reliably earn your UAV with its normal loadout.

ORBITAL CARE PACKAGE 500: SUPPORT CAPABLE

A CARE PACKAGE CALLED IN FROM ORBIT CONTAINING A RANDOM SCORESTREAK THAT HAS A CHANCE OF BEING THE MAP SCORESTREAK.

The Orbital Care Package does precisely what it says on the box: it drops a care package from orbit at a target location of your designation. It takes roughly seven seconds from the time you call it in to when the package lands and you can pick it up. Without the Hidden modification, the package shows up to the enemy team on their mini-map while active. Expect alert opponents to track you down and either hijack your package or attempt to take you out. The Trap upgrade works quite well to punish such thieving foes…

The care package can potentially award you any streak up to the Paladin, though by default, it is weighted toward cheaper options. Because you have no control over how the streaks are modified, this isn't as well suited for a specific build as a Scorestreak that you choose and modify. Still, you can take Better Odds and/or Double Tap to improve your chances at better items. The care package is ultimately a decent way to explore higher streaks that you have difficulty earning normally, especially if you take the Support modification.

FAST PICKUP +50
Pickup your own care package faster.

DRONE DELIVERY +50
Adds thrusters allowing it to seek you out before landing.

A module that is by turns amusing, useful, and dangerous, Drone Delivery causes the care package to actually lift itself up on thrusters and follow you on the map until it reaches your destination. It then hovers helpfully and lets you pick up your goodies. It's quite a sight to see a care package floating by. But there is a downside, and it is a big one: you are giving your enemies a bloodhound that freely tracks you down.

It is possible to use Drone Delivery as bait to get enemies to pursue you to a defensible position. But be careful: this is a risky tactic, unless your care package is trapped, as well…

HIDDEN +100
Care package does not appear on enemy radar.

Care packages normally serve as a beacon for enemies. This upgrade helps reduce the chances of you being hunted if you drop your care package in a safe place behind friendly lines.

DOUBLE TAP +100
Allow double tap to change the package contents.

If you dislike your first item, reroll it to another. This slightly increases your chances of getting a more expensive streak, letting you swap out an undesirable streak immediately.

TRAP +150
The package will explode if the enemy team tries to capture it.

You or a teammate can pick it up safely, leaving behind a trapped package. This is a nasty surprise for the enemy, and it can score you multiple kills if too many foes get greedy. Don't drop trapped packages in really obvious places: canny opponents won't take the bait if you drop them on the central Momentum flag every time…

BETTER ODDS +200
Increases the chance of getting better items.

A direct increase to the odds of getting higher Scorestreaks, Better Odds can also be combined with Double Tap for the best possible odds of a high-end streak. This is a pricy upgrade given the randomness inherent in care packages, so think carefully before adding it without a Support upgrade.

SUPPORT +600
Points earned toward this streak retain through death.

A very expensive support upgrade, this version of Support allows you to earn any streak in the game, but at the cost of slow acquisition. If you find that you struggle to achieve high streaks normally, this is a good way to experiment with streaks you might have difficulty earning otherwise. Load up with Support, Double Tap, and Better Odds, and you have a decent shot at getting a mid to high-tier streak, though you won't be able to earn many of these in a match.

REMOTE TURRET 550: SUPPORT CAPABLE

A DEPLOYABLE, MANUALLY CONTROLLED, HIGH POWERED TURRET.

The Remote Turret places a remotely controlled machine gun turret that covers a frontal arc of roughly 180 degrees and lasts for a full minute. With modifications, you can improve this targeting radius to a full 360 degrees, change its weapon to rockets or a laser, or make it an autonomous AI-controlled weapon.

The Remote Turret is ideal for defending objective areas and chokepoints, but you may need to add Heavy Resistance if you expect the enemy team to attempt to take it out with equipment. With the 360 Turret Head and Sentry upgrades, the turret becomes an expensive but powerful defensive tool, capable of locking an area down for your team while it is active.

Place the turret carefully, where enemies cannot easily attack from behind cover, and it can completely deny access to your opponents while it is active. The Remote Turret cannot be locked on by secondary Launchers, but it can be stunned for five seconds by a Stun Grenade (if in AI-controlled Sentry mode) or cause your screen to white out (if you are manually controlling it).

ROCKET TURRET +100

Fires rockets. Replaces Machine Gun or Directed Energy Turret.

This upgrade causes the turret to fire powerful rockets. These offer less suppression than continuous machine gun fire, but you have almost guaranteed kills if they strike anywhere near a target.

DIRECTED ENERGY +100

Fires a controlled laser. Replaces Machine Gun or Rocket Turret.

This upgrade functions similarly to the Machine Gun Turret in functionality, but it offers increased sustained damage output for a slight price premium.

360 TURRET HEAD +100

Turret can spin 360 degrees.

This very useful upgrade allows the turret to cover a full 360 degrees of terrain, particularly powerful when the turret is carefully placed.

RIPPABLE +100

Adds ability to rip off the turret head and be carried on the battlefield.

If you don't want a turret, but you do want a powerful weapon, take this upgrade, and you can dominate the battlefield for a while with a powerful handheld turret weapon. Just be careful—this is a pricy weapon to use, and you can still die just as easily as normal while using it. (If anything, you're going to attract more attention if you start spraying lasers and rockets everywhere.)

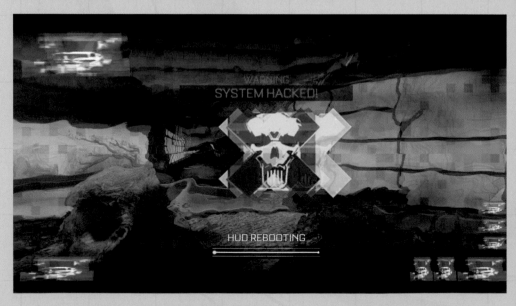

HEAVY RESISTANCE +100

Adds flashbang and concussion immunity.

This upgrade is useful only if you know with certainty that the enemy team regularly uses Stun Grenades. Otherwise, skip this module in favor of others.

SENTRY +200

Turret will be a sentry when not remote controlled.

The most dramatic upgrade to the turret, this causes it to become AI-controlled, automatically firing on hostile targets. This should be your default module. Alongside the 360 Turret Head, this allows you to completely lock down a section of the map with careful placement. Back up your Sentry by covering it from a distance, and you can create a very tough defensive position.

The Sentry upgrade is especially useful in objective modes. You can place it to cover an objective directly, or cover a flank or rear approach to guard your back.

SUPPORT +600

Points earned towards this streak retain through death.

The final Support streak, this allows you to get your turret up and running guaranteed. Best paired with Sentry, possibly with either 360 Turret Head or one of the weapon upgrades, this gives you one guaranteed Sentry every match (and likely several). In objective modes, this is a very strong combination, as it is the only directly lethal streak that can use the Support module.

SYSTEM HACK 600

AN AUTONOMOUS CYBER ATTACK THAT DISABLES ENEMY HUD, RADAR, AND RETICLES.

System Hack shuts down enemy HUDs, minimaps, and reticles, obscuring their screens for the duration of the hack. With modifications, the System Hack can be greatly extended in duration and modded to disable enemy equipment, Exo Suits, and Scorestreaks.

System Hack is an odd streak in that its effects are necessarily immediately visible. Much like the UAV (particularly with the Scrambler upgrade), it is a very powerful team support streak.

Getting hit with a System Hack is no fun at all, and it's all but guaranteed death for anyone involved in a firefight. On top of that, for the duration of the hack, the team using System Hack has an edge in combat, distinct from the information advantage that the UAV grants.

DISABLE EQUIPMENT +50

Kills all active enemy electronic-based equipment and disables its usage for the duration of the device.

This is a cheap upgrade, but it's hard to know how effective it is. Since you don't know precisely which loadouts your opponents are using, this module may be very powerful, or do nothing at all. If you do see frequent evidence of equipment usage in your favored modes, use this module.

FLASH +50

Flashbangs all enemies for a short time.

This cheap upgrade adds even more disorientation when the System Hack is fired. System Hack can already cause enemy players to experience enough of a disruption to their HUD to lose a firefight. However, Flash guarantees that they are helpless when it is triggered.

This upgrade is most useful when playing with an organized team. You can call the hack immediately before a teammate makes a key objective play, running for a flag or goal, or pushing on an enemy position.

ASSIST POINTS +50

Earn assist points for teammate kills.

A nice upgrade for the price, this is basically free points, much like the UAV upgrade. If you have room for this mod, take it.

EXTENDED TIME +150 x2

**Increase the amount of time the device is active.
Can be taken twice.**

A strong but expensive upgrade, this extends the duration of the System Hack. You need to decide if the extra time is worth the risk of not earning the hack in the first place.

DISABLE EXO SUIT +200

Disables the usage of Exo movement for the duration of the device.

A very, very powerful module, this enhancement causes System Hack to nullify the entire enemy team's Exo movement for the duration of the hack. This gives your team an enormous mobility advantage, particularly devastating in modes like CTF and Uplink, but strong in any mode due to the importance of Exo movement.

While this is active, you can freely clear and secure rooftops, raining down fire on enemies below who cannot reach you. Even on the ground, you have an edge in evasion with Boost Dodges, quick jumps, and dashes. This is a costly upgrade, but it's well worth the price.

DISABLE STREAKS +400

Kills all active enemy scorestreaks and disables their usage for the duration of the device.

A very expensive upgrade, this is a one-shot answer to every Scorestreak in the game. Because of this upgrade's cost, if you do intend to run this, it is best to hold the hack in reserve until the enemy team deploys something truly lethal. That way, you can destroy it instantly (alongside reaping all the usual benefits of a hack). One problem with this is that you may end up sitting with the hack in your streak list for an extended period of time. Using it defensively may result in using it less than you can normally.

This is a strong upgrade if the opposing team has multiple players capable of earning high streaks, but in most casual public matches, you can handle streaks with secondary Launchers or stealth Perks.

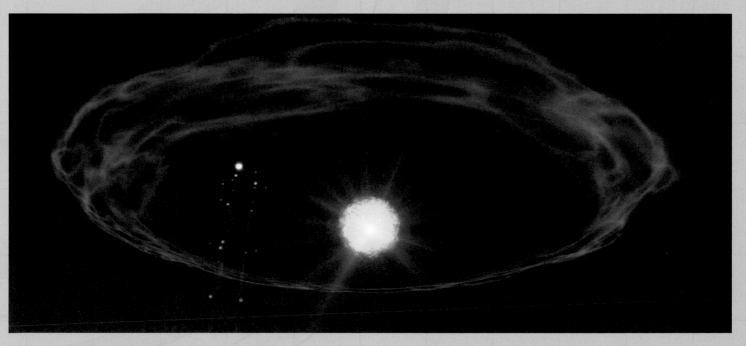

XS1 VULCAN 600

A MANUALLY CONTROLLED BURST OF HIGH-POWERED DIRECTED ENERGY DEPLOYED FROM SPACE.

The Vulcan is an orbiting satellite energy weapon, and activating it grants you a single burst of energy that you can direct across the battlefield, frying any enemy unfortunate enough to be in the open. Extra modifications improve the area of devastation or grant additional shots beyond the first.

The Vulcan works best on maps with little overhead cover, as the beam strikes straight down from the sky and can be blocked by any building rooftops or other overhead cover.

This streak is particularly powerful in objective modes if used in coordination with your team. You can cover an attack or escape perfectly with a Vulcan beam, even using the basic streak with no modules attached. You're spoiled for choice with the Vulcan's modifications, as they are all quite good.

EXTRA TIME +100
Double the burst duration.

A very nice upgrade, this extends the suppression effect of the Vulcan, and combined with Extra Bursts, can keep an objective area locked down for an extended period of time, or provide perfect cover for teammates near an objective.

EXTRA BURST +150 x2
Add another burst. Can be taken twice.

A moderately priced but very strong upgrade, this allows you to use the Vulcan more than once. Given that you're paying a quarter of the normal price for another full-strength shot, this is good value for its cost.

LIGHT SHOW +200
Adds three rotating lasers.

Another powerful offensive upgrade, this adds multiple secondary beams that orbit the primary beam. Whether you prefer to use Overcharge or Light Show (or both), you gain extra lethality in the blast zone. The cost increase for Light Show is significant, so consider whether you may get more benefit from Extra Bursts and Extra Time.

OVERCHARGE +100
Increase the beam width.

Overcharge significantly increases the radius of the blast, ensuring that any enemies caught near the impact point are fried, as well. You don't absolutely need this upgrade to take down targets near the impact point, but it can score you some extra kills that you might not have earned without it.

MISSILE STRIKE 650

A MANUALLY GUIDED AERIAL MISSILE.

The Missile Strike grants you manual control of a single guided missile with a decent blast radius and the ability to activate booster rockets, speeding its descent. With upgrades, the Missile Strike becomes considerably nastier, gaining additional homing missile strikes and a special detonation for the primary missile.

CLUSTER MISSILE +50

Primary missile splits into multiple spiraling missiles for concentrated area damage.

Mutually exclusive with Hellfire Missile.

Cluster Missile causes the missile to split into several spiraling missiles that spread out and saturate a wide area with explosions. This is ideal for hammering the entire area around a key objective, but it is less effective at focusing on multiple targets that are spread out.

HELLFIRE MISSILE +100

Primary missile splits into multiple targeting missiles.

Mutually exclusive with Cluster Missile.

Hellfire Missiles split into several auto-targeting missiles that seek out enemies within the strike zone and terminate them. This upgrade is very powerful on maps with little overhead cover, but less so when there are a lot of buildings or hard cover that enemies can flee into.

EXTRA MISSILE +100 x2
Adds an additional single target missile to fire. Can be taken twice.

This upgrade lets you add up to two additional missiles that break off and target single players. This is particularly nasty when combined with Hellfire or Cluster Missiles, as it allows you to quickly pick off two isolated targets, then bomb the main area you're concerned with (or that has the highest concentration of targets). Keep in mind that if you don't score extra kills with this module consistently, you should spend the points elsewhere.

NANO SWARM +150
Primary missile leaves behind a swarm of Nanobots.

A powerful upgrade for objective modes, this causes the primary missile strike to leave behind a globe of Nanobots that damage and eventually kill any hostile enemy who enters the affected area. The Nano Swarm persists for a short time, but while it is active, it's almost impossible for the enemy team to enter an objective area covered by it (barring specific Perk usage).

BOMBING RUN 725

A MANUALLY TARGETED AERIAL BOMBING RUN.

The Bombing Run unleashes a directed bombardment of the battlefield, cutting a swath of destruction across the map. Use the Bombing Run to deny an entire strip of the map to the enemy team. This is particularly relevant in modes like Uplink and Capture the Flag, where your team may need a clear path to a specific goal. However, it can also be useful in objective modes with outdoor objectives vulnerable to the bombing.

It is possible to destroy the bombers with a secondary Launcher, but you must be extremely fast to target and fire before they drop their payload.

A friendly player on your team can join the Bombing Run as a support bomber, firing a single guided missile onto the battlefield!

FLARES +50
Add ability to shoot flares to ward off enemy missiles.

A cheap but marginal upgrade, bombers are generally fairly difficult to react to. If you find that hostile players begin to wise up to Bombing Runs and start actively targeting them, start slotting this mod.

STEALTH +100
Airstrike is hidden on the enemy radar.

Note that the Bombing Run is still announced to the enemy team; they just can't see it on the mini-map. In objective modes, smart opponents are going to assume you're dropping it on or near the objective (which you probably are), so this upgrade is a bit less useful in those situations.

ADDITIONAL BOMBER +300
Call in an additional bomber.

Although expensive, this upgrade adds even more area saturation to the Bombing Run. The cost increase pushes Bombing Run into very pricy territory, so don't take this module unless the map and game mode you're playing specifically suit its use; you need clear, open terrain for the bombers to devastate the enemy team.

CARE PACKAGES +400
Drop care packages instead of bombs close to the chosen site.

Get three care packages per bomber dropped on the battlefield, resulting in a shower of gifts! This upgrade is very expensive, even more so if you choose to take another bomber, but it is a gambler's joy. If you luck out with several powerful streaks, you can swing a match in your team's favor with one streak.

XS1 GOLIATH 775

A MANUALLY PILOTED SUIT OF ADVANCED ARMOR WITH HEAVY WEAPONS.

The Goliath drops a care package from orbit containing a powerful suit of Exo armor, armed with a rotary mini-gun and the potential for a variety of explosive munitions. The Goliath has a set amount of armor that small arms fire from the enemy team can deplete.

A single secondary Launcher hit is lethal to the Goliath.

To suit up in a Goliath, approach the care package, and hold the Reload button to enter it. Once inside, you can self-destruct the suit to eject early (useful if you get heavily damaged). The Goliath comes equipped with a mini-gun by default. Fire it in short bursts to avoid overheating (firing in this manner also maintains high accuracy).

RECON +50
Equips Goliath with a rechargeable Exo Ping device.

Extremely useful and cheap, this upgrade gives you the ability to use Exo Ping and locate hostile players who lack stealth Perks to avoid your scans. Use Recon to track down players and terminate them.

TROPHY +50
Mobile Trophy System on suit.

A powerful and cheap upgrade, this protects you from incoming explosives that can potentially destroy your Exo Suit instantly. It's especially recommended if you see the enemy using secondary Launchers often. The Trophy module for the Goliath lasts as long as the Goliath is alive.

UNDERBARREL ROCKET +100
Underbarrel rocket launcher

A powerful one-shot kill on other players, this is a useful upgrade, as it simply increases your instant lethality. It is also especially nasty near crowded objectives.

HOMING ROCKETS +100
Rocket pack on shoulder that can shoot multiple missiles on a locked target.

This upgrade fires four missiles that automatically lock and track a nearby player. This is a mean upgrade; even players using Exo movement can be tracked and blasted with ease. Pair this with the dumbfire rocket, and you have a walking engine of destruction.

WARBIRD 850

For 30 seconds, you can pilot the Warbird, saturating the enemy team with aerial machine gun fire. This is an expensive but very powerful streak. If left unchecked by the enemy team's secondary Launchers, you can completely shut down their ability to fight in the open and provide perfect cover for your team near objectives.

A friendly player on your team can join the Warbird in the air, marking targets in a similar manner as the Recon Drone and aiding your ability to find and eliminate hostiles.

AGGRESSOR +50

AI controlled Warbird. Seeks out enemy targets.

Mutually exclusive with Defender.

If you prefer to stay in the fight while your Warbird works for you, take this upgrade. It patrols the map while firing on the enemy team.

DEFENDER +50

AI controlled Warbird. Stays near player, providing cover fire.

Mutually exclusive with Aggressor.

The defensive option, Defender causes the Warbird to follow you around the map, giving you cover fire from the enemy team. This is particularly nice in deathmatch modes and in objective modes on offense. One option is to earn this streak while on defense, then switch to offense while it is active, returning to defense to rack up the points again more easily.

EXTRA FLARE +100

Add an extra flare to ward off more enemy missiles.

Extra Flare is potentially very useful or entirely useless, depending on how the enemy team plays. Keep an eye on how many secondary Launchers you see used and how often you see streaks taken down to determine if you should burn the points on this module.

CLOAK +150

Adds Cloak ability to Warbird.

A marginal upgrade for the cost, while the Cloak makes it harder to spot and track, it's not particularly stealthy once it starts firing!

EXTRA TIME +200

Increases Warbird time in the air.

This gives you an extra 15 seconds in the air. It pushes the Warbird's cost up to a high level, but you're getting 50% more time in the air for a fraction of the cost of a full Warbird…

WARBIRD WINGMAN +200

Joining player mounts additional MG Turret.

A pricy upgrade, Warbird Wingman gives you a second pair of eyes and another trigger finger to mow down the enemy team. Keep in mind that this is effectively taking two players out of the fight on your team. It's vital that you both do a good job of suppressing the enemy team, or your remaining teammates may find themselves fighting outnumbered on the ground.

ROCKETS +300

Adds rockets as an alternate weapon.

Although it is very expensive, this upgrade gives you even more offensive firepower. The rockets are instantly fatal to any target near the blast, and you can use them to clear out an objective area even quicker than your machine guns.

PALADIN 950

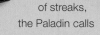

A MANUALLY CONTROLLED WEAPON SYSTEM ABOARD AN ORBITING PALADIN GUNSHIP.

The king of streaks, the Paladin calls in a droneship that orbits the battlefield for 40 seconds. Take the controls and saturate the battlefield with fire from above. The Paladin is very expensive and very powerful. Earning it requires dedication, especially with upgrades, but on any map that is even remotely open, it is a lethal streak that can completely suppress the enemy team.

WINGMAN +200

Joining player mounts additional MG Turret. Replaces default ability.

Though expensive, Wingman is one of the most fun upgrades in the game. If you can get yourself and a buddy in the Paladin, it's well worth the cost. It's also extremely painful for the enemy team…

EXTRA TIME +200

Increase the amount of time in the air.

This upgrade raises the Paladin's time in the air to 55 seconds. Proportionally, this is a worse value than the Warbird's upgrade, but the Paladin can lay down a more devastating barrage of fire while it is in the air. Also, suppressing the enemy team for almost a full minute can clinch a match.

105MM CANNON +300

Add a 105mm turret.

EXTRA FLARE +100

Add an extra flare to ward off more enemy missiles.

The Paladin only has one flare by default, and a single Stinger hit can destroy it. Pay very close attention to enemy secondary Launcher usage, and use this module if you see them used frequently.

SLEIGHT OF HAND +150

Time to reload turrets is shorter.

This upgrade speeds up reloads and lets you rain down even more firepower on the battlefield.

LASER GUIDED ROCKET +200

Add a turret that fires laser guided rockets.

This adds an additional rocket weapon, useful for flushing out targets from cover where they think they are safe. Guide the rocket into a doorway or window, and eliminate the enemy.

The 105mm Cannon fires an incredibly powerful shell that is instantly lethal to anyone in the blast radius. This is expensive, but it rewards you with the most lethal controlled weapon in the game. The blast is so large that you can use it to take out targets hiding under hard cover—aim near openings or doorways, and the blast will do the rest.

MULTIPLAYER GAME MODES

The gameplay modes in Multiplayer matches of *Call of Duty®: Advanced Warfare* define your goals and your path to victory in every match. Beyond that, they also heavily influence your choice of loadout. Depending on the map and the mode, different weapons and equipment become more or less useful. It's important to tailor your classes to your preferred modes. Using the correct tools for the job is just as important when it comes to your overall Class as it is when choosing weapons for combat.

OVERTIME!

Call of Duty®: Advanced Warfare has stopwatch-style overtime in objective matches. If you end a match tied, you go on to play a final round. Whichever team scores (or completes an objective first) sets the time for the opposing team to beat. If the other team can score in less time, they win; otherwise, they lose.

NEW MODES

UPLINK

A heavily team-focused mode, somewhat similar to a one-flag CTF-style game, Uplink challenges both teams to secure a Satellite Drone and score points in the opposing team's goal. You earn one point for throwing the Drone into the goal, and two points for touching it while carrying the Drone. The goals are always aerial, so Exo movement is a must to reach them. You are naturally exposed when going for a two-point score, so there are times where only throwing the Drone is a wiser plan.

You can also pass the Drone to teammates by targeting them, or manually throw the Drone at an enemy. Why do that? To force the enemy to drop their weapon in order to catch the Drone so you can shoot them, of course…

Picking up the Drone gives you an armor bonus, granting you a bit of added protection to help you survive the hail of incoming fire you can expect while running it.

Uplink heavily rewards teamplay. It is vital to have fast-moving classes for offense, both for carrying the Drone and escorting the carrier. Intercepting opposing players closing in on your carrier is critical for clearing a path.

Defense wins games in Uplink. Having a pair of defenders patrolling near the goal at all times can shut down the enemy team's offense if the defenders are using suitable weapons and equipment. Defenders can also run (and reliably earn) high-end Scorestreaks because they can potentially earn so many points for downing the constant assaults on the goal.

Offensive players, particularly the Drone carrier, should have low Scorestreaks, support streaks, or no streaks at all. Instead, put points into mobility, stealth, and awareness tools.

MOMENTUM

Momentum tasks both teams to capture a central contested flag point. Scoring kills speeds the capture of the point, and once it is captured, another flag closer to the enemy team's side of the map is activated. There are five flags in total. If the last flag of a team is captured, they lose the match. Long-time veteran *Call of Duty®* players may remember the "War" mode. Momentum is a modern remake.

Momentum conflicts play out very similar to Domination, with a few key differences. First, every flag is just as hot as the B point in Domination. With only a single flag to focus on, it is incredibly dangerous and difficult to hold the flag down long enough to score a capture.

Momentum differs from Domination slightly in that scoring kills speeds the flag capture. It is doubly important to take down the enemy team near the flag, both to clear the area of danger and to speed the capture before reinforcements can arrive.

Beware of explosive Classes bombarding you while fighting on the flag. If you plan on tackling the point directly, it is very important to have at least one Heavy Shield user and defensive Perks and equipment.

Because players tend to fixate on the currently active flag, on many maps, it is very possible to bypass the flag and flank the enemy team. Clear them out, and buy time for your team to capture the flag. This is particularly important if you are fighting to a standstill on the flag itself. Disrupting the enemy line can be enough to shift the match in your favor.

Think of flanking attacks as similar to doing an A or C run in Domination, where you seek to flip the flags and spawns, shifting the balance of a match.

DEATHMATCH MODES

Classic warfare-style deathmatch modes are pure combat. If you don't want to worry about any objective more complex than picking up an occasional Dog Tag, these are the modes for your mood.

FREE FOR ALL

Fight for sole glory as the victor in an arena with everyone out to kill you. FFA matches are intense cat and mouse games, with roaming players constantly pressuring defensive players trying to stake out a corner of the map as their own. With Exo movement, FFA is fast-paced and intense. Targets bounding across rooftops and dodging in close quarters combat (CQC) battles make for a chaotic battlefield.

Unlike Team Deathmatch or Kill Confirmed, which focus on maintaining a positive kill/death ratio to win, you can die quite a bit and still come out the victor in FFA if you can maintain a rapid pace of kills. Generally, there are two viable tactics for winning FFA matches. Either roam and kill at great speed, or lock down one area of the map, slaughtering anyone who attempts to get anywhere near you.

TEAM DEATHMATCH

This is the most elemental of all game modes. Fight with your comrades to defeat your enemies, and score more kills than deaths to win. One note about TDM: while it may be the simplest of all game modes, it is not an easy game mode. With no objectives to focus players around (not even Dog Tags to bait players with, like in Kill Confirmed), TDM is highly fluid and mobile. Expect to encounter enemies almost anywhere on a map.

This equates to campers and snipers hiding out in buildings or behind cover on rooftops. Aggressive players use rapid Exo movement to close distance. Cunning defensive players score kills and then relocate, waiting for a revenge rush. You'll encounter players using all of these tactics and many more.

TDM is all about controlled aggression. You want to score kills, but giving up kills is damaging to your team. Always try to engage with an edge, whether it's using stealth Perks to flank the enemy team, fighting at long range against players with no long-range answer, or using terrain and Exo movement to get into CQC fights with a close-range Class.

If a situation looks unfavorable, don't engage or get out. Try to fight near your teammates whenever possible. If you don't see any friendly blips on your mini-map (especially if you see death indicators on your HUD), it's likely that enemies are very near or all around you, and friendlies are not. Use Exo movement, and get away safely to fight under better conditions.

KILL CONFIRMED

Very similar to TDM, Kill Confirmed causes any downed player to drop a Dog Tag. If you pick it up, you get a bonus score and confirm the kill. If an enemy picks it up, they deny you the kill and the points.

Kill Confirmed is also an excellent mode for stringing together multiple Scorestreaks. If you can chain kills and collect Dog Tags with a fast-moving CQC Class, you can often manage to call in the heavy artillery.

Kill Confirmed somewhat disadvantages long-range Classes, as they can have a hard time confirming kills. However, nearby teammates can confirm your kills, so you can still win a match as long as you have several aggressive players near the front lines.

OBJECTIVE MODES

CAPTURE THE FLAG

Classic Capture the Flag: two flags, two bases. Steal and capture the enemy flag to score. Defend your own flag, or you cannot capture while it is away. CTF gains new life with Exo movement in the mix. The incredible speed and agility gained from Exo usage allows for incredibly swift flag runs and interceptions.

Bring your highly mobile Classes for offense. Much like Uplink, run higher streaks on defense to punish overly aggressive players who don't check their corners. The flag makes delicious bait, after all... Also, like Uplink, defense wins games. Having a pair of defenders guard the flag area (not necessarily the flag itself) while the rest of the team plays offense works extremely well.

DOMINATION

Capture the A, B, and C flags to score. Win by holding two flags and locking the enemy team at the third. Domination is fast-paced, with action constantly flowing around the capture points. The B flag is often a madhouse, featuring constant attacks and switches.

A and C can be either quiet or busy, depending on how the level is laid out. Linear maps with the flags in a line often have more conflict over B and fewer flips on A and C. Triangular or irregular layouts frequently have constantly shifting flags.

Domination rewards many playstyles. You can play defense around a point and rack up a huge score, play offense and capture flags with defensive Classes, or sneak rear flags to shift the battlefield.

Halftime in Domination causes teams to switch sides at the halfway mark, giving both teams an equal shot at uneven terrain on any map.

HARDPOINT

A returning favorite, Hardpoint challenges you to control shifting areas ("hardpoints") around the map. Each hardpoint requires that friendly teammates stand inside it to score with no enemies present. If an opponent enters the hardpoint, you get a "Contested" warning, alerting you to an immediate enemy threat even if you don't spot them. Hardpoints shift around the map, moving the conflict all over the level even more than Momentum does.

It is equally important to hunt and intercept players heading for the hardpoint as it is to secure the hardpoint itself. If you can block off a fresh spawn of enemies from even approaching the hardpoint, you can secure a full hold of a hardpoint to get a significant score advantage.

Be wary of having your entire team standing in the hardpoint itself. You become vulnerable to explosive assaults and Scorestreaks. If you see too many players stacked up (especially in confined areas or smaller hardpoints), evac and find a nearby vantage point to guard the hardpoint from.

Hardpoints cycle in a fixed order, so it's important to recognize when a point is lost and move into position for the next one ahead of time. Securing a strong hold on a new hardpoint area before it appears can reward you with a full or nearly full hold.

BOMB MODES

Intense modes with no respawns or limited respawns, these modes challenge your team to play both offense and defense, switching between the bomb planters and the bomb defusers.

It is also possible (and quite common) to win by killing all players on the opposing team before they plant the bomb. If the bomb is planted, you must defuse it before it detonates, even if the team goes down.

SEARCH & DESTROY

S&D challenges you to plant the bomb, defuse it, or kill all players on the opposing team. You get just one life, played out over multiple rounds, with halftime switching between the two teams on offense and defense. S&D demands sharp situational awareness, fast movement, and keen map knowledge. Avoid using high Scorestreaks in S&D, as the points are better spent elsewhere.

Informational Perks and equipment are powerful, as is stealth gear. Both can give you an edge in hunting or avoiding detection. If you enjoy the tension of knowing you're the last person standing on your team and there are three angry players hunting you, this is the mode for you.

SEARCH & RESCUE

S&R plays identically to S&D, with one very important exception: it has Kill Confirmed-style Dog Tags that you can use to revive friendly teammates or keep enemy players down. This changes the tactics significantly. Where S&D encourages smart, aggressive play whether solo or together, S&R heavily favors teams that pair up in groups and revive each other.

It also makes long-range kills much more difficult to secure, as an enemy downed in a distant window can easily be revived before you can collect their Dog Tag. Just like Kill Confirmed, close-quarters Classes (when the maps permit their efficient use) are highly effective for downing targets and securing their Dog Tags.

PARTY MODES

When you want to take a break from high-stress matches, relax with some entertaining bonus modes.

GUN GAME

Progress through a variety of weapons, unlocking a new weapon each time you kill another player. Knife other players to knock them back a weapon. Prove your mastery of every weapon class, and chain kills to secure a decisive advantage.

INFECTED

Dodging the infected with Exo movement? Scary indeed. Survivors face off against the infected, and each kill from an infected grows their ranks by one. Can you be the last soldier standing?

Infected is also unique in that it gives the infected players the Tactical Insertion equipment. Using it allows you to set your spawn point anywhere on the map as you see fit. Survivors get an Exo Shield and one Explosive Drone, whereas infected spawn with Tactical Insertion and a Spike Grenade.

EXO SURVIVAL

Exo Survival mode pits you and up to three other players against countless waves of enemy soldiers, drones, Dobermans, and ASTs. The rounds get increasingly more difficult, with more hostiles and the occasional objective round. Objective rounds force you and your team to move out and gather Intel, defuse bombs, collect Dog Tags, or defend a specific point on the map.

Players advance to the next level by completing Round 25. At that point, you return to Round 1 with tougher enemies.

THE BASICS

GAME SETUP

Before starting a game of Exo Survival, you can change the following options in Game Setup. Note that your character starts with no upgrades whether you start at the beginning or Join-In-Progress, making it much tougher to start on a later round.

Map	Choose among 13 Multiplayer maps
Difficulty	Regular, Hardened, Veteran (private or local matches only)
Starting Wave	1, 5, 10, 15, 20
Support Drops	Enabled, Disabled

CHOOSE A CLASS

As a game starts, each player is asked to choose from three classes: Light, Heavy, or Specialist. They vary in speed, armor, boost abilities, weapon type, and Class Scorestreak. You can switch your class at any time at an Exo Upgrade Station.

LIGHT EXO

Speed	Fastest
Armor	Lowest
Boost Abilities	All
Guns	Pistols, Submachine Guns, Assault Rifles
Starting Ability	Exo Hover
Class Scorestreak	UAV

This guy is quick, with his Exo dodges and fast movement, but he is the easiest to go down. His UAV Class Scorestreak allows the team to get a heads-up on where the enemy is coming from.

HEAVY EXO

Speed	Slowest
Armor	Most
Boost Abilities	Boost Jump
Guns	Pistols, Heavy Weapons
Starting Ability	Exo Shield
Class Scorestreak	XS1 Goliath

The Heavy Exo is the tank of the group with high armor, but it is the slowest class and can only perform a limited Boost Jump. These guys cause the most damage with their heavy weapons and XS1 Goliath Scorestreak.

SPECIALIST EXO

Speed	Normal
Armor	Normal
Boost Abilities	Limited
Guns	Pistols, Shotguns, Sniper Rifles
Starting Ability	Exo Cloak
Class Scorestreak	Remote Turret

The Specialist is average in speed and movement and more limited on boost abilities than the Light Exo. His Class Scorestreak of a Remote Turret is great for watching a second entrance when playing solo. The choice of shotguns and sniper rifles allows them to fight from a variety of distances.

GAME PLAY

Once the first round begins, enemies pour into the area. Take them all down, as the last five are counted down on the left side of your HUD—just above the round number.

Once you defeat all the foes, a 45-second counter begins until the next round. This gives the team time to visit the Weapon and Exo Upgrade Stations and make purchases. You can skip this time if each player double-taps the Use button.

This continues until the entire team is wiped out, though a downed player can be revived if a teammate gets to him in time.

UPGRADE POINTS

Upgrade Points are earned as you play through Exo Survival, which you can in turn use at the Armories to purchase new weapons and upgrades. Two points are given for finishing each round and completing an objective. One point is given for each Support Drop.

UPGRADE STATIONS

Each map contains a Weapon and Exo Upgrade Station. These allow players to purchase new equipment and upgrades. You can use Upgrade Points to buy new weapons, gun attachments, and Exo improvements. Many items are unavailable until later rounds.

Here is a quick rundown of the categories available for purchase from the Armories. Full lists with costs and round availability can be found later in the chapter.

WEAPON UPGRADE STATION

Weapons	A list of various weapons, with availability dependent on your class.
Weapon Optics	A list of various sights.
Weapon Attachments	A list of various weapon attachments.
Exo Launcher	Choose from various types of Exo Launchers.
Refill Ammo	Refill all bullet ammo.

EXO UPGRADE STATION

Exo Class	Change your Exo Class.
Exo Stats	Upgrade your Exo Weapon Proficiency, Armor, and Exo Battery.
Exo Ability	Choose your Exo ability such as Cloak, Hover, etc.
Scorestreak Upgrades	Purchase modules to upgrade and enhance your Scorestreaks.

WEAPONS

Players begin equipped with a pistol and primary weapon, along with four Frag Grenades. You can purchase new weapons at the Weapon Upgrade Station, as well as optics and attachments. Depending on your class, you are limited to certain types of weapons. A purchased gun replaces the one that you currently have equipped, so be sure you switch to the one you want to give up before accessing the computer.

Grabbing the Weapons Free Perk from a Support Drop allows you to purchase any weapon you want.

Refer to the Upgrade Stations section of this chapter for a full list of the available weapons, attachments, and Exo Launchers.

OPTICS AND ATTACHMENTS

Optics and attachments are available at the Weapon Upgrade Station for purchase. Only certain upgrades are available for each gun, and they can be replaced before the game is over by purchasing a new one.

Optics enhance your sight when aiming down sight. For the most part, this involves zooming in on the target, though the Target Enhancer highlights enemies.

Attachments improve an attribute of the weapon, such as fire rate, recoil, round capacity, accuracy, and more. When you find a gun you like, improve on it with an optic and attachments.

EXO LAUNCHERS

Each class starts with Frag Grenades, but you can purchase a different launcher from the Weapon Upgrade Station. Some types cannot be bought until you have reached a certain round. Grenades are fired from a launcher on your wrist by pressing the Grenade button.

Available launchers are Frag, Stun, Threat, Semtex, Contact, and Spike. The Stun and Threat Grenades are good for managing a group of enemies, while the rest are all about doing damage.

EXO STATS

At the Exo Upgrade Station, select Exo Stats to upgrade three stats of your Exo Suit. These aren't available until later rounds, but they are well worth putting your points into.

The stats and what they do are listed here. For cost and round availability, refer to the tables later in the chapter.

Weapon Proficiency	Increases weapon damage, fire rate and/or speed.
Armor	Decreases damage taken.
Exo Battery	Increase the maximum capacity of your Exo Suit battery, increasing duration of Exo Abilities such as Cloak and Hover.

EXO ABILITIES

A player can have one Exo Ability equipped at a time. Each class starts with a specific ability, but you can purchase a different one from the Exo Upgrade Station with Upgrade Points. Press the Exo Ability button to use your selected ability.

The Exo Abilities available in Exo Survival are as follows. Each one costs one Upgrade Point. For round availability, refer to the tables later in the chapter.

Exo Cloak	Visually conceal yourself for a short duration.
Exo Hover	Hover in place for a short duration.
Exo Shield	A quick-deploy shield is attached to your Exo's arm.
Exo Stim	Temporarily generate health beyond normal levels.
Exo Trophy System	Destroy up to two incoming enemy projectiles.

DOWNED BUT NOT OUT—BLEEDING OUT

When you are downed in Exo Survival, you are not dead. Instead you bleed out for a good amount of time while waiting for a teammate to revive you. You can continue to fight off hostiles with your pistol. If you see a downed teammate, represented by a plus icon, move over to him, and hold the Use button to get him back on his feet.

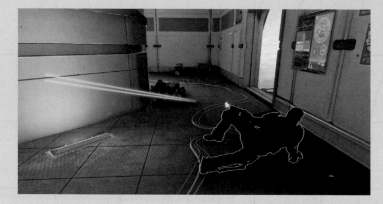

If a round is completed during this time, downed players are brought back into the game. If you bleed out and teammates are still alive, you enter Spectating View until the next round starts. Once all players have bled out, the game is over.

When playing solo, you are revived automatically one time.

AMMO RESUPPLY

Sometimes, a killed enemy will drop an Ammo Resupply, which looks like a box floating above the corpse. Picking this up refills all players' ammo reserves. It is best to reload all weapons before picking it up to get those few extra bullets.

SCORESTREAKS

Each class has a specific Scorestreak that they start with, and you can add up to three more to your arsenal by collecting Support Drops. You can then upgrade these at the Exo Upgrade Station. Current Scorestreaks are shown on the right side of the screen. Press up and down on the D-pad to scroll through them. Press Right to activate the one you want to use. Each Scorestreak has a cooldown meter above it that must fill up before you can use it again.

Many of the Scorestreaks are manually controlled. By holding down the Use button, you can Exit back to your character. This cancels out of the attack if nothing has been done yet.

You can have up to four Scorestreaks at a time, including the Class Scorestreak. For costs and the specific round required for each upgrade, refer to the tables later in the chapter.

AERIAL ASSAULT DRONE

A small AI-controlled aerial drone with on-board machine guns.

Upgrades

Rockets	Adds a rocket launcher onto the drone.
Hardened	Increases drone health but decreases movement speed.

BOMBING RUN

A manually targeted aerial bombing run. With a Bombing Run activated, you decide both where it will hit on the map and from which angle. If the circle is red, you cannot use the bomb there. Move it around until it turns green, then press the Fire button to send the bomber out.

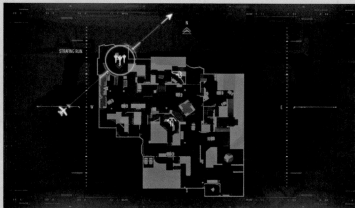

Upgrades

Additional Bomber	Call in an additional bomber.

MISSILE STRIKE

A manually guided aerial missile. As soon as you activate it, the missile starts descending toward the ground. Steer it with the Right Stick, and give it a boost with the Fire button.

Upgrades

Cluster Missile	Primary missile splits into multiple spiraling missiles for concentrated area damage.
Hellfire Missile	Primary missile splits into multiple targeting missiles.
Nano Swarm	Primary missile leaves behind a swarm of Nanobots.
Extra Missile	Adds an additional single-target missile to fire.

REMOTE TURRET

A deployable AI-controlled, high-powered turret that the player can also choose to control manually. Once activated, you must place the turret. If it is red, you cannot place it there. Once blue, press the Fire button to place the gun. Standing next to it, hold the Use button to carry the gun. When away from it, hold the button to manually use Remote Sentry. When using the Sentry, the Aim button zooms in, while the Fire button shoots the gun.

Upgrades

Rocket Turret	Fires rockets. Replaces Machine Gun or Directed Energy Turret.
Directed Energy	Fires a controlled laser. Replaces Machine Gun or Rocket Turret.
Rippable	Adds ability to rip off turret head and carry on the battlefield.
360 Turret Head	Turret can spin 360 degrees.

UAV

An unmanned aerial vehicle that shows enemies on the mini-map.

Upgrades

| Extra Time | UAV lasts longer. |
| Threat Detection | Points out enemies with each sweep of the UAV. |

WARBIRD

A remotely piloted aerial attack vehicle. With a view from the Warbird above, use the Aim button to zoom in and the Fire button to fire the weapon. Press Up on the D-pad to toggle between FLIR (Forward Looking Infrared) and OPT (Optical) views. The machine gun can overheat if you fire it for too long. With the Wingman upgrade, other players receive an onscreen message saying that they can defensively support the Warbird by holding the Use button.

Upgrades

Rockets	Adds rockets as an alternate weapon.
Warbird Wingman	Joining player mounts an additional MG Turret.
Aggressor	AI-controlled Warbird that seeks out enemy targets.
Defender	AI-controlled Warbird stays near player, providing cover fire.

XS1 VULCAN

A manually controlled burst of high-powered directed energy deployed from space. The Aim button zooms, while the Fire button releases the Rapid Charge. With the view from above, find a concentration of enemies, and fire the energy weapon as you sweep through the enemies. There is a six-second charge time before you can use the weapon.

Upgrades

Extra Time	Double the burst duration.
Overcharge	Increases the beam width.
Light Show	Adds three rotating lasers.

SUPPORT DROPS

Below your mini-map, a blue bar fills as you kill enemies. When it completely fills up, a container drops nearby for each player. At this point, anyone can grab what is inside. One player can even grab all of them if he wants to be greedy. Inside, you receive a selection of four random Scorestreaks or Perks to choose from. The map depicts the locations of these drops via a circular yellow icon with a question mark.

There are many possible locations for the Dog Tags, with the 10-20 randomly selected from them.

DEFEND

Objective: Kill 10 enemies near Defend location (Defense Kills)
Time Limit: One round

A Defend icon appears on the map. You must kill 10 enemies near this location to complete the objective. You must be near the Defend area, but the enemy can be farther away. If the hostile is outlined in yellow, you score the Defense Kill.

PERKS

Perks give an added stat boost, such as more explosive damage, increased Exo ability battery life, unlimited sprint, and more. They are only received from Support Drops. Once selected, an icon representing the perk is shown next to the Upgrade Points along the bottom of the screen. With some luck and surviving for a long time, you can have all of the available Perks active at once.

Perks

Danger Close	Do more explosive and Scorestreak damage.
Fast Hands	Reload while sprinting. Swap weapons, use Exo Abilities, and use the Exo Launcher faster.
Flak Jacket	Take less explosive damage. Cancel Frag cooking with weapon switch. Reset fuse when throwing back Frags.
Gung-Ho	Fire while sprinting and sliding.
Hardline	Reduces cooldown on built-in Class Scorestreaks.
Overcharged	Increase Exo Ability battery life. Concuss nearby enemies with boost slams.
Toughness	Flinch less when shot.
Unlimited Sprint	Unlimited sprint.
Weapons Free	Remove restrictions on weapon types per class. All weapons unlocked.

DEFUSE EMP BOMBS

Objective: Defuse three bombs
Time Limit: 2 minutes

Three EMP Bombs are scattered throughout the map. The locations are randomized from 8-10 different spots, which you can view by pausing the game. Find one of the circular bombs, and hold the Use button until it has been defused. This takes a while to do, so you are vulnerable. Make sure you are safe before attempting to defuse a bomb.

OBJECTIVES

If there is a required objective, a message appears on screen at the start of a round. This objective can be to Gather Intel, Collect Dog Tags, Defuse Bombs, or Defend a specific location. Complete the task to earn two Upgrade Points. Fail, and you are penalized. Objectives occur every three rounds.

COLLECT DOG TAGS

Objective: Collect 10 (1 player)/15 (2 players)/20 (3 or 4 players) Dog Tags
Time Limit: 2 minutes

Dog Tags are littered around the map, and your team must run around and collect them. The required number differs based on the number of players in the game. You can see their locations on the mini-map and on the full map when paused. You only have two minutes to get them all, so get moving.

GATHER INTEL

Objective: Gather five Intel
Time Limit: One round

As you kill enemies, some will drop Intel. Approach one, and hold the Use button to pick it up.

PENALTIES

If you fail to complete an objective before the timer runs out or the round ends, you are penalized with one of the following events.

ENEMY SENTRIES ONLINE

Several sentry turrets pop up around the map, firing at the players whenever nearby. You can destroy these turrets.

NANO SWARM STRIKE

A red sphere shows up nearby, causing a player harm if he enters it. This does not appear on the map and goes away after causing a certain amount of damage.

SMOKE STRIKE

Smoke fills your surrounding area, obscuring your vision. Smoke continues to fill in as you move away.

SYSTEM HACKED

When hit with System Hacked, your Exo is rebooted. The mini-map, Scorestreaks, Exo Abilities, and the Exo Launcher are unusable. The Armories are also offline, and there is no break between rounds. The screen is also distorted a bit, making using your guns a little tougher.

An EMP Grenade from an EPM3 enemy causes your HUD to reboot, which restricts you just the same, but for a much shorter time.

WEAPONS JAMMED

When weapons are jammed, your primary weapons are disabled. Extra enemies attack, and the next round starts immediately.

FLIPPING A MAP

Once you complete Round 25 on any map except for Riot, you return to Round 1, but the enemies become a little tougher. As long as you survive the waves of enemies, this process repeats continuously.

SCORING

Performing actions earns points toward your Survival score. This list gives all of the possible actions that score points.

SCORE

Action	Score
Kill Assault	150
Kill AST	500
Kill Beamer	150
Kill Cloaked	150
Kill Doberman	100
Kill Drone	100
Kill Drone Handler	200
Kill Elite	175
Kill EPM3	200
Kill Grunt	100
Kill Gunner	125
Kill Heavy Beamer	200
Kill Launcher	250
Melee Hit	50
Shoot Appendage	10
Shoot Head	30
Shoot Torso	20
Any Hit on AST	10
Directed Energy Damage	4
Headshot Kill	50
Melee Kill AST	+50
Collect Dog Tag	200
Defense Kill	+100
Defuse Bomb	1000
Gather Intel	300
Destroy Enemy Sentry	200

ROUND PERFORMANCE

After each round, a score is calculated based on the following criteria:

ROUND SCORE

Round Time	The less time a round takes, the better the score.
Kills	Number of kills tallied during the round. 50 points per kill.
Upgrade Points	Total Upgrade Points earned by the team. 500 points per Upgrade Point.
Support Drops	Number of Support Drops earned. 500 points per Support Drop.
Head Shots	Number of head shots. 50 points per head shot.

ENEMIES

SOLDIERS

Soldiers come in many types. There are Grunts, Gunners, EPM3s, Drone Handlers, Cloaked soldiers, Elites, Beamers, Assaults, Heavy Beamers, and Launchers. These guys all have their own Exo Suits, and as the rounds go by, they use them much more efficiently. Eventually, they even use Exo Shield to great effect.

Use a Threat Grenade on Cloaked enemies to reveal their locations. Some enemies have their own personal drone. These little guys target a player, dive at him, and explode, although you can avoid this. Watch out, as soldiers will throw different kinds of grenades your way. As usual, you can return these grenades.

DRONES

Drones are small flying turrets that fire at their targets from above. They will attack from afar and can be tough to hit at long range. It is possible to take cover inside a building and still get a shot on these guys.

DOBERMANS

Dobermans are dogs that jump at the player with a bite attack. They are low to the ground and tougher to hit than the soldiers. They cannot jump onto a roof, so you can take refuge there while taking these guys down.

ASTs

Enemy soldiers equipped with an AST mech suit deal a lot of damage with their heavy weapons and are tough to take down. Stay on the move to avoid their gunfire. You can also fight them from a rooftop, as they will not follow you up there.

GENERAL STRATEGIES

Playing solo, you won't find too many places where you can dig in and defend by yourself. If you have a turret, you may be able to hold out for a little while in a location with two openings, but the sentry won't last long.

Use everything at your disposal and stay on the move to avoid being surrounded when fighting alone.

With a team, set up in a building or other structure, and protect the entrances. Use Remote Turrets to help out. You can use other Scorestreaks to hit enemies as they stream toward your locations. You must eventually move out to complete objectives and grab Support Drops. Use a Heavy Exo to perform the duty of grabbing the drops, as he can withstand more damage.

THE UPGRADE STATIONS

WEAPON UPGRADES

You can purchase weapons at the Weapon Upgrade Station, but are limited to types available to the class you selected. Also available at these stations are optics, attachments, and Exo Launchers. You can also refill your bullet ammunition at any time for one Upgrade Point.

The cost and round unlocked information is listed below. A round of 0 means that it is available from the start.

WEAPONS

	Weapon	Description	Cost	Round Unlocked
Pistols	Atlas 45	Semi-automatic. Best in class handling.	1	0
	MP443 Grach	Two-round burst. Best in class range.	2	6
	PDW	Fully automatic machine pistol. Best in class fire rate.	2	12
	RW1	Break-action handheld railgun. Best in class damage.	3	20
Submachine Guns	KF5	Fully automatic. First five rounds in each magazine have increased damage. Best in class range.	1	0
	MP11	Fully automatic. Best in class mobility.	1	2
	ASM1	Fully automatic. Firing over time increases accuracy and lowers fire rate. Best in class damage.	2	7
	SN6	Fully automatic. First three rounds of burst fire faster. Best in class accuracy.	2	12
	SAC3	Fully automatic. Akimbo only. Best in class fire rate.	3	19
	AMR9	Five-round burst. Allows underbarrel attachments. Best in class handling.	3	24
Assault Rifles	Bal-27	Fully automatic. Fires faster over time. Best in class fire rate.	2	0
	AK12	Fully automatic. Best in class mobility.	2	5
	ARX-160	Three-round burst. Best in class range.	2	8
	HBRa3	Fully automatic. First three rounds of a burst fire faster. Best in class handling.	2	11
	IMR	Four-round burst. Prints rounds to ammo reserve. Best in class damage.	3	17
	MK14	Semi-automatic. Best in class accuracy.	3	25
Shotguns	Tac-19	Pump-action directed energy weapon. Best in class mobility.	1	0
	Bulldog	Semi-automatic. Best in class damage.	2	6
	S-12	Fully automatic. Best in class fire rate.	3	16
Sniper Rifles	MORS	Bolt-action railgun. Best in class handling.	1	0
	Lynx	Semi-automatic. Best in class range.	2	9
	NA-45	Semi-automatic two-round fire system. Primer (first round) explodes when the Catalyst (second round) hits nearby.	2	13
	Atlas 20mm	Semi-automatic. Shoulder mounted with no hip fire. Best in class damage.	3	24
Heavy Weapons	EM1	Constant beam of directed energy. No ammunition, but can overheat. Best in class damage.	1	0
	Pytaek	Fully automatic. Reduces recoil over time. Best in class accuracy.	1	3
	XMG	Fully automatic heavy machine guns. Akimbo only. Aim and Fire shoot the two guns separately. Increased fire rate and accuracy in lockdown mode. Press Left on D-pad to enter lockdown mode.	2	10
	EPM3	Semi-automatic directed energy. No ammunition, but can overheat. Best in class range.	3	15
	Ameli	Fully automatic. Slow reload. Best in class fire rate.	3	19
	MDL	Grenade launcher.	3	23

WEAPON OPTICS

Optic	Description	Cost	Round Unlocked
Red Dot Sight	Precision sight.	2	0
Auto Focus Sight	Sight automatically zooms when aiming down the sights and not moving.	2	3
ACOG Scope	Enhanced zoom.	2	5
Target Enhancer	Advanced optics with built-in threat detection.	3	10
Variable Scope	4x magnifier with attached red dot sight.	3	14
Hybrid Sight	Scope with multiple zoom levels.	2	0

WEAPON ATTACHMENTS

Attachment	Description	Cost	Round Unlocked
Laser Sight	Increased hip fire accuracy.	2	4
Extended Mags	Increased round capacity in each magazine.	2	7
Rapid Fire	Increased fire rate.	2	11
Foregrip	Vertical foregrip for reduced recoil.	2	15
Stock	Move faster when aiming down the sights.	3	19
HeatSink	Extends firing time before overheating.	3	22

EXO LAUNCHER

Launcher	Description	Cost	Round Unlocked
Frag Grenade	Cookable Frag Grenades.	1	0
Stun Grenade	Blinds, disorients, and slows enemies. Can be manually detonated.	1	0
Threat Grenade	Temporarily shows enemies through walls. Can be manually detonated.	1	4
Semtex	Timed sticky explosive.	1	8
Contact Grenade	Grenade that detonates on contact with any surface.	1	12
Spike Drone	A lethal thrown drone that returns on command.	2	16

EXO UPGRADE STATION

Your Exo can be upgraded at the Exo Upgrade Station. Here, you can change your class, improve Exo stats, change your Exo ability, and upgrade Scorestreaks.

The cost and round unlocked information is listed below. A round of 0 means that it is available from the start.

EXO CLASS

Class	Description	Cost	Round Unlocked
Light Exo	Fastest movement speed, full range of boost abilities, lowest armor. SMGs and Assault rifles. UAV Class Scorestreak.	0	0
Heavy Exo	Slowest movement, limited boost abilities, highest armor. High damage, heavy weapons. XS1 Goliath Scorestreak.	0	0
Specialist Exo	Normal movement, limited boost abilities, normal armor. Shotguns and sniper rifles. Sentry Gun Class Scorestreak.	0	0

EXO STATS

Stat	Description	Cost	Round Unlocked
Weapon Proficiency	Increases weapon damage, fire rate, and/or spread. Max stat is 10.	2 (1-3) 3 (4-6) 4 (7-8) 5 (9-10)	5
Armor	Decrease damage taken. Max stat is 10.	2 (1-3) 3 (4-6) 4 (7-8) 5 (9-10)	10
Exo Battery	Increases the maximum capacity of your Exo Suit battery, increasing duration of Exo Abilities such as Cloak and Hover. Max stat is 5.	2 (1-3) 3 (4-5)	15

EXO ABILITIES

Ability	Description	Cost	Round Unlocked
Exo Shield	Quickly deploy a portable shield attached to your arm.	1	0
Exo Hover	Hover in place for a short duration.	1	3
Exo Cloak	Visually conceal yourself for a short duration.	1	7
Exo Trophy System	Destroy up to two incoming enemy projectiles.	1	13
Exo Stim	Temporarily generate health beyond normal levels.	1	17

SCORESTREAK UPGRADES

Scorestreak	Upgrade	Description	Cost	Round Unlocked
UAV	Extra Time	UAV lasts longer.	3	2
	Threat Detection	Paints enemies with each sweep of the UAV.	3	7
XS1 Vulcan	Extra Time	Doubles the burst duration.	3	6
	Overcharge	Increases the beam width.	3	17
	Light Show	Adds three rotating lasers.	3	22
Remote Turret	Directed Energy	Fires a controlled laser. Replaces machine gun or Rocket Turret.	3	4
	Rocket Turret	Fires rockets. Replaces machine gun or Directed Energy Turret.	3	9
	360 Turret Head	Turret can spin 360 degrees.	3	14
	Rippable	Adds ability to rip off the turret head and carry it on the battlefield.	3	19
Missile Strike	Extra Missile	Adds an additional single-target missile to fire.	3	3
	Cluster Missile	Primary missile splits into multiple spiraling missiles for concentrated area damage.	3	8
	Hellfire Missile	Primary missile splits into multiple targeting missiles.	3	13
	Nano Swarm	Primary missile leaves behind a swarm of Nanobots.	3	18
Bombing Run	Additional Bomber	Calls in an additional bomber.	3	7
Aerial Assault Drone	Rockets	Adds a rocket launcher onto the drone.	3	10
	Hardened	Increases drone health but decreases movement speed.	3	15
Warbird	Rockets	Adds rockets as an alternate weapon.	3	7
	Warbird Wingman	Joining player mounts additional MG Turret.	3	12
	Aggressor	AI-controlled Warbird seeks out enemy targets.	3	17
	Defender	AI-controlled Warbird stays near player, providing cover fire.	3	25

THE MAPS

There are four tiers of maps in Exo Survival. These maps are unlocked as follows:

Tier	Maps	When Unlocked
1	Bio Lab, Retreat, Detroit, Ascend	Unlocked from start.
2	Horizon, Comeback, Terrace, Instinct	Complete 50 rounds in Tier 1 maps.
3	Greenband, Solar, Recovery, Defender	Complete 75 rounds in Tier 2 maps.
4	Riot	Complete 100 rounds in Tier 3 maps.

BIO LAB

Atlas modular bioengineering facility in the heart of Monument Valley. Its fast, vertically oriented combat enhances survival.

Several labs offer locations to fight within. Protect each entrance as you keep the enemies away. Explosive containers are moved around Building 08 along a rail. You can use these to your advantage by shooting them with hostiles nearby. However, they can also take you out if you are not careful. Watch out for Cloaked soldiers, as they can be especially tough to see outside in the snow.

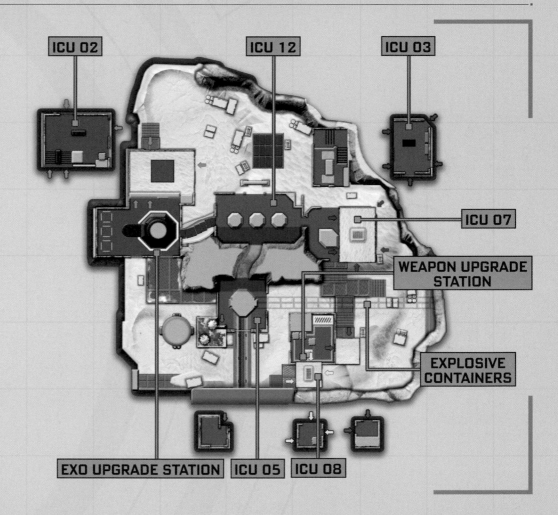

ICU 02 ICU 12 ICU 03 ICU 07 WEAPON UPGRADE STATION EXPLOSIVE CONTAINERS EXO UPGRADE STATION ICU 05 ICU 08

RETREAT

Atlas retreat in the middle of the Guilin Mountains. Utilize your Exo Suit to its fullest to flow throughout this map.

Many of the buildings in this resort are wide open with glass walls, making you quite vulnerable. A cave on the north side can be defended by a team when they are not needed elsewhere. Take advantage of rooftops and canopies to escape danger on the ground.

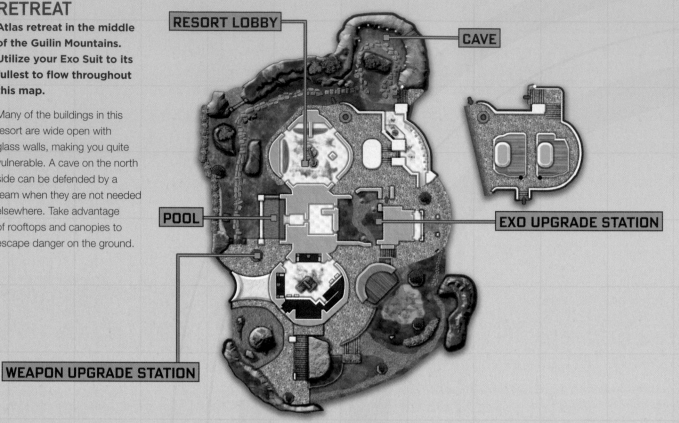

RESORT LOBBY

CAVE

POOL

EXO UPGRADE STATION

WEAPON UPGRADE STATION

DETROIT

Downtown Detroit. Progress quickly through the open main street, or seek safety inside the buildings of the outer lanes.

Buildings surround the wide open streets of Detroit, with numerous locations to dig in. A narrow trailer on the west side can be protected fairly easily, but watch out for incoming grenades. The school hallway has only two ways in, making it a prime location to spend some rounds. Using a Bombing Run can prove difficult because of narrow outdoor streets and a monorail overhead.

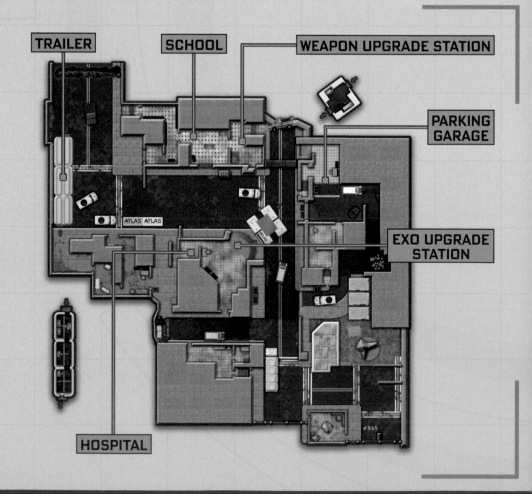

TRAILER

SCHOOL

WEAPON UPGRADE STATION

PARKING GARAGE

EXO UPGRADE STATION

HOSPITAL

ASCEND

Space elevator platform in the Gulf of Mexico. Long top deck sightlines countered with a close-quarter bottom deck.

The rainy Ascend map is a good mix of indoor and outdoor areas, with many levels to fight from. You can use the narrow underground pathways with limited access to fight off waves of hostiles.

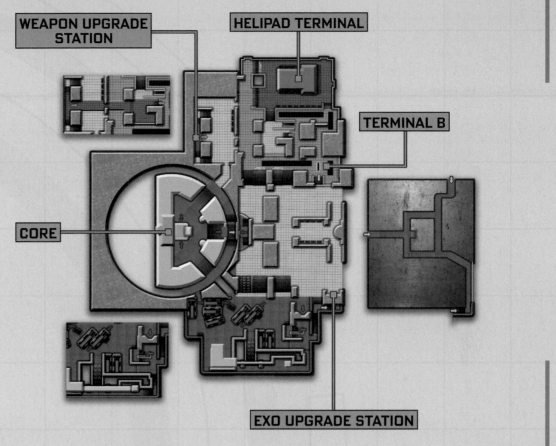

WEAPON UPGRADE STATION

HELIPAD TERMINAL

TERMINAL B

CORE

EXO UPGRADE STATION

HORIZON

Atlas drone facility in the Icelandic Highlands. The chaotic center hangar is home to intense engagements.

Centered around the hangar, this map contains a lot of indoor areas that you can use to set up in, such as Mission Control in the northeast corner. A control room that overlooks the hangar has limited access.

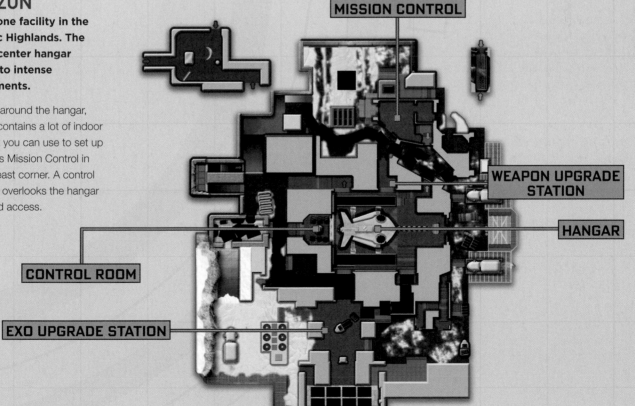

MISSION CONTROL

WEAPON UPGRADE STATION

HANGAR

CONTROL ROOM

EXO UPGRADE STATION

COMEBACK

Downtown Lagos. Maintain the high ground to dominate this circular map.

Comeback is centered around the power station, which is a great location for teams to set up in. The Upgrade Stations are close by, and there are only two entrances. A couple upstairs rooms near the northwest and southeast corners offer nice spots for smaller teams to hole up in. Many rooftops offer escape from those hostiles who do not jump up with you.

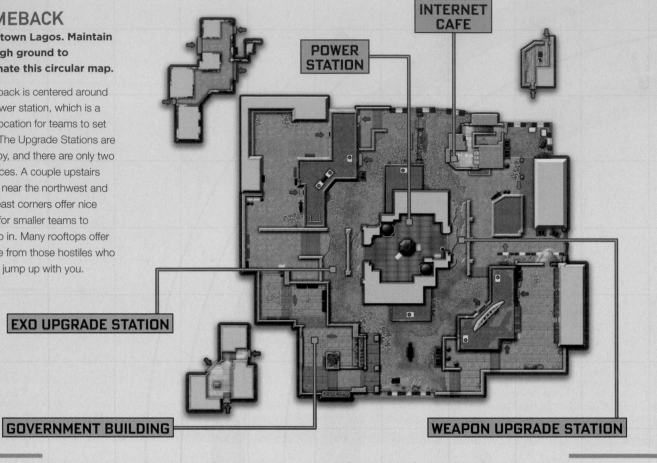

POWER STATION

INTERNET CAFE

EXO UPGRADE STATION

GOVERNMENT BUILDING

WEAPON UPGRADE STATION

TERRACE

Atop the picturesque cliff tops of Santorini, Greece. Dynamic lanes around an enclosed center allow for a great Exo experience.

This map is centered around the resort lobby in the middle of the area. There are some great locations for teams to dig in throughout this resort. A narrow tunnel at the top of the map is relatively easy for a team to protect. Well-placed turrets can assist in the process. Another good spot is the pathway from the west side to the pool area.

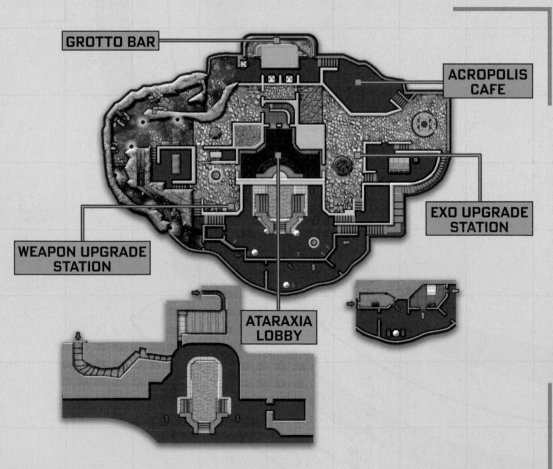

GROTTO BAR

ACROPOLIS CAFE

EXO UPGRADE STATION

WEAPON UPGRADE STATION

ATARAXIA LOBBY

INSTINCT

A mining operation in a South American stepped pyramid. Open terrain and a contested center allow for fast action.

This mostly outdoor map is about as wide open as it gets. A cave in the far-north corner offers a great location for teams to hole up in. Bigger teams can use the entire indoor area on the northeast side. The Exo Upgrade Station is a long way from the cave, though, so be quick between rounds. You can also defend a raised pathway on the south side, but you are vulnerable to drones. It is also possible to last a good while behind the Exo Upgrade Station. This small area behind the structure only has one way in.

CAVE

DRILL

EXO UPGRADE STATION

WEAPON UPGRADE STATION

GREENBAND

A high-rise park in Seoul, South Korea. Clean lanes and quick flanks make for great tactical combat.

Buildings on each side of the map offer protection from drones and give teams a good location to fight within. Smaller teams can defend a long hallway on the far-north side. Be careful when jumping over walls, as holes in the middle of the map make for a quick death.

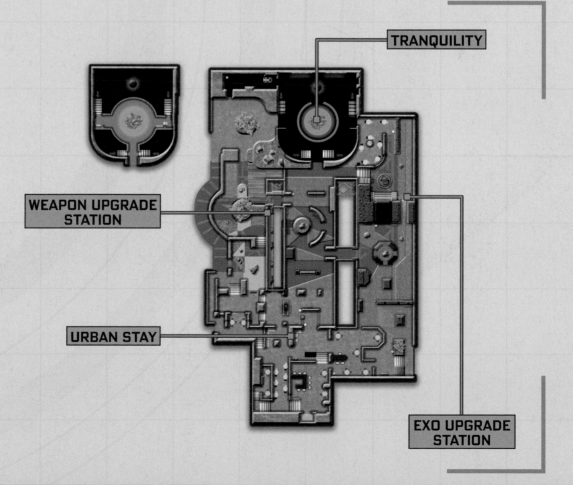

TRANQUILITY

WEAPON UPGRADE STATION

URBAN STAY

EXO UPGRADE STATION

SOLAR

Solar array near New Baghdad. Rooftop gameplay with mixed sightlines for diverse combat experiences.

The Solidae complex centers around a pool of shallow water, with some interesting rooftops and walkways to explore. A big pipe leads from the water up to a small room, where a team can fortify with Remote Turrets and fight off attacks. A big warehouse on the west side gives teams a bigger area to hole up in.

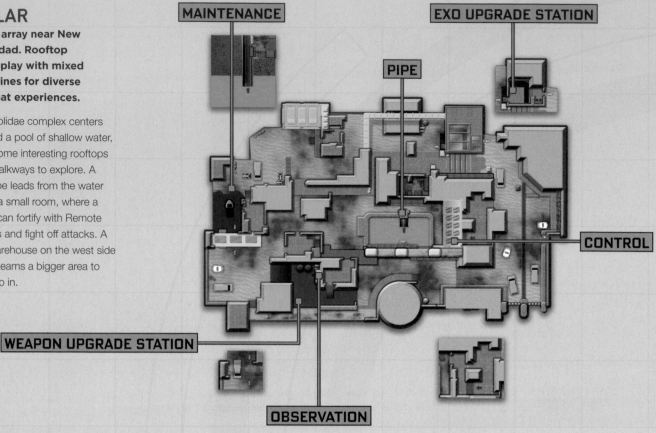

MAINTENANCE

EXO UPGRADE STATION

PIPE

CONTROL

WEAPON UPGRADE STATION

OBSERVATION

RECOVERY

Observatory straddling a volcano rim in Hawaii. Fast gameplay with dynamic chokepoints.

Unlike in Multiplayer, the gates do not open on this map, so all gameplay takes place on the east side of the doors. Mostly made up of outdoor area, a structure in the southeast corner offers up a good location for smaller teams to fight from.

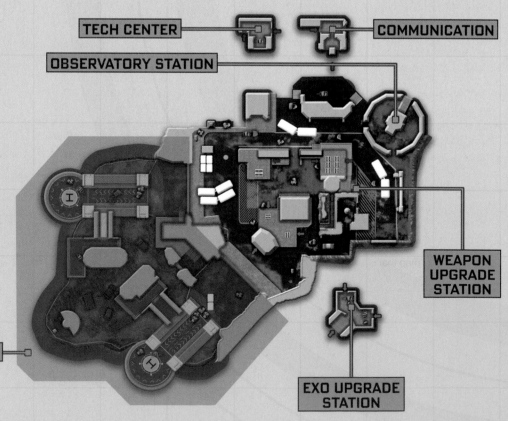

TECH CENTER

COMMUNICATION

OBSERVATORY STATION

WEAPON UPGRADE STATION

INACCESIBLE IN SURVIVAL

EXO UPGRADE STATION

DEFENDER

Domestic air defense base centered around a directed energy anti-air weapon. Features a close-quarter cut-through center, allowing for quick flanks and a fast pace.

Located next to the Golden Gate Bridge, this map offers up well-fortified bunkers with an open beach area. At Round 5, waves flood the beach side. When flooded, a narrow pipe is still accessible by diving underwater. This pipe connects to the central anti-air weapon building.

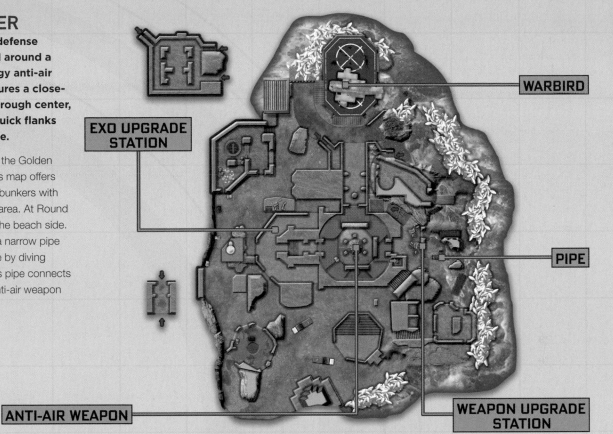

WARBIRD

EXO UPGRADE STATION

PIPE

ANTI-AIR WEAPON

WEAPON UPGRADE STATION

RIOT

A rioted prison with clear lanes for head-on-head combat.

The prison grounds is a mix of long indoor hallways and huge outdoor areas, along with rooftops that you can use to escape trouble. The cell block offers a decent-sized room with limited entrances. The prison yard is wide open and a great place to lure enemies to their doom with a Bombing Run or other devastating Scorestreak.

This is the only map that does not flip once you complete Round 25.

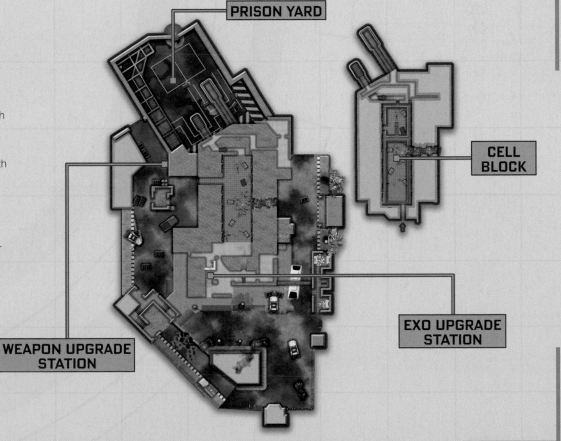

PRISON YARD

CELL BLOCK

EXO UPGRADE STATION

WEAPON UPGRADE STATION

MULTIPLAYER MAPS

The exclusive illustrated maps in this section are meant to give you a clean and clear overview of the layout of each Multiplayer map in *Call of Duty®: Advanced Warfare*. The section displays two versions of each map: one with a clean layout and no markings (to give you the best view possible), and another with all objective locations marked. Use these maps to get a sense of how and where spaces connect, where you can make use of elevated terrain, and where you need to watch for hostile players using long sight lines.

MAP SCORESTREAKS

Some levels include special "streaks" that are entirely map-specific. You can earn these special streaks from a care package or steal them from your enemies. Once activated, they trigger a map-wide benefit for your entire team. Typically, this results in very bad things for your opponents.

DYNAMIC EVENTS

Several levels have special events that occur partway through the match, changing the layout of the map (sometimes completely). In the case of Recovery, you actually transition from one side of the map to the other permanently! These events are generally fairly straightforward; just be aware of their presence and how they impact the fight.

ASCEND

Ascend takes place beneath a massive space elevator, with open lanes above and catwalks snaking beneath.

Map Scorestreak:
Auto-Turrets. Gain control of the automated turrets on this level to devastate the opposing team.

Ascend consists of a multi-level central area, two opposing ends of the map with differing terrain, and a tight interior space directly beneath the space elevator itself. You can transition quickly between anywhere in the center to the space elevator, or to either end of the map.

There are quite a few elevated vantage points on the edges of the map, but there are fewer in the center and the space elevator. Beware of rooftop defenders when you approach either side of the map.

When moving through the center of the map, be aware of the catwalks below. While multiple routes across the main level break up the sightlines, enemies can sneak under from below. In objective modes, have someone monitor the catwalks below for hostiles.

The space elevator room is particularly dangerous. Be careful entering it, as you can expect a nasty close-quarters fight to erupt. Whenever possible, try to enter from a direction your opponents won't suspect, or throw grenades to clear a path.

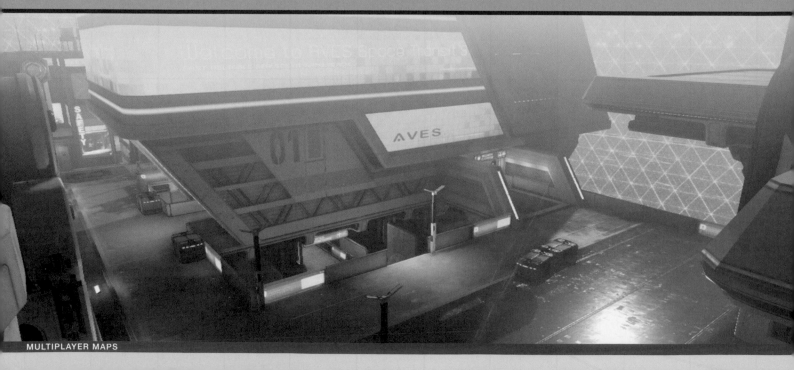

ASCEND: OVERVIEW

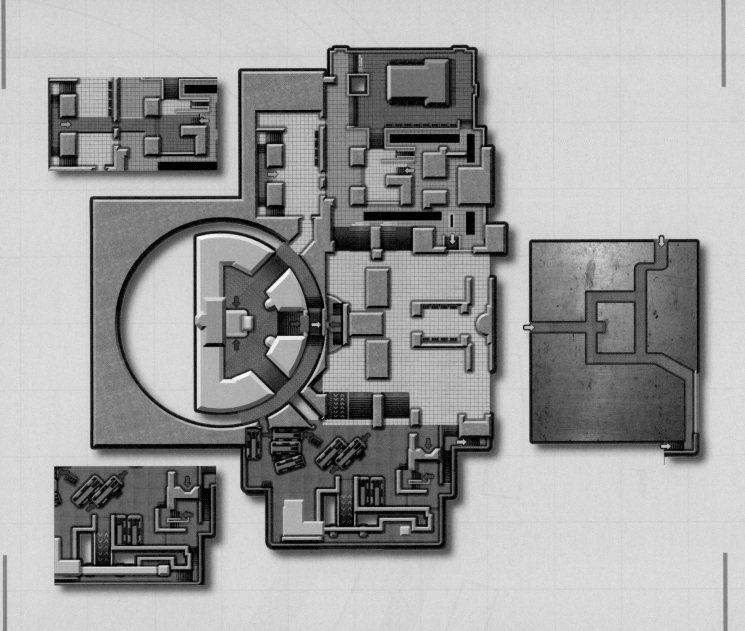

ASCEND: OBJECTIVE

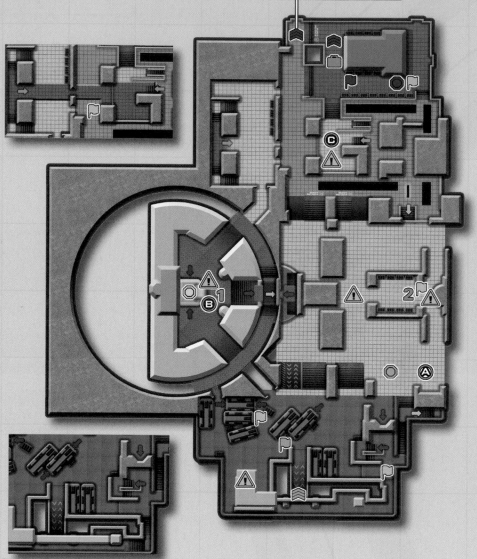

S&D, S&R, AND DOMINATION SPAWN

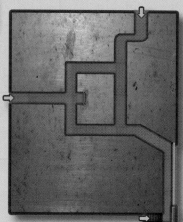

 SPAWN POINT	UPLINK SATELLITE	Ⓐ Ⓑ Ⓒ DOMINATION CONTROL POINT
MOMENTUM FLAG	S&D BOMB	⬆ ⬆ ⬆ ⬆ CONNECT TO SAME-COLORED ARROWS ON MULTI-LEVEL AREAS
CTF FLAG	1 2 S&D/S&R TARGET	
UPLINK GOAL	HARDPOINT	

BIO LAB

Set in a wintry research facility, Bio Lab contains a mix of medium-range sightlines and interior combat, with a fair amount of elevated positions around the outer edges of the level.

Map Scorestreak:

None. However, you can detonate moving containers of hazardous material to kill any enemies nearby!

Bio Lab is divided into three connected exterior areas and one larger central facility. The titular Bio Lab facility in the center of the map connects to all parts of the level, so you can stick to CQC on the interior if you prefer, or you can transition to the outer areas and rooftops outside as needed.

The outer areas have longer sightlines and more elevated positions. Keep a sharp eye out for distant enemies behind cover or on rooftops when you're moving out in the open. Hugging the walls of the Bio Lab or other adjacent buildings when moving is advisable.

BIO LAB: OVERVIEW

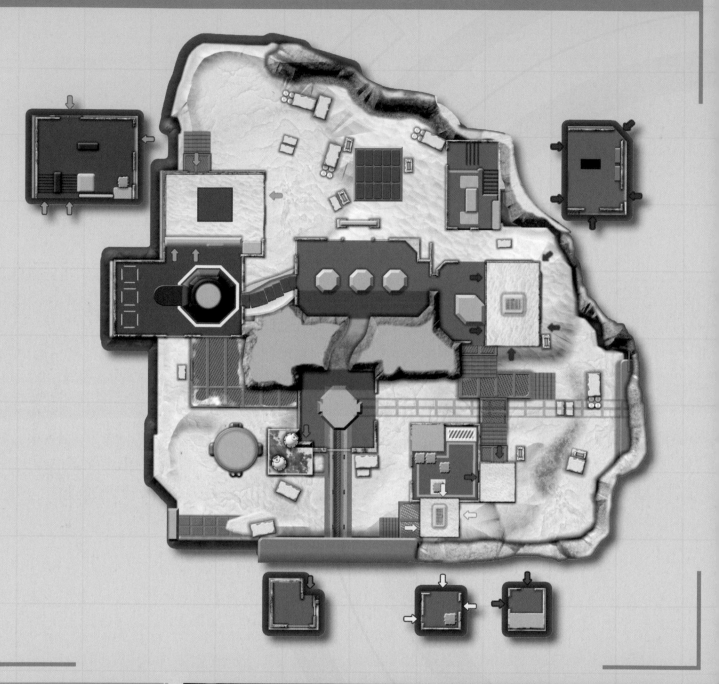

HELI-DELIVERY

The area directly around the B Domination point on the map is unusual—partway through the level, a massive helicopter delivers a new piece of the map! It drops off a small, multi-level building, moving the B point from the ground to the inside of this small structure. The new building creates some line of sight blocking for the outer area around it, and once it is placed, it remains for the rest of the match.

BIO LAB: OBJECTIVE

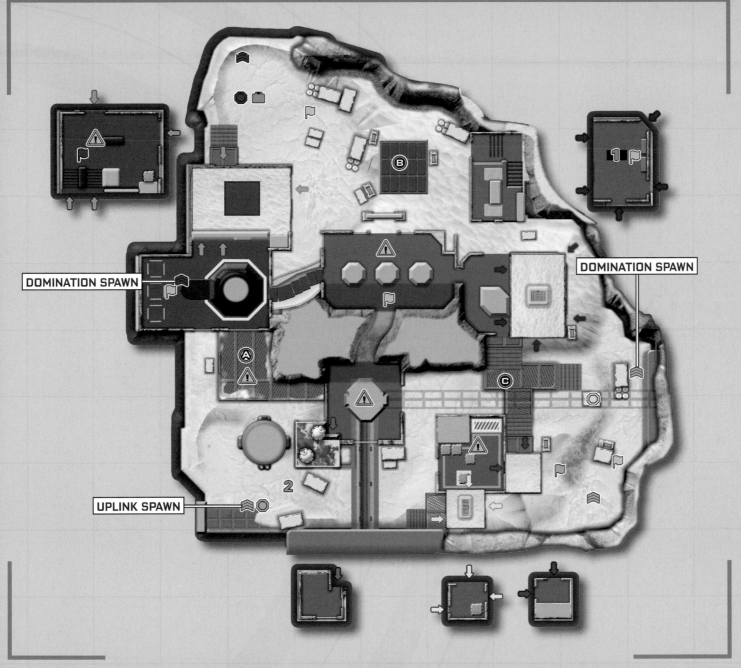

DOMINATION SPAWN

DOMINATION SPAWN

DOMINATION SPAWN

UPLINK SPAWN

	SPAWN POINT	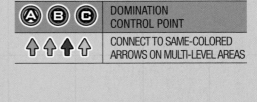	UPLINK SATELLITE	Ⓐ Ⓑ Ⓒ	DOMINATION CONTROL POINT
	MOMENTUM FLAG		S&D BOMB	⬆⬆⬆⬆	CONNECT TO SAME-COLORED ARROWS ON MULTI-LEVEL AREAS
	CTF FLAG	1 2	S&D/S&R TARGET		
	UPLINK GOAL	⚠	HARDPOINT		

COMEBACK

A circular level set in the slums of Lagos, centered around a new power station constructed in the middle of the map, Comeback features steep elevation changes from the outer edges to the center.

Map Scorestreak:

Call in a barrage of fire from a pair of powerful walker tanks. This powerful Map Scorestreak can devastate the opposing team and suppress them for some time, giving you a chance to secure objectives or a lead.

Comeback is anchored by the center power station located at the bottom center of the map. In the corners, rooftops and buildings give vertical positions and cover for players to move around the edges of the level. The ground transitions between the outer sides of the level are dangerous, as enemies on the rooftops or in the buildings can see players moving around out in the open. Use Exo movement to cross the spaces quickly.

The power station itself only has two entrances, and when objectives require you to enter it, expect it to turn into a hotly contested firefight. Bring explosives or explosive resistance.

Most of the sight lines on Comeback are medium range at best. Most long-range shots can only be taken on the outer edges, and all of the building interior and power station fights are close-quarters. A medium- to short-range loadout can thrive here.

Comeback is a smaller map, so expect constant contact with the enemy, and fast-paced combat.

COMEBACK: OVERVIEW

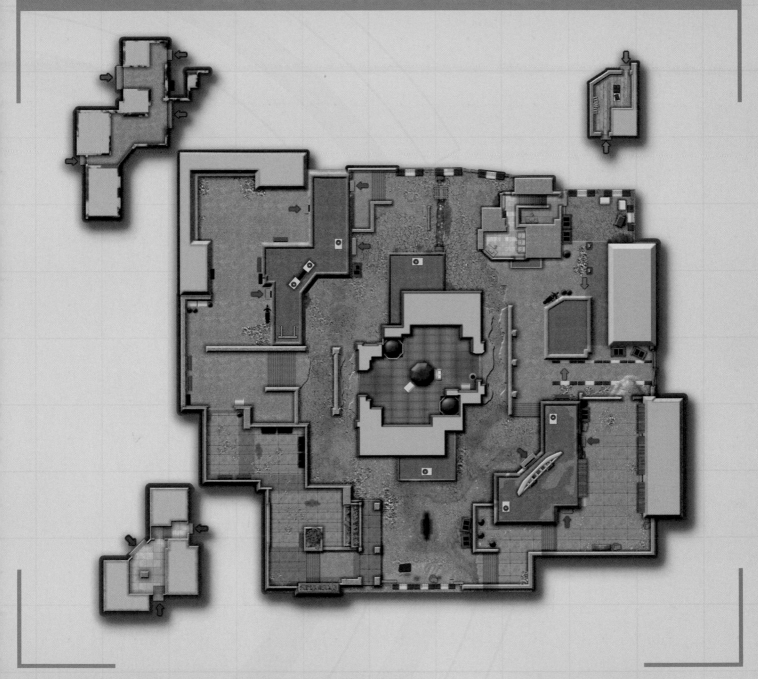

COMEBACK: OBJECTIVE

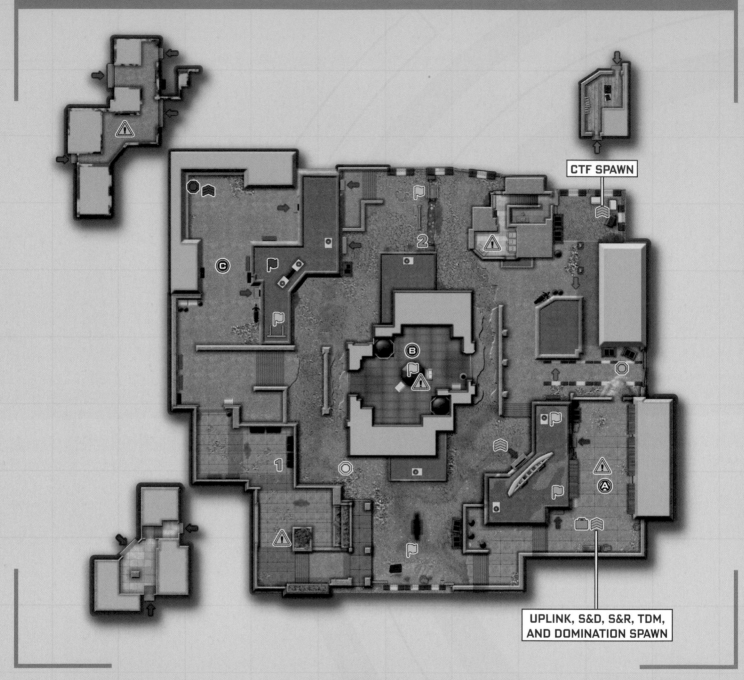

CTF SPAWN

UPLINK, S&D, S&R, TDM,
AND DOMINATION SPAWN

	SPAWN POINT		UPLINK SATELLITE	Ⓐ Ⓑ Ⓒ	DOMINATION CONTROL POINT
	MOMENTUM FLAG		S&D BOMB	↑↑↑↑	CONNECT TO SAME-COLORED ARROWS ON MULTI-LEVEL AREAS
	CTF FLAG	1 2	S&D/S&R TARGET		
	UPLINK GOAL	⚠	HARDPOINT		

DEFENDER

A dilapidated shoreline base, Defender takes place in and around massive concrete bunkers, with combat transitioning in and out of the buildings.

Map Scorestreak:

Laser Air Defense. Activating the massive defense turret in the center of the map causes it to rise up from its building and shoot down any hostile enemy aerial Scorestreak support. The movement of the turret also opens up lines of sight in the room it was contained in, making the central building even more dangerous to move through.

Defender is a flexible medium-sized map focused around a huge central structure housing the turret. There's also a beach on one side of the level and multiple smaller bunkers and buildings around the edges. Defender has a lot of combat lanes and sight lines, as well as many elevated positions that you can reach with a quick Boost Jump. It is possible to move both quickly and unseen if you're careful strafing around the outer edges, but be wary about passing through the central building. Although it allows fast access to any part of the map, its central location also means that you can expect a lot of traffic, particularly if an objective is located within.

Be wary of jumping onto the bunkers if you're uncertain of enemy positions. You can expose yourself to fire unnecessarily, and many of the rooftops have little or no cover for you to evade incoming fire.

DEFENDER: OVERVIEW

TSUNAMI WARNING!

Partway through the match, a massive wave crashes into the shoreline, obliterating any players unfortunate enough to be in the area and covering the shore in seawater for the remainder of the match. This also has the effect of making the lower access tunnel to the central bunker a bit slower to use, as you must swim through the water to reach it.

Use Exo movement to skip the water if you're moving down on the shore after the wave hits.

DEFENDER: OBJECTIVE

CTF SPAWN

SPAWN POINT	UPLINK SATELLITE	DOMINATION CONTROL POINT
MOMENTUM FLAG	S&D BOMB	CONNECT TO SAME-COLORED ARROWS ON MULTI-LEVEL AREAS
CTF FLAG	S&D/S&R TARGET	
UPLINK GOAL	HARDPOINT	

DETROIT

Set in the streets of metropolitan Michigan after a massive nuclear disaster, Detroit features a mix of open street fighting and very close-quarters combat inside the buildings around the street.

Map Scorestreak:

Rail Turret. A manually controlled turret is attached to the tracks above the streets, and you can move freely along the street and fire at any hostiles you spot. If the enemy gets this Map Scorestreak, stick to the buildings and avoid it!

Detroit is a fairly small map where conflict is fast and intense. Out in the streets, you have straightforward lines of sight but little cover. Be careful staying in the open for any extended period of time. It is safer to use the back alleys and buildings around the street to navigate the level, peeking out from the windows and alleyways to pick off players in the streets. When objectives force you into the streets, strike quickly from the edges of the level, secure the objective, and get back in cover as swiftly as possible.

If you expect to spend the majority of your time in the CQC areas of the map, bring a short-range setup to get an edge over anyone using mid-range builds.

DETROIT: OVERVIEW

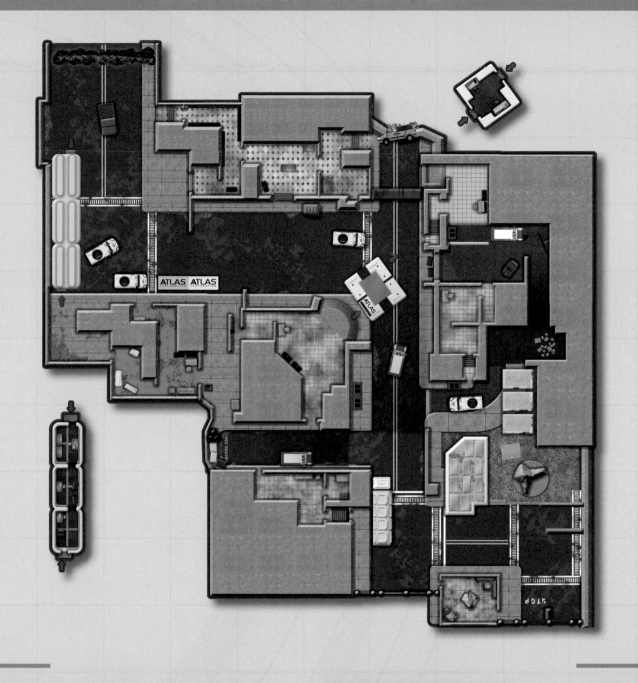

DETROIT: OBJECTIVE

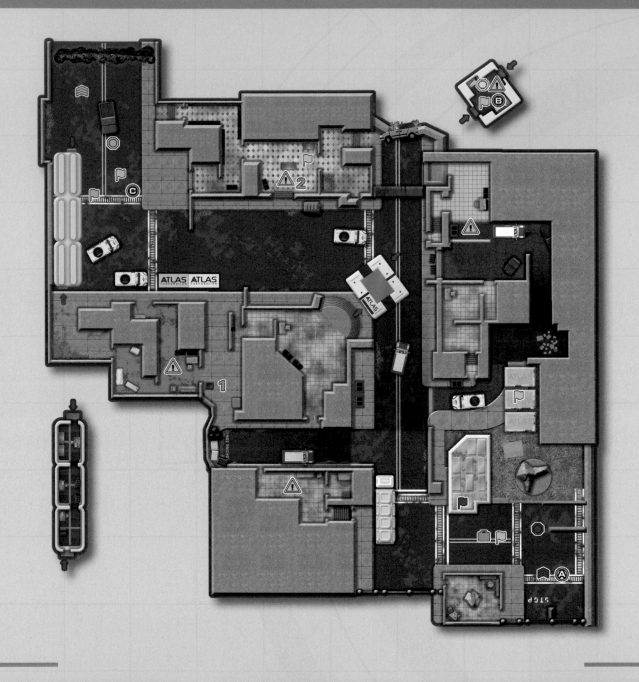

SPAWN POINT	UPLINK SATELLITE	Ⓐ Ⓑ Ⓒ DOMINATION CONTROL POINT
⚑ MOMENTUM FLAG	🧰 S&D BOMB	⬆⬆⬆⬆ CONNECT TO SAME-COLORED ARROWS ON MULTI-LEVEL AREAS
⚑ ⚑ CTF FLAG	1 2 S&D/S&R TARGET	
⬡ ⬡ UPLINK GOAL	⚠ HARDPOINT	

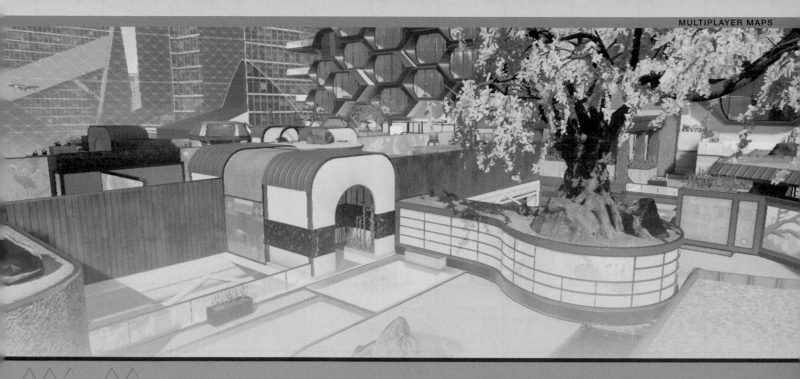

GREENBAND

Set in a beautiful rooftop garden in a major downtown Korean city, Greenband features three cleanly divided lanes of fire, with dangerous falls between them.

Map Scorestreak:
None.

Greenband is an intense map, with few places to hide from your enemies anywhere in the middle of the map. The three lanes of the map offer large chunks of cover, but anyone using Exo movement from the air can easily spot you. Use the available cover when engaging opponents on the ground. Get up on the rooftops only briefly to sight new targets, and then drop down again to pursue them. Avoid staying atop anything in the middle of the level, as this makes you an easy target for snipers and long-range gunners.

The edges of the level have two small interior areas, though only a pair of Hardpoints forces you near them in objective modes. Otherwise, you can use them as hard cover when you seek to attack an enemy objective that is nearby in the center of the map. One of the outer lanes in the middle of the map has a raised rock garden. This is the only elevated position with meaningful cover, so expect hostiles to use this area for sniping and long-range cover fire.

Mid- to long-range weaponry is preferred for tackling targets in the center lanes. However, it is definitely possible to use SMGs and short-range weaponry if you use Exo movement carefully and use the available cover to shield yourself from long-range players as you move through the map.

GREENBAND: OVERVIEW

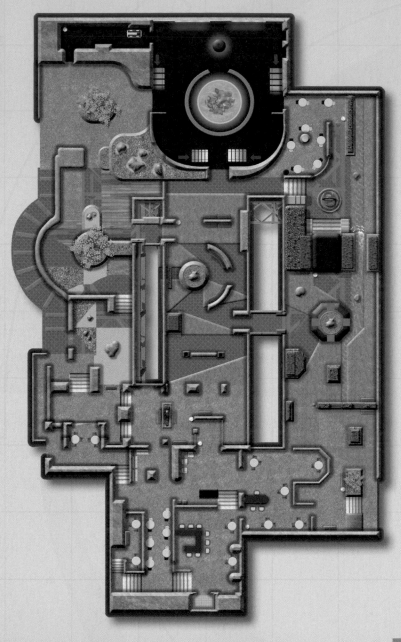

GREENBAND: OBJECTIVE

SPAWN POINT	UPLINK SATELLITE	Ⓐ Ⓑ Ⓒ DOMINATION CONTROL POINT
MOMENTUM FLAG	S&D BOMB	⬆⬆⬆⬆ CONNECT TO SAME-COLORED ARROWS ON MULTI-LEVEL AREAS
CTF FLAG	1 2 S&D/S&R TARGET	
UPLINK GOAL	⚠ HARDPOINT	

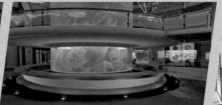

HORIZON

An Atlas drone facility set in the Icelandic Highlands, Horizon features incredibly intense combat focused around a central drone hangar, mixed with lane combat on the outer edges around the hangar.

Map Scorestreak:
None.

A complex map, Horizon has indoor and outdoor combat in and around the central drone hangar. There are a lot of routes around the outer edges of the level, with sightlines broken up by bits of cover and exposed to the occasional rooftop vantage point. Be very, very careful if you pass through the central hangar, accessible from all four sides of the map. It is impossible to keep yourself covered from every angle. Stay out of it unless you have teammates to cover you, you're forced to fight there over an objective, or you must use it to quickly reach another part of the map or flank an enemy.

The outer edges of the map support a variety of playstyles. You can move aggressively to get into close range, or hang back and pick off targets as they expose themselves. Just be wary about staying in any one place for long, as there's always at least one flanking route for opponents to reach you.

HORIZON: OVERVIEW

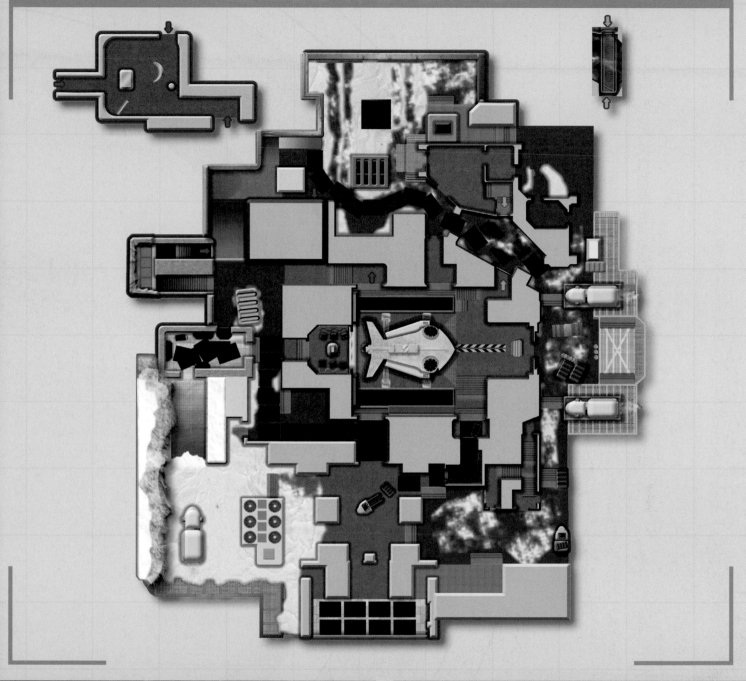

HORIZON: OBJECTIVE

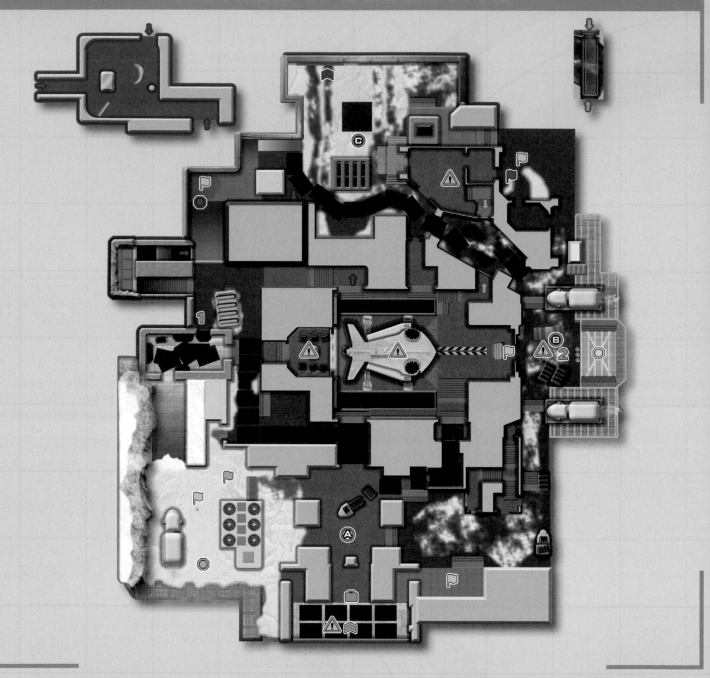

SPAWN POINT	UPLINK SATELLITE	DOMINATION CONTROL POINT
MOMENTUM FLAG	S&D BOMB	CONNECT TO SAME-COLORED ARROWS ON MULTI-LEVEL AREAS
CTF FLAG	1 2 S&D/S&R TARGET	
UPLINK GOAL	HARDPOINT	

INSTINCT

Set in South American ruins being despoiled by mining operations, Instinct has steep elevation changes from one end of the map to the other, anchored around a central ruin structure.

Map Scorestreak:
None.

Instinct can be a challenging level to move through safely, as there is a huge no man's land below the central ruin stairs. If you are anywhere in the open down there, you are at risk from enemies in elevated positions. Use Exo movement to move through that space quickly, and avoid lingering in the open as much as possible. The upper portions of the level closer to (and beneath) the massive pyramid have more cover. You can fight in and around those more safely, as long as you are aware of enemy positions and likely avenues of assault.

In objective modes, all of the objectives flow in an arc from the area under the pyramid, down one edge of the map, and back along the edge of the lower area toward the C domination point. If combat is heavily focused on one side of the level, use the other side to flank the opposing team. If they're distracted by an objective, you can often ambush them by quickly moving in from the opposite side of the level.

Be wary of standing on the top of the central ruins. It's a tempting power position to snipe players far below, but it puts you in danger from many angles that you cannot cover. If you go up there, take a shot, and then get back down.

INSTINCT: OVERVIEW

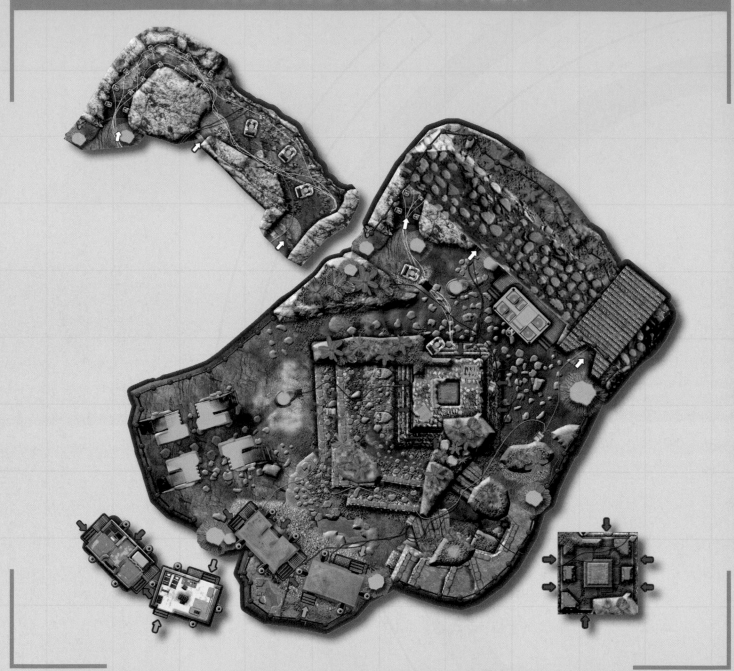

INSTINCT: OBJECTIVE

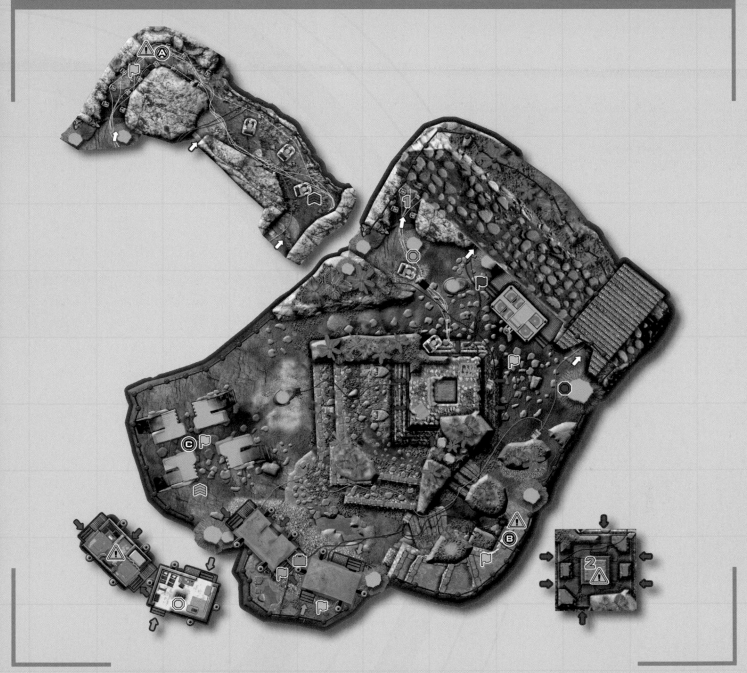

		SPAWN POINT		UPLINK SATELLITE	Ⓐ Ⓑ Ⓒ	DOMINATION CONTROL POINT
		MOMENTUM FLAG		S&D BOMB	⬆⬆⬆⬆	CONNECT TO SAME-COLORED ARROWS ON MULTI-LEVEL AREAS
		CTF FLAG	1 2	S&D/S&R TARGET		
		UPLINK GOAL	⚠	HARDPOINT		

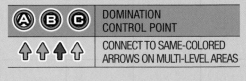

RECOVERY

A volcano observatory in Hawaii, Recovery is a highly unusual level that transitions partway through the match from one side of the map to another—permanently!

Map Scorestreak:
None.

The most unique map event in the game occurs on Recovery. Partway into a match, the volcano begins to spew toxic gases into the complex. When this occurs, warnings sound, and brightly lit evacuation arrows guide you to the outer area of the map, beyond the blast doors. Once the blast doors are sealed, you can no longer access the first half of the map!

This event turns Recovery into a two-stage map: one part is fought closest to the volcano's heart, the other takes place outside the blast doors on the edge of the volcano. The first half of the map has numerous rooftops and small interior areas, with multiple routes between the different objective targets. The second half is more open, with wide open helicopter pads and exposed grassy areas.

Spend some time exploring Recovery in a private match. That way, you can get an edge over players who aren't used to the map transition.

Combat on Recovery is generally medium distance, though the first half of the map is a bit friendlier to short-range builds than the second half. You can even change classes if you find that the map shift disrupts your favored build.

RECOVERY: OVERVIEW

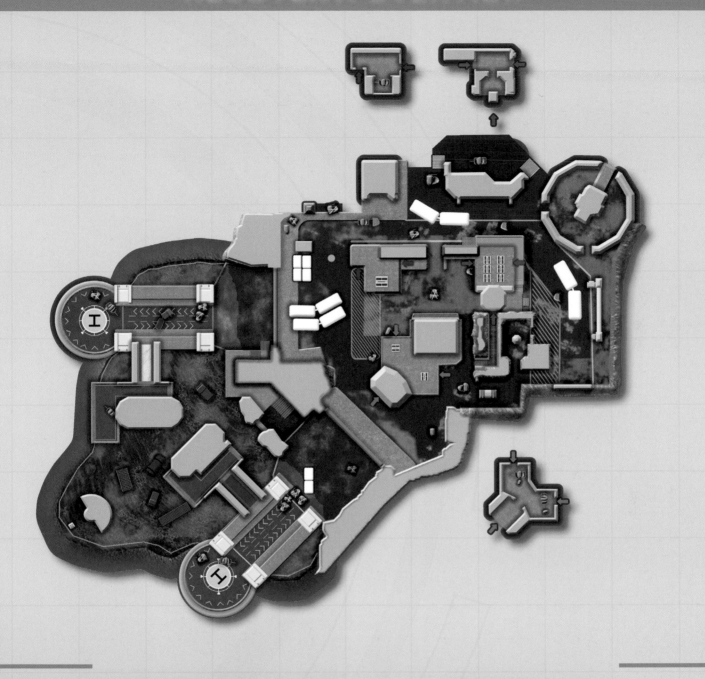

RECOVERY: OBJECTIVE

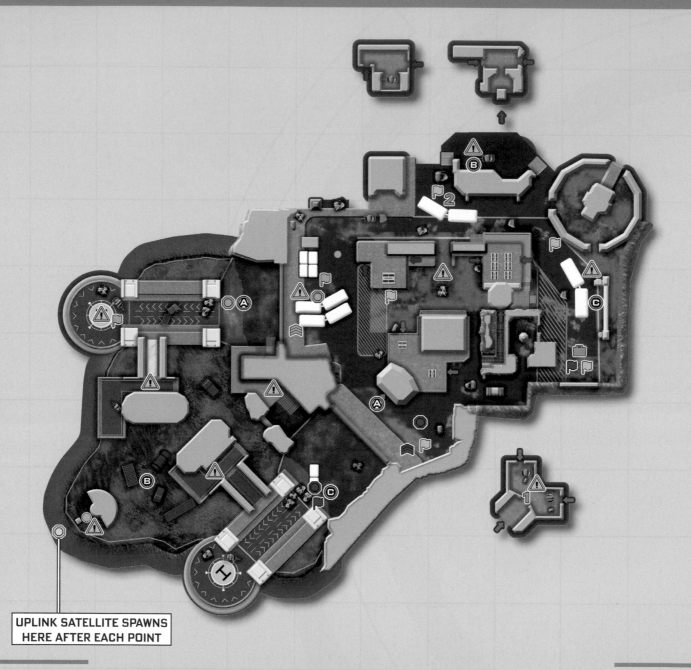

UPLINK SATELLITE SPAWNS
HERE AFTER EACH POINT

⋙ ⋙	SPAWN POINT	
⚑	MOMENTUM FLAG	
⚑ ⚑	CTF FLAG	
⬡ ⬡	UPLINK GOAL	

⬡	UPLINK SATELLITE
💼	S&D BOMB
1 2	S&D/S&R TARGET
⚠	HARDPOINT

Ⓐ Ⓑ Ⓒ	DOMINATION CONTROL POINT
⬆⬆⬆⬆	CONNECT TO SAME-COLORED ARROWS ON MULTI-LEVEL AREAS

   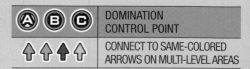

RETREAT

An Atlas retreat in the Guilin Mountains, Retreat is a beautiful level with complex connectivity. Almost any room or area in the level has multiple points of entry. To survive, watch your back and stay alert.

Map Scorestreak:
None.

This beautiful resort is home to some dangerous sightlines on the outer areas and a lot of complex interconnected areas in all parts of the map. If you are an aggressive, fast-moving player, you can do extremely well on this level by taking advantage of the buildings and transitional areas to constantly flank your opponents.

If you prefer to fight at long range or play defensively, you need to communicate with your teammates or use Scorestreaks and equipment that can give you an informational edge. Stay aware of enemy positions constantly, as losing track of the enemy team is fatal on Retreat.

You can use any range of weapon effectively on Retreat as long as you control the engagement distance, play to your strengths, and deny your foes the ability to use theirs.

RETREAT: OVERVIEW

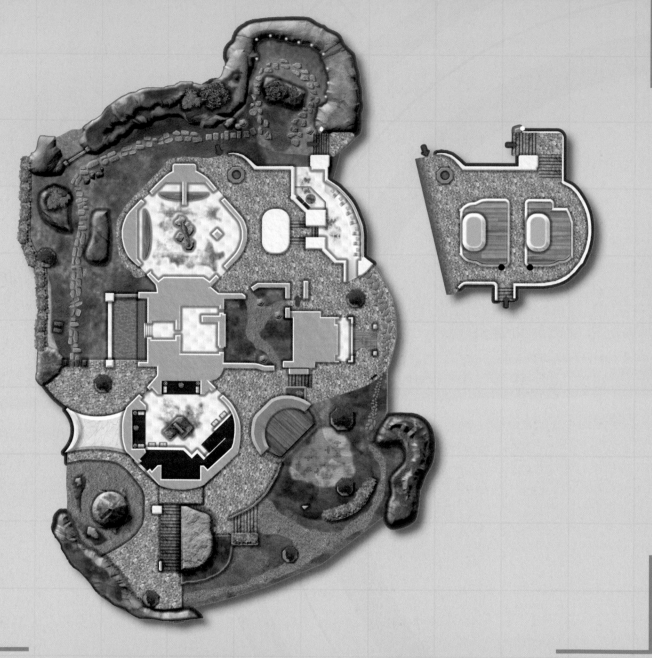

RETREAT: OBJECTIVE

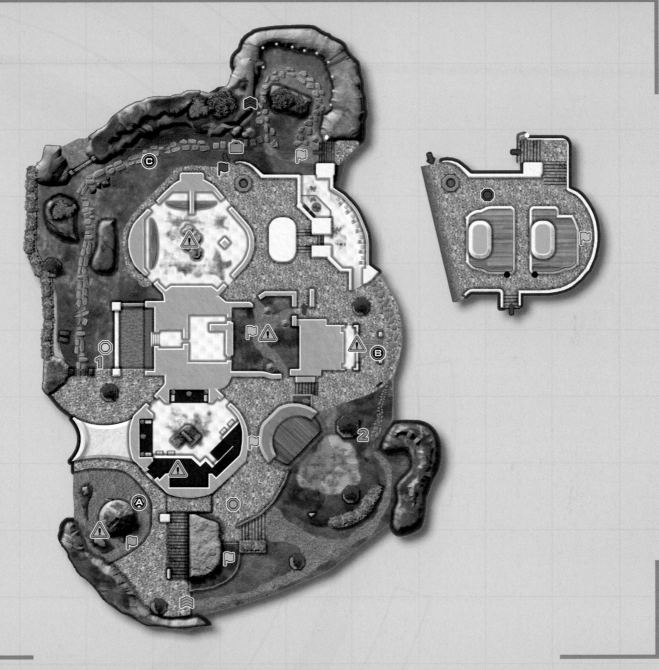

	SPAWN POINT		UPLINK SATELLITE	A B C	DOMINATION CONTROL POINT
	MOMENTUM FLAG		S&D BOMB	↑↑↑↑	CONNECT TO SAME-COLORED ARROWS ON MULTI-LEVEL AREAS
	CTF FLAG	1 2	S&D/S&R TARGET		
	UPLINK GOAL		HARDPOINT		

RIOT

Set after a riot, this prison facility features a mix of interior combat within the central prison structure and clean lanes of combat on the outer edges.

Map Scorestreak:
Sensor Network. Once this prisoner control system is activated for your team, all enemy players get lit up by the tracking system. This gives your team a massive information advantage for the duration of the Map Scorestreak.

A clean and straightforward map, Riot has three central lanes and two distinct outer edge areas near the team spawns: one inside the prison yard, and the other in front of the prison. The three lanes through the middle are on the left and right outside of the prison, and inside the prison itself.

The outer areas have quite a few rooftops that provide easy line of sight across the entire lane. When you round a corner to either side, be prepared for lurking players. The central prison has some medium-range lines of sight across the interior, but it isn't difficult to force a short-range fight if you enter from the sides or flank from the rear.

RIOT: OVERVIEW

RIOT: OBJECTIVE

	SPAWN POINT		UPLINK SATELLITE		DOMINATION CONTROL POINT
	MOMENTUM FLAG		S&D BOMB		CONNECT TO SAME-COLORED ARROWS ON MULTI-LEVEL AREAS
	CTF FLAG	1 2	S&D/S&R TARGET		
	UPLINK GOAL		HARDPOINT		

SOLAR

A solar array near New Baghdad, Solar is another cleanly divided three-lane map, with several routes between the lanes and quite a few power rooftop positions that can cover the lanes.

Map Scorestreak:

Solar Reflection Tower. Gain control of the central solar tower, and incinerate the opposing team with a directed blast of raw energy. The beam from the tower moves fairly slowly. Try to get it into position near the greatest number of enemies, or use it to control a key objective area for the duration of the Map Scorestreak.

Although this is another clean three-lane map, be wary of the central area, which is overlooked by multiple rooftops and has little in the way of cover. There is a tunnel where you can sneak in from the side, and it provides limited protection from enemies lurking above. Your best bet for surviving the middle is to either cover it from the rooftops yourself, or only enter the center for objectives, with teammates covering you.

The two outer lanes have slightly more disrupted line of sight, though both still have plenty of rooftop coverage. Use your Exo movement to traverse them quickly or evade attackers if the pressure gets too heavy. There are only a few places where you can transition from the outer lanes to the center. If you stay alert to enemy movements, you can shut down any attempts to cross over.

The areas around the team spawns are quite small, but you can use them to flank around opponents who are camping around the central area. Long-range weaponry can thrive here if you stay mobile and keep your distance. Fighting in CQC is harder, as you must work to get into short range safely.

SOLAR: OVERVIEW

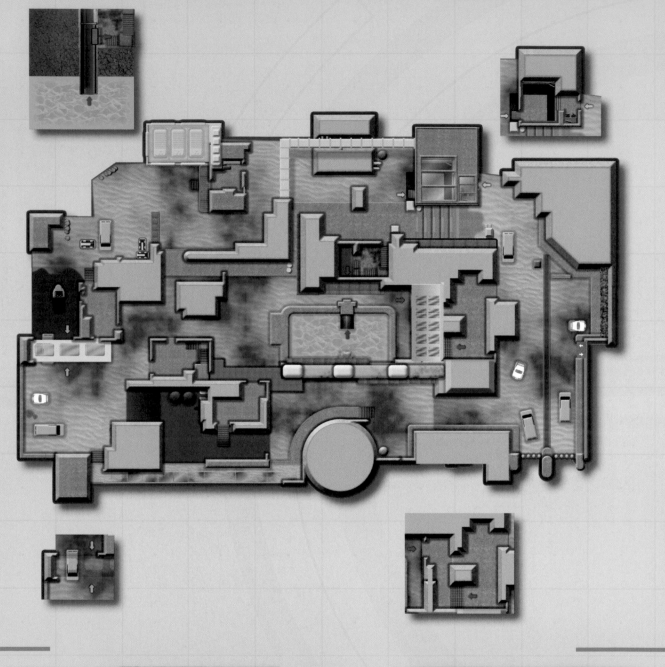

SOLAR: OBJECTIVE

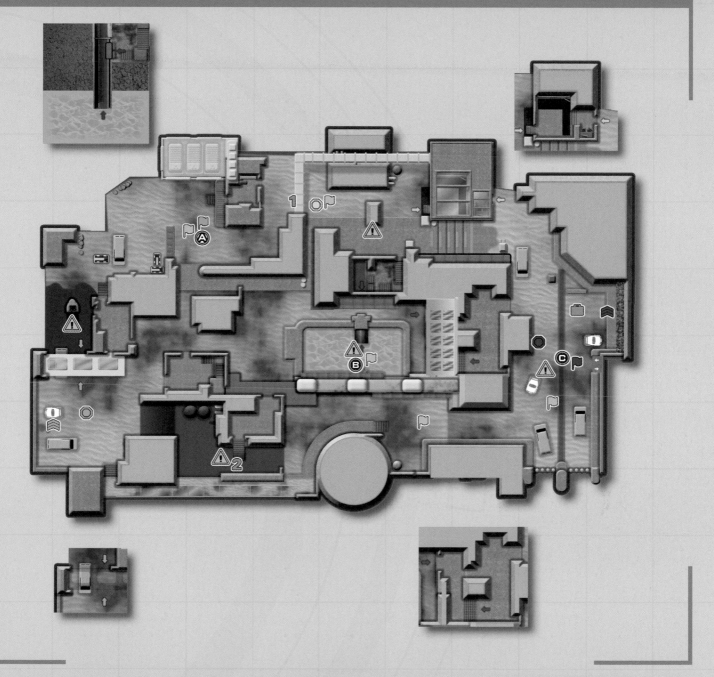

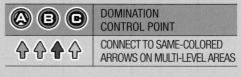 SPAWN POINT	UPLINK SATELLITE	Ⓐ Ⓑ Ⓒ DOMINATION CONTROL POINT
MOMENTUM FLAG	S&D BOMB	⇧⇧⇧⇧ CONNECT TO SAME-COLORED ARROWS ON MULTI-LEVEL AREAS
CTF FLAG	1 2 S&D/S&R TARGET	
UPLINK GOAL	⚠ HARDPOINT	

TERRACE

Set in Santorini Greece on the cliffside, Terrace has steep elevation changes from the top of the map to the bottom, with combat flowing around a central building. Use your Exo movement to flow through this map effectively.

Map Scorestreak:
Sniper Drone.

An extremely vertical map, Terrace has three "lanes" that are arranged vertically, with an upper, central, and lower area. Exo movement is absolutely vital on this level, as you must move between different elevations and lanes quickly. However, be very careful with your Exo movement. You make a tempting target while you're hanging in the air, and there are a lot of vantage points that can cover the different lanes.

Use the small interior areas and hallways to transition from one place to another in cover. Be careful about exposing yourself on the ledges overlooking the swimming pool on the bottom tier.

The outer edges near the spawns on the central level have quite a few objective targets near them, and the buildings provide both cover and elevation. Consequently, expect a lot of intense fighting around them.

TERRACE: OVERVIEW

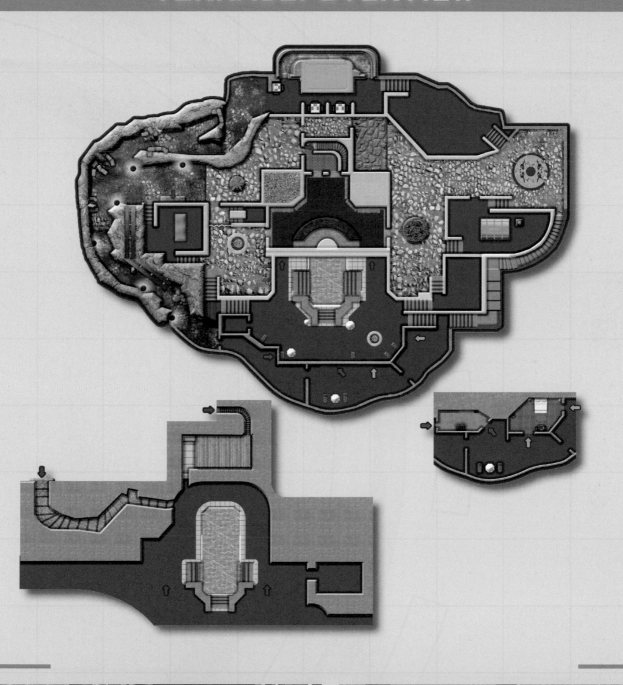

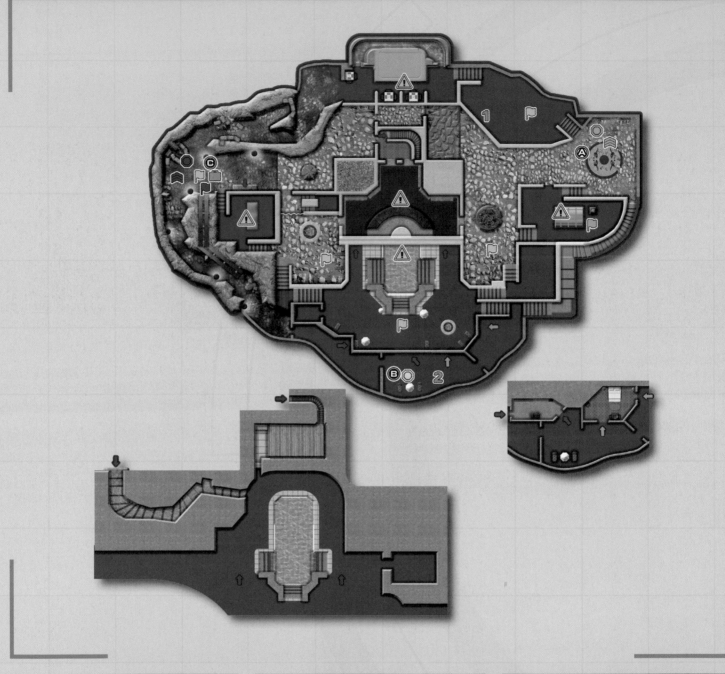

SPAWN POINT	⯃ UPLINK SATELLITE	Ⓐ Ⓑ Ⓒ DOMINATION CONTROL POINT
⚑ MOMENTUM FLAG	💼 S&D BOMB	⬆⬆⬆⬆ CONNECT TO SAME-COLORED ARROWS ON MULTI-LEVEL AREAS
CTF FLAG	1 2 S&D/S&R TARGET	
⬡ UPLINK GOAL	⚠ HARDPOINT	

CALL OF DUTY®
ADVANCED WARFARE

BRADYGAMES OFFICIAL STRATEGY GUIDE

FREE Searchable & Sortable eGuide

Go to www.primagames.com/code
and enter the unique code found at the back
of this guide!

POWER CHANGES EVERYTHING

BEAT THE CAMPAIGN

We lead you step-by-step through the entire game from start to finish, including all Intel locations.

MASTER EVERY NEW FEATURE

We break down all the new innovations and cutting-edge arsenal additions, including potent exoskeletons, specialized drones, directed energy weapons, and much more. Learn everything that's new and gain the advantage over your opposition!

BUILD THE PERFECT LOADOUT

Our winning Create-a-Class advice helps you custom tailor your loadout for the game modes, the maps, the team roles, and the play styles you want to employ.

THERE'S MORE!

Achievement and Trophy rosters, unlockables, gripping artwork, and much more!

DOMINATE IN MULTIPLAYER

We provide pro-level tactics for solo and team-based play. Every game mode, including Exo Survival, unbeatable weapon analysis, perks, ranking up, challenges, scorestreaks, and much more!

KNOW THE LEVELS

Exclusive, highly detailed SP and MP maps depict every level in the game. We reveal weapon and ammo positions, collectible locations, SP campaign and MP objectives, and more!

BRADYGAMES

SLEDGEHAMMER GAMES™

ACTIVISION.

www.bradygames.com   www.sledgehammergames.com   www.activision.com

ARM YOURSELF FOR WARFARE

LIMITED EDITION
GAMING HEADSETS

TOURNAMENT GRADE
GAMING HEADSET

GAMING HEADSET

PREMIUM GAMING HEADSET

CALL OF DUTY
ADVANCED WARFARE

Written by Phillip Marcus, Michael Owen, Jason Fox, and Will Murray

Maps illustrated by Darren Strecker and Michael Tumey

DK/BradyGames, a division of Penguin Group (USA) Inc.
800 East 96th Street, 3rd Floor
Indianapolis, IN 46240

ISBN: 978-0-7440-1564-5

Printing Code: The rightmost double-digit number is the year of the book's printing; the rightmost single-digit number is the number of the book's printing. For example, 14-1 shows that the first printing of the book occurred in 2014.

17 16 15 14   4 3 2 1

Printed in the USA.

CREDITS

TITLE MANAGER
Tim Fitzpatrick

BOOK DESIGNERS
Tim Amrhein
Dan Caparo

PRODUCTION DESIGNER
Tracy Wehmeyer

COPY EDITOR
Angie Lawler

BRADYGAMES STAFF

VP & PUBLISHER
Mike Degler

ASSOCIATE PUBLISHER
Andy Rolleri

LICENSING MANAGER
Christian Sumner

MARKETING MANAGER
Katie Hemlock

DIGITAL PUBLISHING MANAGER
Tim Cox

OPERATIONS MANAGER
Stacey Beheler

ACKNOWLEDGMENTS

BradyGAMES sincerely thanks everyone at Activision and Sledgehammer Games for their partnership, support, and collaboration throughout this project, and for their gracious hospitality hosting our authors. Very special thanks to Lindsay Friedman, Matt Wellman, James Bonti, Mike Mejia, James Lodato, Alicia Mandeville, Zach Betka, Angel Garcia, Jeremy Le, Teddy Hwang, Matthew Kerbel, Andrew Hoffacker, Adrian Devally, Fiona Ebbs, and Angel Garcia—without your generous assistance, this guide would not be possible. Thank you!

PHILLIP MARCUS: A big thank you to the team at Activision for making us welcome during a busy time: Jason Ades, Angel Garcia, Teddy Hwang, Jeremy Le, and Matthew Wellman. As ever, creating a guide takes a small village. Thanks to Tim Fitzpatrick for helming the rudder in stormy waters, Tim Cox, Leigh Davis, Tracy Wehmeyer, and my compatriots, Jason Fox, Michael Owen, Will Murray, Darren Strecker, and Michael Tumey. And most importantly, all my love to my wife Daphne.

JASON FOX: I'd like to thank the fine folks at Activision for hosting us for another *Call of Duty* guide. In particular, I'd like to thank Angel Garcia for helping us with internal build commands and talking through some of our analysis work, Jeremy Le for hosting us in his bunker, and Teddy Hwang for his tireless IT help while on site. Thanks to our gracious host Matt Wellman. As always, a big thanks to Phil, Michael, Will, Darren, and Tumey for camaraderie while on-site. Finally, as with every one of these guides, a big thanks to my wife Lindsey and my kids Jake and Ellie for putting up with this gaming thing.

WILL MURRAY: This project was a blast to work on due to the awesome people working over at Activision! I'd like to thank Jeremy who helped us out in the bunker, even letting us into the secret snack stash. A big thank you to Matt Wellman, not only for taking care of getting us in and out of the building, but for opening the doors late at night to get my laptop cable for me! The screenshots were made much easier with the help of Angel and his secret list of camera commands. I'd also like to thank Pete for sitting down and helping us out with PvP shots; he's got some mad *Call of Duty* skills! A big thanks to Jason for helping power through all the screen shots in our few days at Santa Monica. Of course, thanks to Phil and Michael for giving me more opportunities and guidance while working on this guide. A special thank you to my beautiful girlfriend Julia, for all her support while I disappear to work on these guides. One last thank you to my Mom and Dad for believing in me and helping boost my confidence in my guide-writing abilities.